# INDIAN POLITICS FROM
# DADABHAI NAOROJI TO GANDHI

K. P. KARUNAKARAN

# INDIAN POLITICS FROM DADABHAI NAOROJI TO GANDHI

A study of the political ideas of Modern India

# GITANJALI PRAKASHAN
New Delhi

First published : July 1975

Printed in India
Dhawan Printing Work 26-A, Mayapuri Phase I New Delhi-110027.

Published by Mrs. Krishna Sondhi, for Gitanjali Prakashan (Opp. Gargi College) Lajpat Nagar-4, New Delhi-110024.

# PREFACE

The first question which faces the student of the political philosophy of the Indian national movement is this : Has modern India made any original contribution to political philosophy? Unlike in the West, in modern India, political philosophy was not recognised as a distinct field of knowledge and it had not created an extensive literature. One is, therefore, tempted to answer this question in the negative. Such an answer is correct only as far as the contribution of political scientists is concerned and not that of the leaders of the national movement.[1] As the evolution of national consciousness in India was different from that of other countries, the Indian leaders were called upon to lead a unique political movement and they reacted to it in a unique way. Their legacy to modern India in the ideological field is the political philosophy of the national movement. As this has not attracted as much attention of the students and scholars as other branches of modern India's political history have done, this is a fertile field for study.

The leaders of modern India were primarily men of action and they did not work out a systematic philosophy. This fact as such, does not reduce the importance of the study of their philosophy.

> The absence of a systematic approach to political philosophy and the limited framework within which political ideas were expressed are not in themselves evidences of a lack of substance or of perception. Many of the greatest contributions to political theory are unsystematic and biased.[2]

1. In this connection the following observation made by an Indian political scientist is worth noting :

'Political Science studies in India present the picture of a rootless growth. Although it is only about thirty years since the branch of the social sciences started attracting the attention of Indian universities, the literature produced so far does not provide any indication of the objectives of these studies. Nor can they be said to have any substantial effect on the shaping of events and ideas which have significantly influenced the life of the Indian people' (S. V. Kogekar and A. Appadorai, *Political Science in India*, Delhi, 1953, 1-2).

2. Norman D. Palmer, 'India and Western Political Thought'. *The American Political Science Review*, 49 (September 1955) 757.

The contribution of Edmund Burke is a typical instance. As Sabine observes in his book, *A History of Political Theory :*

> It is perhaps stretching a point to say that Burke had a political philosophy at all. His ideas are scattered through his speeches and pamphlets, all called out by the stress of events, though they have the consistency that is the stamp of a powerful intelligence and settled moral convictions. Certainly he had no philosophy other than his own reaction to the events in which he took part and little knowledge of the history of philosophy.[3]

This is true of many leaders of modern India also. Their ideas are scattered through many speeches and writings and the resolutions of the organisation they led and all of them were called out by the stress of events. But they not only reacted to the political events but moulded some of them too. The strategy and tactics of the national movement were completely worked out by them and in this respect they were more original than a political thinker who only reacted to events.

Another question which we have to answer before we proceed with this study is this : What is meant by the term 'political philosophy'? As the differences of view among many authorities indicate, it is difficult to arrive at a precise definition of the term but not to describe its form and substance. The author of the book, *Politics and Vision* notes :

> Turning......to the subject-matter of political philosophy, even the most cursory examination of the masterpieces of political literature discloses the continual re-appearance of certain problem topics. Many examples could be listed, but here we need mention only a few such as the power relationships between rulers and ruled, the nature of authority, the problems posed by social conflict, the status of certain goals or purposes as objectives of political action, and the character of political knowledge. No political philosopher has been interested in all of these problems to the same degree, yet there has been a sufficiently widespread consensus about the identity of problems to warrant the belief that a continuity of preoccupation has existed.[4]

3. George H. Sabine, *A History of Political Theory* (New York, 1949) 618.

4. Sheldon S. Wolin, *Politics and Vision* (London, 1961) 3.

It is in this broad sense that the term 'political philosophy' is used in this study.

As we are concerned with the political philosophy of the national movement, the goals or purposes accepted by it as objectives of political action become an important part of the study. These objectives were of a limited character and primarily concerned with such matters as the spreading of the concept that India was a nation, the extension of political rights of the people and achievement of freedom of the country. In the period we are surveying, there was not much discussion in India on many other fundamental questions of political philosophy. The field of study of the political philosophy of the Indian national movement is, therefore, not wide, but it is complex because the leaders of the movement, as we noted earlier, being primarily men of action rather than of thought, had given expression to their ideas not always in a consistent and systematic manner.

Moreover, some of them were faced with the fact that even the politically conscious people of India in the nineteenth and early twentieth century did not have any specific conceptual framework within which political ideas were expressed. They had to create one and the attempt to create it itself led to a great controversy in the country. The debate around the question, whether India was a nation or not, was a typical example of this kind of controversy.

According to one scholar, nationalism itself is a political philosophy.[5] In this sense, one can say that one important feature of the political philosophy of many of the modern Indian leaders was nationalism itself.

It is difficult to give a single definition of the word 'nationalism' which is acceptable to all. The following definitions of the terms 'nation', 'nationality' and 'nationalism' given by various scholars are reproduced here because they throw much light on their meanings and indirectly on the nature and scope of the study. An author, who has made a deep study of the march of

---

5. 'One of the most explosive political philosophies is nationalism. It is also one of the greatest forces of civilization' (Flicks Green, ed., *European Ideologies*; New York, 1948, 541).

many Asian countries from their position of dependencies to that of independent nations, observes :

> The nation is a community of people who feel that they belong together in the double sense that they share deeply significant elements of a common heritage and that they have a common destiny for the future.[6]

The same author adds :

> Since the state is, in modern times, the most significant form of organisation of men and embodies the greatest concentration of power, it is inevitable that there should have been, and should still be, a great and revolutionary struggle to secure a coincidence between state and nation. The nation seeks to take over the state as the political instrument through which it can protect and assert itself.[7]

J. H. Carlton, who devoted most of his adult life to the study of nationalism, writes :

> Nationalism is now obviously a world-wide phenomenon, vitally affecting both the material and intellectual development of modern civilisation. It tends more and more to influence the economic and spiritual as well as the political relationships of mankind.[8]

According to J. S. Mill,

> A portion of mankind may be said to constitute a Nationality if they are united among themselves by common sympathies which do not exist between them and any other which make them co-operate with each other more willingly than with other people, desire to be under the same government, and desire that it should be a government by themselves or a portion of themselves exclusively.[9]

One aspect of nation and nationalism which is stressed by the two authors quoted above is the desire of the people concerned to have a government of their own which would be more or less exclusively controlled by them. The Indian national move-

6. Rupert Emerson, *From Empire to Nation* (Cambridge, Massachusetts, 1960) 95.

7. *Ibid.*, 96.

8. J. H. Hayes Carlton, *Nationalism : A Religion* (New York, 1960) vii.

9. J. S. Mill, *On Liberty and Considerations on Representative Government* (Oxford, 1948) 291.

ment was the outward expression of this desire of many people of the country.

The period for this study is 1885-1921. Its importance lies in the fact that almost all the main trends of the national movement are reflected in this period. Some of the early leaders of the Indian national movement like Dadabhai Naoroji and Surendranath Banerjea were very influential in the first decade of the twentieth century and Gopal Krishna Gokhale, another leader, championed their view, for a greater part of this period. Bal Gangadhar Tilak, Bepin Chandra Pal, Lajpat Rai and Aurobindo Ghose entered the political scene during 1905-1908 as the exponents of a new political philosophy. Among the Indian Muslims one can see the influence of various individuals like the Aga Khan, Muhammad Ali Jinnah, Maulana Muhammad Ali and Abul Kalam Azad, each with his own distinct political views. M. K. Gandhi emerged as a national leader towards the end of the period and broke fresh ground in Indian politics. Ideas such as socialism, internationalism and Asian resurgence, which found favour with Indian politicians later, appeared on the Indian horizon during 1918-1920. A study of the Indian national movement during 1885-1921, therefore, touches, though it does not cover, the major elements in its political philosophy.

As the national movement of this period is influenced by many developments of an earlier period we begin our study with a background chapter. It discusses, among other things, the political impact of the British administrative system, the constitutional developments and the political significance of the social and religious reform movements. The next chapter gives an account of the impact of liberalism on the early phase of the Indian national movement. The third chapter is a study of the political philosophy of 'Extremism' which emerged as a new factor in Indian politics at the beginning of the twentieth century. In contrast with it was the moderate approach of the early leaders of national movement. The fourth chapter is concerned with religion as a factor in the political thinking of a large section of the people during this period. The fifth chapter explains the emergence of Gandhi as the national leader of the country and the philosophical basis of the non-cooperation movement he led against the British government during 1920-1921. The concluding chapter makes an assessment of the various schools of political thought which dominated the national movement during 1885-1921 and notes the new ideas which appeared in the Indian political horizon towards the end of that period. The seventh chapter deals with the evolution of Indian politics in the Gandhian era.

In the preparation of this study, I was given encouragement and help by many individuals. For reasons of space, only a few are mentioned here.

I am grateful to Prof. V. K. N. Menon who gave me valuable suggestions regarding the nature and scope of the study. The continuous guidance I received from him has made its mark on every chapter.

Mrs. Urmila Phadnis and Mrs. Susheela Kaushik were kind enough to go through the manuscript carefully and suggest many improvements. I acknowledge with gratitude the great help rendered by them in preparing it for the press.

This book is based on my earlier publication entitled "continuity and change in Indian Politics".

# CONTENTS

# CHAPTER I

# BACKGROUND

AMONG the many factors that have contributed to the origin and growth of the Indian national movement, none is more important than the nature and character of the British rule in the country. We shall begin this study with a brief survey of the political and administrative policies of the British rulers and an assessment of the political significance of the social and religious movements which made a profound impact on the political movements which followed them.

## EXPANSION OF BRITISH POWER IN INDIA BEFORE 1857

The nature of the origin and expansion of British power in India is as important as the fact of that expansion.[1] The East India Company came into being with the Charter of 1600. Until 1760 they were primarily traders enjoying some important mercantile privileges and holding sundry factories on or near the coast. In that year they assumed responsibilities of territorial sovereignty over Burdwan, Midnapore and Chittagong. With the grant of *diwani* by the Mogul Emperor to the Company, they became practically sovereign over Bengal, Bihar and Orissa. During the next phase, the Company expanded its territorial

1 British authority in India may be traced historically to a twofold source. It is derived partly from the British Crown and Parliament, partly from the Great Mogul and other native rulers of India. In England, the powers and privileges granted by the Royal Charter to the East India Company were confirmed, supplemented, regulated and curtailed by successive Acts of Parliament, and were finally transferred to the Crown. In India concessions granted by, or wrested from native rulers gradually established the Company and the Crown as territorial sovereigns, in rivalry with other country powers; and finally left the British Crown exercising undivided sovereignty throughout British India, and paramount authority over the native states. — Sir C. Ilbert, *The Government of India* (Oxford, 1907) 1.

power to the vast parts of the Indian subcontinent. In this period it also began to share its sovereignty over India in diminishing proportions with the Crown, and gradually began to lose its mercantile privileges and functions. The system prevailing then was often referred to as one of double government.

The nature and character of the British administration in India was determined as much by the political ideas prevalent in the United Kingdom in this period as by the structure of the Government of India. As R. C. Dutt, a civil servant and a well-known author says in his book, *England and India*:

> ...the administration of India is determined by the currents of opinions in England, that progress in India is stimulated by English progress, and that the history of India under British rule is shaped by those great influences which make for reforms in Europe. This is a fact which is often overlooked by the historians of India, but Indian history is unintelligible to us without this explanation. From the time of the great Pitt to the time of Mr. Gladstone, English influences have inspired the rulers of India; English history and Indian history have run in parallel streams.[2]

Although the author's contention that the history of the two countries ran on parallel lines is an exaggeration, at least in regard to the influence of political ideas in the two countries, there is no doubt that the policy of the British administrators in India and the thinking of the Indian leaders were tremendously influenced, even when they were not fully governed, by the political and other ideas prevalent in England.

LIBERAL AND SCIENTIFIC CULTURE OF THE WEST

The eighteenth century was the age of enlightenment in Europe and it produced such great philosophers as Locke, Berkeley and Hume in England and Rousseau, Voltaire and Leibniz in the Continent. The progress in sciences which this period witnessed transformed the generally held view of the nature of the material world. Many of the medieval concepts were replaced by ideas which arose from national and scientific modes of thinking.

2 R. C. Dutt, *England and India: A Record of Progress During a Hundred Years* 1785-1885 (London, 1897) 120.

A very great deal of good, undoubtedly, was done, suffering mitigated, injustice avoided or prevented, ignorance exposed, by the conscientious attempt to apply scientific methods to the regulation of human affairs. Dogmas were refuted, prejudices and superstitions were pilloried successfully. The growing conviction that appeals to mystery and darkness and authority to justify arbitrary behaviour were all too often so many unworthy *alibis* concealing self-interest or intellectual indolence or stupidity, was often triumphantly vindicated.[3]

These developments did not take place simultaneously in the eighteenth century India. She had to wait for the social and political awakening of the nineteenth century to gain an experience even remotely akin to it. By the time, in England, from where India had received some of these ideas, liberalism had become a great intellectual force. For England, 'the nineteenth century is the epoch of liberal triumph; from Waterloo until the outbreak of the Great War no other doctrine spoke with the same authority or exercised the same widespread influence.'[4]

As the most dominant political doctrine of Great Britain during the period of the expansion of her power to India, liberalism demands the close scrutiny of the student of modern India. More than one definition is given to it. 'In a general way, liberalism comprehended a belief in the power of reason to regulate the conduct of life, in critical views of dogmatic beliefs, and in an experimental attitude toward problems in government and society.'[5] Some authors emphasise certain specific aspects of liberalism, such as individualism. One of them says:

Liberalism is premised upon the assertion of the absolute moral worth of each individual. It is the political expression of a comprehensive *weltanschauung,* of an intellectual climate of opinion that has pervaded all realms of thought since the Renaissance. It is the theory of political order based upon individualism.[6]

3 Isiah Berlin, *The Age of Enlightenment* (New York, 1956) 20.
4 H. J. Laski, *The Rise of European Liberalism* (London, 1947) 237.
5 J. S. Schepiro, *Liberalism and the Challenge of Fascism* (New York, 1949) 1.
6 John H. Hallowell, *The Decline of Liberalism as an Ideology* (London, 1946) 21.

Other definitions, such as the one following, focus attention to the appeal to the reason inherent in liberalism:

> The essential elements of the liberal *weltanschauung* were the appeal to reason, the belief in happiness as the end, belief in liberty of opinion and conduct, toleration, natural rights, equality and faith in progress. Faith in the liberated reason of each individual is the way to it all—the individual thought of as autonomous and largely self-sufficient.[7]

## LIBERALISM AND THE EARLY PHASE OF THE BRITISH ADMINISTRATION IN INDIA 1818-58

The fact that the British administrators in India before 1859 were drawn from a country where liberalism was the dominant political doctrine had made its mark on their policy in India. This does not, however, mean that British political ideas were mechanically or automatically applied to India as and when they were popular in Britain. The British administrators came to India with some political ideas which they acquired during their education or their period of training in Great Britain. Since then, owing to changed circumstances, new ideas began to spread among the people at home in Britain. The administrators in India did not always keep pace with these new ideas, nor were they influenced by them. Moreover, the situation they had to face in India had its own unique features and they had to respond to them. The following comment of Lord Morley on the Indian Viceroy of the latter period applied to earlier British administrators as well: 'The Indian Viceroy is not bound to know political philosophy or juristic theory or constitutional history; he is first and foremost an administrator and the working head of a complicated civil and military service.'[8] While functioning in this capacity, the British administrator was not eager to show allegiance to a particular political theory. However, in the earlier phases of British administration, India did provide a ground for implementing some of the liberal ideas prevalent in England in this period.

For the purpose of examining these liberal trends in the early

7 F. R. Pennock, *Liberal Democracy: Its Merits and Prospects* (New York, 1950) 13.
8 J. V. Morley, *Recollections* (London, 1918) II, 151-2.

phase, we may start with 1818 when, after the defeat of the
Marathas, the British East India Company became supreme
over the whole of India, southeast of the Sutlej. 'The realisation
of the fact that Britain was now responsible for the government
of all India led men to take a new view of the functions of
government. It helped to give birth to new political aims and a
new and deeper sense of responsibility for the welfare of the
Indian peoples.'[9] This development of new methods and ideas
in relation to the British administration and policy in India
was stimulated by the liberal current in England, where the
cause of reform gathered momentum since 1818. In this period

> the missionaries of English civilisation in India stood openly
> for a policy of 'assimilation.' Britain was to stamp her image
> upon India. The physical and mental distance separating
> East and West was to be annihilated by the discoveries
> of science, by commercial intercourse and by transplanting
> the genius of English laws and English education. It was the
> attitude of English liberalism in its clear, untroubled dawn,
> and its most representative figure in both England and India
> was Macaulay.[10]

Before this trend began to exert its influence, some British
administrators in India were hesitant in introducing social reforms based on liberal and other Western ideas. They thought
that the attempt to interfere with Indian social usages and
religious beliefs would provoke hostility against the British
government in the country and endanger it. Referring to this
dilemma of the early British administrators of India, a writer
says:

> The new spirit showed itself in two ways, which often came
> into conflict. On the one hand there was a far more respectful
> study and appreciation of Indian law and custom than has
> been shown since the time of Warren Hastings. This showed
> itself in the first place in a remarkable reaction against the
> blind eagerness to introduce English ideas and methods, es-
> pecially in landholding and in law, which had marked the
> period following Warren Hastings. Metcalfe viciously criticis-
> ed Cornwallis' Permanent Settlement... as a grave injustice

9 Ramsay Muir *The Making of British India* 1756-1858 (London, 1915)
276.

10 Eric Stokes, *The English Utilitarians and India* (Oxford, 1959)
xiii-xiv.

to the actual cultivators, and in the land settlement which he carried out in the Delhi district departed absolutely from Cornwallis' principles.... Alongside of this new anxiety to understand and make the best of Indian traditions, was an equally strong conviction that it was the duty of the British government to introduce into India the best results of western civilisation. This conviction often came into conflict with the other, though the two points of view were by no means irreconcilable.[11]

This apparent conflict was resolved in favour of introducing progressive measures. The Government of East India Company decided to abolish *sati*, i.e. the practice of Hindu widow immolating herself on the funeral pyre of her deceased husband and in 1835 the government decided to introduce western education in India. Another step taken by the government in the same year was the withdrawal of the restrictions on the press. It released liberal and progressive forces in the country. It is significant that the Act of 1835 also added a fourth or legal Member to the Governor-General's Council. His duty was to codify the Indian laws.

In this period there were also proclamations of high ideals in regard to India by British authorities. For instance, the India Act of 1833, among other things, stated:

And be it enacted, that no native of the said territories, nor any natural-born subject of His Majesty's resident therein, shall, by reason only of his religion, place of birth, descent, colour or any of them, be disabled from holding any place, or employment under the said Company.[12]

Another was the following statement of Macaulay in the House of Commons on 10 July 1833:

It may be that the public mind of India may expand under our system till it has outgrown that system; that by good government we may educate our subjects into a capacity for better government; that, having become instructed in European knowledge, they may in some future age, demand European institutions.... Whenever it comes, it will be the proudest day in English history.[13]

11 Muir, n. 9, 277-8.
12 A. B. Keith, ed., *Speeches and Documents on Indian Policy*, 1750-1921 (London, 1922) 273.
13 *Ibid.*, 265.

These attempts to popularise liberal ideas in India, which the British administrators made, meant spreading a belief in the power of reason to regulate the conduct of life and in developing critical views of dogmatic beliefs. Other aspects of liberalism like an experimental attitude towards problems in government were not relevant to the situation in India in that period. But the spread of liberal ideas in regard to social and religious matters had its repercussions in the political field, because social, religious and political activities of the people could not be separated and maintained in watertight compartments indefinitely. By the time the social, religious and political awakening in India was leading to the birth of a national movement in the country, the British administrators' Indian policy was moving away from its early liberal leanings. Many new features in the domestic situations in Great Britain and India and in the international field contributed to this development.

NEW FACTORS IN BRITISH RULE IN INDIA AFTER 1858

Within India the most important event was the uprising of the Indian army against the British authority in 1857. After that year, such subjects as education of the natives of India did not continue as favourites in discussions among Englishmen interested in India. Instead they began to speak the language of firmness. The 1857 Mutiny, with its tale of massacres and reprisals, engendered bitterness and widened the gulf between Englishmen and Indians.

While the character of British administration in India changed in this manner, Britain herself was experiencing considerable changes in her internal social and economic life and these changes were making themselves felt in her external relations.

This determining influence of English history extends beyond character to the broad fashioning of British policy. However confused the surface of events, the tide of British policy in India moved in the direction set by the development of the British economy. The Industrial Revolution and the reversal it brought about in the economic relations of India with Britain were the primary phenomena. A transformation in the purpose of political dominion was the main result. Instead of providing a flow of tribute—a conception which survived at least until the end of the eighteenth cen-

tury—the British power in India came to be regarded after
1800 as no more than an accessory, an instrument for ensuring
the necessary conditions of law and order by which the poten-
tially vast Indian market could be conquered for British industry. This transformation of economic purpose carried with
it a new, expansive, and aggressive attitude.... [14]

The close connection between the great expansion of British
trade and finance in the second half of the nineteenth century
and the attitude of British politicians towards the colonies and
empire was evident in many of their speeches. Disraeli very often
emphasised the economic value of India and the Suez Canal as
the route to the East. Joseph Chamberlain was another exponent of this view. In a speech delivered on 25 March 1896 he
said:

What is the greatest of our common obligations?   It is the
Imperial defence. What is the greatest of our common interest? It is Imperial trade and those two are very closely connected. Imperial defence is largely a matter of ways and
means, and ways and means are dependent upon the fiscal
and other commercial arrangements you may make; and
therefore, the conclusion to which I arrive is this—that if the
people of this country and the people of colonies mean what
they have been saying and if they intend to approach this
question of Imperial unity in a practical spirit, they must
approach it on its commercial side.[15]

This 'commercial side' of the Empire was particularly important to Britain since the seventies of the nineteenth century
when she was experiencing what was often referred to as the
second Industrial Revolution. In this period British industry
was shifting from cotton to iron and steel, which led to a rush
for concessions to develop overseas territories, to build railways
and bridges and to find cheap labour and new markets. No more
was it possible for the British government to get rid of the
colonies, as some of their officials wanted to do in an earlier
period because they thought that the colonies were expensive
encumbrances in a world where all trade was to be free. In this
period some important developments were taking place in other
parts of the world which made the concept of free trade out of

14 Stokes, n. 10, xiii.
15 George Benett, ed., *The Concept of Empire—Burke to Attlee* 1774-
1947 (London, 1953) 316-7.

date. The increasing commercial and imperial rivalry between
the industrially advanced countries was one of them. Indicative
of the mood of the times was the following statement by Joseph
Chamberlain to assert his claim as the Secretary of State for
Colonies:

> These qualifications are that, in the first place, I believe in
> the British Empire and in the second place, I believe in the
> British race. I believe that the British race is the greatest of
> governing races that the world has ever seen. I say that not
> merely as an empty boast, but as proved and evidenced by
> the success which we have had in administering the vast domi-
> nions which are connected with these small islands.[16]

In this concept of Empire India occupied a central place.
Lord Curzon, the Viceroy of India during 1898-1905, told the
Royal Societies' Club, London, in 1898: 'India has always appeared to me to be the pivot and centre—I do not say the geographical, but the political and Imperial centre— of the British
Empire.'[17] On another occasion, while addressing an Indian
audience, he developed this view still further:

> The past year has, moreover, been one which has conspicuous-
> ly demonstrated the part that is played by India in the
> Imperial system. It was the prompt despatch of a contingent
> of the Indian army a year ago that saved the colony of Natal.
> They were Indian regiments who accomplished the rescue of
> the Legations at Peking. We have rendered this service to the
> Empire in a year when we have been distracted by famine
> and plague, and weighed down by our own troubles. If our
> arm, reaches as far as China in the East, and South Africa in
> the West, who can doubt the range of our. influence, or the
> share of India in Imperial destinies?[18]

## AUTHORITARIAN ELEMENTS IN BRITISH
## ADMINISTRATION IN INDIA

When these developments were taking place in the international field, and Britain's economic stakes and strategic interests
in India were gradually becoming more important, and thus
making a change in the British attitude towards the question

16 *Ibid.*, 315.
17 Sir Thomas Raleigh, ed., *Lord Curzon in India* (London, 1906) I, 8.
18 *Ibid.*, 30.

of the continuation of the political domination over India, some new political ideas were appearing in Great Britain. The total effect of all these was the weakening of the liberal trends in the British administration in India. This was reflected in the following statement made by Macaulay when he advocated the reorganisation of the body of laws and judiciary in India:

A code is almost the only blessing—perhaps it is the only blessing which absolute governments are better fitted to confer on a nation than popular governments. The work of digesting a vast and artificial system of unwritten jurisprudence, is far more easily performed, and far better performed by few minds than by many.... This seems to me, therefore, to be precisely that point of time at which the advantages of a complete written code of laws may most easily be conferred on India. It is a work which cannot be well performed in an age of barbarism—which cannot without great difficulty be performed in an age of freedom. It is the work which especially belongs to·a government like that of India—to an enlightened and paternal despotism.[19]

This extract from Macaulay's speech was an exceptional one among his utterances in that it betrayed a certain authoritarian spirit. But towards the close of the nineteenth century the British administrators' statements became very outspoken as regards to the authoritarian nature of the British rule. A typical conception of the 'Foundations of the Government of India' was as follows:

The English in India have been by circumstances committed to an enterprise which is in reality difficult and dangerous to the last degree, though its difficulties and dangers have thus far been concealed by the conspicuous success which has attended their efforts. That enterprise is nothing less than the management and guidance of the most extensive and far-reaching revolution recorded in history. It involves radical change of ideas and institutions of a vast population which has already got ideas and institutions to which it is deeply attached. The only method of conducting this revolution to a good end is by unity of action and policy, communicated from a central authority to a small number of picked local officers, the central and local authorities being supported by a military force sufficient to give them practically undisputed executive power, and the whole body being regulated by known laws

19 Keith, n. 12, 263-4.

impartially administered. By these means the tremendous change now in progress may be carried out in a quite orderly and gradual way, with what specific results no one can tell, but it may be hoped with good ones unless the ideas on which all European civilisation is based are essentially wrong. If, however, the authority of the government is once materially relaxed, if the essential character of the enterprise is misunderstood and the delusion that it can be carried out by assemblies representing the opinion of the natives is admitted, nothing but failure, anarchy and ruin can be the result.[20]

The British policy and attitude is rightly summed up as follows:

The Government of India was increasingly regarded as a white man's burden rather than as a call to creative effort or the preparation for a new era.... With vision and hope laid aside there remained the task of keeping order and dealing justice, of devising improving measures and exercising fostering care.... Thus the sixties and seventies, though prosperous and materially creative, were spiritually somewhat barren.[21]

## RIPON'S VICEROYALTY—A LIBERAL INTERLUDE

Under Lord Ripon, there was a short interlude of the British administrator's liberal attitude and policy towards India. Ripon was the nominee of Gladstone who, during the British elections of 1880 said: 'I cannot tell you how dishonouring to England I consider to have been the Government of India during the last three years.'[22] Lord Ripon took a series of steps in pursuance of a liberal policy towards India. One among them was the repeal of Lytton's Vernacular Press Act, which gave considerable freedom to the Indian newspapers and another was the establishment of a system of self-government by setting up, in 1882, elected municipalities in towns and District Boards in rural districts. Another one of his measures was the unsuccessful attempt to promulgate the controversial Ilbert Bill, the main feature of which was the removal of the absolute race disqualification from Indian judges in mofussil—the disqualification based

20 Fitzjames Stephens, 'Foundations of the Government of India, *Nineteenth Century*, 49 (October 1883) 566.
21 V. A. Smith, *The Oxford History of India* (Oxford, 1958, 3rd edition) 683.
22 S. Gopal, *The Viceroyalty of Lord Ripon* 1880-1884 (London, 1953) I.

on the view that the Indian was, as such, incapable of fairly trying a European subject. Owing to the organised opposition of Englishmen in India, Ripon could not implement this measure, although the British Cabinet was unanimous and firm in its support to him.

Ripon could not implement any spectacular programme in India.

Every measure that he has brought forward has been defeated in detail; and so powerful has the Civil Service been that they have forced the Home Government into an abandonment, step by step, of all his Indian policy. This they have effected in part by open opposition, in part by covert encouragement of English lay element, in part by working through the English Press.[23]

There is, however, no doubt that Ripon did fulfil some positive functions.

Ripon's sad failures bore within them the seeds of eventual success. He had sought to impart real content to abstract doctrines and remote sentiments. The effect was not lost on the imagination of the class which was the custodian of national forces in India.[24]

In the years immediately following Ripon's Viceroyalty the liberal elements in Britain's administration did not make much headway.

... while this new current of thought existed and made its impact on India before 1900 it was a minority opinion in both countries. Gladstonian liberalism went into eclipse for twenty years with the defeat of Home Rule and the new ideas had not more than a scanty following amongst officials in India itself. The Viceregal backing which obtained under Bentinck was lacking except for a time under Ripon, and there was never a 'pressure group' of young civilians such as that constituted by Charles Trevelyan Macaulay, and their friends.[25]

IMPACT OF ADMINISTRATIVE UNIFICATION ON INDIA

When we turn from the ideas and policies of the British administrators and the constitutional developments in India,

23 W. Sawen Blunt, *India under Ripon — A Private Diary* (London, 1901) 315.

24 *Ibid.*, 316.

25 Smith, n. 21, 684.

which were based on them, to another aspect of the British rule we find that the record is not so barren and fruitless. This aspect is Britain's introduction of various institutions like an efficient state apparatus, new legal system and judiciary, modern education and press.

The first and foremost among them is the administrative machinery and state apparatus which Britain established and perfected in the country.

Perhaps the most important characteristic of British administration was its impersonality. It did not fundamentally change character with changes in Secretaries of State or Viceroys, and its strength or weakness at any particular time never depended on one man, as did that of all previous empires in India. It was in fact a machine which had to be tended, but the tempo or performance of which did not vary very much with the mood or personality of the tender.[26]

Another feature of the administrative system was the consolidation of the power of the government. This took place at two levels: one, at the centre, where the Government of India emerged as a power which could make itself felt throughout the country and the other at district level where the representative of the government functioned as the symbol of the mighty state whose orders could not be challenged by any other authority.

Under British rule the people of India began to be subjected to the influence of an efficient and powerful government, bent on introducing uniformity in many spheres. Race, language, religion and social conditions might continue to separate, but political association under one rule began to weld the people of India together.[27]

This administrative unification had its important effects in many other fields. As one of the British administrators of this period remarked:

The consolidation of India under the Queen is not a mere question of the mechanism of government. The old Customs' lines, which strangled internal trade and divided province from province, have been swept off the map of India during the second half of Her Majesty's reign.... While India thus

26 Sir Percival Griffiths, *The British Impact on India* (London, 1952) 227.
27 *Ibid.*, 243.

has been compacted and knit together by the ties of government, by the fibres of trade, and by bands of iron and steel from railway centres in every province, its population has been incorporated under a system of common codes. Each race retains its domestic law and the special conditions of each Presidency are provided by local legislation. But the protection of person and property, with the punishment of offences against either, the transaction of commerce, the business of daily life of man and man, are placed under the sanctions of a common law.[28]

The only exception to these administrative measures promoting the unity of the country was the retention of the native states ruled by the princes as separate political entities. These princes owed allegiance only to the British Crown and not to the Indian government and the Viceroy dealt with them in his capacity as the Crown Representative and not as the Governor-General of India. But this separation of the powers of the Crown Representative from those of the Governor-General was more or less a legal fiction, because the economic, fiscal and administrative control of the states by the Central Government made them a part and parcel of a united India.

Another important factor in the development of the administrative system was the high standards maintained in the recruitment of the Civil Service. After 1853 new recruits to the high levels of the Indian Civil Service were enlisted by competitive examinations. Gradually India was equipped by a highly trained professional Civil Service, characterised in the main by efficiency and integrity.

The most important achievement of this efficient administrative system was the ensuring of peace and the establishment of law and order throughout the country, without which no political progress even at a later stage was possible.

INTRODUCTION OF NEW LEGAL SYSTEM AND COURTS

It was not just the maintenance of internal peace that was achieved by the British, but the establishment of a sound and effective administration of justice on modern lines. In pre-British India there was no coherent, precise and well defined body of laws which were uniformly accepted throughout the

28 W. W. Hunter, *The India of the Queen* (London, 1908) 17-8.

country and which were enforced by a well-organised system of courts.[29] Apart from the variety of the different schools of justice, there was the difficulty arising from the fact that neither the main body of Hindu nor of those of the Muslims were suited to the needs of the modern age.[30]

Although the problems arising from the differences in the personal laws of the two communities and the ill-defined nature of the laws of the Hindus were complex, it was in relation to the law of crime that radical reforms were urgent. Before British rule the Muhammadan law of crime was administered in vast parts of the country.

> Many of its rules were fundamentally opposed to the western conceptions of natural justice, order, progress and the good of the society.... Many changes were introduced into it from time to time so much so that in 1860, when the modern Indian Penal Code came into force, the prevailing Muhammadan Law of Crimes—or rather the Anglo-Muhammadan Law—had become detached from its base in the Muhammadan jurisprudence.[31]

According to the original Muhammadan jurisprudence the punishment for certain offences were very cruel and primitive;

29 Addressing the House of Commons, Macaulay, whose contribution to the development of new legal system in India was considerable, said as early as 10 July 1833: 'I believe that no country ever stood so much in need of a code of laws as India, ... I said, that there were many points of analogy between the state of that country after the fall of the Mogul power, and the state of Europe after the fall of the Roman Empire. ... As in Europe then, so in India now, there are several systems of law widely differing from each other, but coexisting and coequal. The indigenous population has its own laws. Each of the successive races of conquerors has brought with it its own peculiar jurisprudence; the Mussalman his Koran and its innumerable commentators. ...' — Keith, n. 12, 260.

30 'The Hindu Law Books were not intended to be a code of laws to be administered by court of the type set up by the British; they do not distinguish between legal, moral and religious precepts, and they conflict. The courts followed the rules in the commentaries, where they conflicted with the rules in the Dharmasasthras; as between conflicting rules in the commentaries they chose that generally accepted in the local area concerned, and applied a similar test in distinguishing legal principles from religious and moral exhortations, but the selected rules had to be such as could be enforced by the procedure of the courts, and some had to be so accepted as to conform to what were regarded as fundamental rules of justice, a process which sometimes almost inverted the rule.' — A. Gledhill, *The Republic of India* (London, 1951) 208.

31 M. P. Jain, *Outlines of Indian Legal History* (Delhi, 1952) 394.

e.g. for adultery, death by stoning or scourging was the penalty
and for theft amputation of hands. The legal system was not
based on modern concepts. One of its principles was that the

> crimes were divisible into two categories: those against God,
> as drunkenness and adultery, as being in themselves crimes of
> a deeper and more atrocious type; crimes against man as
> murder and robbery.... The latter, though in fact equally
> ruinous to the peace of the society, were given up to the
> *discretion* or *caprice* of individuals; they were regarded as
> private injuries to be taken care of by the persons injured.
> These offences were punished by the state but the basic notion
> was to secure satisfaction for the injured rather than to afford
> protection to others.[32]

These were the systems of jurisprudence which the British
government in India inherited and which they altered in many
ways. The introduction of the English system in some fields
and the modifications of the indigenous system in other fields
which British rule accomplished did not start on a precise date.
The first few steps in this direction were undertaken when the
East India Company took over the administration of the Province of Bengal and when it began to govern the natives by
their laws and the Englishmen by English laws.

This system did not work out smoothly. Then came the
Charter Act of 1833, which made provisions for the establishment of an all-India legislature, the creation of the new office
of the Law Member and for the appointment of a law commission for India.

In accordance with this act a law commission was constituted
and Macaulay was appointed Law Member of the Council.
Their work bore fruit only after twenty years. A cumulative
Civil Procedure Code was passed in 1859 and an Indian Penal
Code was enacted in 1860. This was the beginning of India's
legal reforms. Later other reforms followed. The Criminal
Procedure Code came into operation in 1862 and an Indian
Evidence Act in 1872. On the basis of the recommendations of
the Indian Law Commission of 1879 the Code relating to the
Negotiable Instruments and in 1882 the Codes relating to Trusts
and Transfer of Property were enacted. In 1882 some revisions

32 *Ibid.*, 397.

were made to the Code concerning companies, Civil Procedure
and Criminal Procedure.

Another important landmark was the constitution of high
courts in 1861. This laid down the foundations of an impartial,
efficient and independent judiciary in India. In spite of the
fact that, owing to the expensive nature of the litigation, the
poorer sections of the people could not always take advantage
of the system of laws and the administration of justice introduced
by the British, no one will deny that they did perform an historically progressive function.[33]

## INTRODUCTION OF MODERN EDUCATION

The impact of modern education on Indian political thinking
is next in importance only to that of the emergence of the
modern state structure and the development of laws and
judiciary in India. Among the British administrators Macaulay
was the most articulate champion of the view that the educational system of the country should be reorganised to suit the
needs of the modern age. In one of his minutes he said:

The question now before us is simply whether when it is
in our power to teach this language (English), we shall teach
languages in which by universal confession there are no books

---

[33] 'Under British rule this principle of the "rule of law" entered so
deeply in the minds and hearts of educated Indians that the occasional
departure from it, under public security regulations in times of emergency,
provoked quite genuine outbursts of indignation and horror. . . . The
second new concept was that of equality before the law. . . . Money, education and position do still, within limits, count with the courts in
England and elsewhere. . . . It is, however, at least true to say that in
India as in England equality before the law is today accepted as the ideal
and some approximation to it results. No such concept would have been
acceptable as between a Brahman and an outcaste in the Hindu period,
or as between Hindus and Muslims under the Moguls. . . .The third
important characteristic of Anglo-Indian law is its firm recognition of the
right of every man to be judged, in a wide range of civil matters, by his
own personal law — whether he be a Hindu, a Muslim, a Parsi or a
Christian. No such principle was recognised in Mogul times, and indeed
there were long periods in which regard was not paid to Hindu law at
all. . . . The fourth and perhaps the most important feature of British
judicial administration in India was the growth of a professional and
therefore trained judicial hierarchy. . . . The growth of the judicial services,
together with the great development of codified law, did much to build
up that confidence in the courts. . . .' — Griffiths, n. 26, 152-3.

on any subject which deserve to be compared with our own; whether, when we teach European science, we shall teach systems which by universal confession, whenever they differ from those of Europe differ for the worse; and whether, when we can patronise sound philosophy and true history, we shall countenance at the public expense medical doctrines which would disgrace an English farrier, astronomy which would move laughter in girls at an English boarding-school, history abounding with kings thirty feet high and reigns 30,000 years long, and geography made up of seas of treacle and seas of butter.... I think it clear that we are not fettered by any pledge expressed or implied; that we are free to employ our funds as we choose; that we ought to employ them in teaching what is best worth knowing; that English is better worth knowing than Sanskrit or Arabic....that it is possible to make natives of this country thoroughly good English scholars, and that to this end our efforts ought to be directed.[34]

Leaders of Indian public opinion like Raja Rammohan Roy also agreed with him on the advantages of Indians learning English. Sir Charles Wood's despatch of 1854 stated that the objective of government's educational policy should be the spread of western knowledge and science. The period between 1854 and 1900 witnessed a rapid westernisation of the educational system in India. Very many agencies, such as the various departments of governments, Indian private enterprise and Christian missionaries were engaged in this task.

The establishment of the universities of Calcutta, Bombay and Madras in 1857 gave a momentum to the educational advancement of the country. The most important function of these universities was the coordination of the work of the affiliating colleges and maintaining a uniform and high standard of education. They had some weaknesses also.

Being 'merely a group of administrative bodies' and having 'no direct contact with real work of learning,' the university could contribute nothing to strengthen the intellectual resources of the college, and little to stimulate free criticism and independent thought among teachers and students. With its uniform curricula and its exaggerated emphasis upon examinations, the system reduced the colleges to much the same pattern.[35]

34 Muir, n. 9. 301
35 **Bhagwan** Dayal, *The Development of Modern Indian Education* (Calcutta, 1955) 357.

There were many other valid criticisms of the educational system under the British in India. One was that it was primarily intended to train Indians for public services and clerical posts under the British. Another was that even this inadequate education did not reach the masses.

In spite of all these defects even the critics of the new educational system would admit that it opened the gates of western thought and literature to the educated Indians and spread among them the ideas of freedom and nationalism.

## EMERGENCE OF A MODERN PRESS

The press was another one of the western institutions introduced into India under the British rule. During the early phase of the British rule there was some kind of censorship of the press in India. In 1818 this was abolished and most of the restrictions on the press were removed. In 1823 some restrictions were again imposed by Adan, the acting Governor-General. It was significant that the Indian leader Raja Rammohan Roy protested against it even at that early date. But his petition to the Supreme Court was rejected and only in 1835 were they removed. But in 1857 a press act, known as the Gagging Act due to its drastic nature, was passed. This act which was promoted by the mutiny operated for only a year. Other restrictions of the press, which followed, were the Press and Registration of Books Act of 1867 and the Vernacular Press Act of 1878. The first restricted the freedem of the printing and publication of books and newspapers and the second imposed serious restrictions on the freedom of the vernacular press. The Vernacular Press Act was repealed in 1882

The attitude of the early British administrators was manifest in the speech Macaulay delivered in 1835, while he was advocating the repeal of restrictions on the press:

It is difficult to conceive that any measure can be more indefensible than those which I propose to repeal.... While the inhabitants of one province are complaining of the tyrannical restrictions which our laws impose on the press, the inhabitants of another province suffer from the irresponsible licentiousness of the press. The editor of a newspaper at Calcutta must have a licence from the government. The editor of a newspaper at Madras may excite his fellow subjects to the most criminal enterprises, or may destroy the peace and honour of private families, with small risk of being convicted before any legal tribunal. The Act which I now propose is intended to remove both evils, and to establish a perfect uniformity in the laws regarding the press throughout the Indian Empire. Should it be accepted, every person who chooses will be at liberty to set up a newspaper without applying for a previous permission. But no person will be able to print or publish sedition and calumny without imminent risk of punishment.[36]

This was a good beginning and throughout the nineteenth century the government's policy did not very much depart from this liberal attitude and Indian press enjoyed considerable freedom except for short periods. After 1908 the position was different because, with the growth of the national movement, the government's attitude towards the press became stiff. But by that time the Indian press had become a power to be reckoned with and had already contributed a good deal to the strength of national movement.

## CONSTITUTIONAL DEVELOPMENTS AND POLITICAL TRAINING

While these changes in the administrative and educational systems and the emergence of a press were conducive to the political awakening in the country very few of the constitutional developments gave political training to the people of the country. The first landmark in the constitutional history since 1833 was the disappearance of the East India Company and the assumption of direct control over India by the British government. The next was the Indian Councils Act of 1861 which provided for the enlargement of the Governor-General's Executive Council and the legislative councils of Madras and Bombay and for the establishment of similar councils in Bengal, the North-Western Provinces and the Punjab. But as both the officials and non-officials in the councils were nominated and their functions were purely legislative, these constitutional developments were not based on representative principles. The Act of 1909 was definitely a constitutional advance, but it is significant that it was also accompanied by official declarations

36 C. D. Dharkar, ed., *Lord Macaulay's Legislative Minutes* (Madras, 1946) 165-7.

that it must not be interpreted as an approach to English parliamentary government.[37] The Government of India Act of 1919 was different. According to an authority on Indian constitutional developments it repudiated the view that parliamentary government was itself repudiated.[38] It laid the foundations for representative institutions in the country and provided some opportunities for political training of some educated Indians.

## THE TOTAL IMPACT OF THE WEST

Although there was no conscious attempt on the part of the British administrators to promote self-government in India there was no doubt that the total impact of the West on the country was such as to help develop political awakening and to create the necessary conditions for the development of a national movement in the country. Among the many factors which influenced the political philosophy of that movement the nature and character of the British government were very important. As we noted, both liberal and authoritarian trends were visible in the British administrators' attitudes towards India. But more important than their attitudes were the institutions they established in the country. The most important among them were a strong government, an efficient civil service, new legal system and judiciary and the universities based on modern concepts of education. Towards the end of the period under survey in this study, i.e. 1905-21, some constitutional developments, which were helpful to the political training of Indians, also took place.

Summing up India's indebtedness to the West, one Indian scholar, who has made a special study of modern Indian culture, observed:

All are agreed that India entered into a new lease of life in the nineteenth century. The spurt of vitality came from the West through various channels like commerce and trade, increased facilities for communication, western learning,

37 As this is not a place to trace the constitutional history of the country, it is not attempted here. For details see R. Coupland, *The Indian Problem* 1833-1935 (Oxford, 1943) and also A. B. Keith, *A Constitutional History of India* 1600-1935 (London, 1936).

38 'Thus, in act as in word, the revolution was effected, the repudiation of parliamentary government was itself repudiated.' — R. Coupland, n. 37, 65.

administrative unity, etc. For the first time, historians assert, an alien civilisation impigned upon every detail of Indian life, changed its pattern and created new values. Thus India's wealth ceased to become treasures; money became capital, goods became commodities, land became a source of monopoly-rent, and the self-sufficiency of rural economy was transformed into the interdependence of urban and world economy. Similarly, the vision of the average Indian, so long closed like that of the frog in the well, was enlarged.... Western philosophy and science introduced reason into daily habits and made Indians realise the meaninglessness of many ancient customs and prejudices.[39]

## PROGRESSIVE CHARACTER OF SOCIAL REFORM MOVEMENT

When educated Indians began to re-examine their ancient civilisation and customs in the light of their modern education and of their knowledge of western science and philosophy they realised that they must at first concentrate on social and religious reforms. For this purpose they organised many social and religious reform movements. The most important among them were: the Brahmo Samaj, the Social Reforms Conference, the Arya Samaj, the Ramakrishna Mission and the Theosophical Society. The broad aims of these movements, which influenced primarily the Hindus, were as follows:

In the social sphere, there were movements of caste reform or caste abolition, equal rights for women, a campaign against child marriage, a crusade against social and legal inequalities. In the religious sphere, there sprang up movements which combated religious superstitions and attacked idolatry, poly-theism and hereditary priesthood. These movements, in vary-ing degrees, emphasised and fought for the principle of in-dividual liberty and social equality and stood for national-ism.[40]

There were similar movements for reform among the Mus-lims, the Sikhs and the Parsis which tackled the problems facing them and which also aimed at reorganising the society on democratic lines and on the basis of the ideas of the 'Ages of Reason, Enlightenment and Liberalism.'

39 D. P. Mukherji, *Diversities* (New Delhi, 1958) 164.
40 A. R. Desai, *Social Background of Indian Nationalism* (Bombay 1954) 210.

The all-India organisation which was exclusively concerned
with social reforms was the Social Reforms Conference which
came into being in 1887 and held many annual sessions since then.
The following demands made by the Conference on various
occasions were indicative of its attempt to promote individual
liberty and social equality and to modernise Indian society:

(1) the reduction of birth, marriage, death and other ex-
    penses according to means;
(2) the gradual raising of the marriageable age;
(3) the remarriage of child widows;
(4) the removal of social disabilities attending sea voyages
    to foreign countries;
(5) the prevention of the disfigurement of child widows
    prevailing in certain parts of India;
(6) Intermarriage between members of the subcastes;
(7) the discouragement of unequal marriages;
(8) the disapproval of the custom of exacting money in
    consideration of the gift of girls in marriage;
(9) the discouragement of polygamy;
(10) the appointment of panchayats to settle religious dis-
    putes between Hindus and Muslims and advising the
    panchayats to promote friendly feeling...;
(11) the promotion of higher female education;
(12) the education and amelioration of the pariahs and other
    outcastes;
(13) widow remarriage, protection of widows and the train-
    ing of widows in useful work;
(14) the abolition of castes;
(15) the recommendation of inter-caste marriage.[41]

Although the Social Conference was apparently a cosmopolitan
and secular organisation, its work was mostly confined to the
Hindus. The Muslim reform movement of the latter half of
the nineteenth century associated with Syed Ahmad Khan and
the Aligarh School stood more or less for the same progressive
reforms as those of the Hindus; but it is significant that even
the social reform movements of the Hindus and the Muslims
did not merge into one stream. One of the reasons
for their remaining separate from one another was that the

41 K. C. Vyas, *The Social Renaissance in India* (Bombay, 1957). These
are extracts from the summary given in the book on pages 152-4. Two
other books which deal with the work of the Social Conference: C. Y.
Chintamony, ed., *Indian Social Reforms* (Madras, 1901) and S. Natarajan.
*A Century of Social Reforms in India* (Bombay, 1959).

social customs of one community were different from those of
the other. Although such evils as low status of women, early
marriage and polygamy were widespread among the Muslims,
they did not suffer from many others like the caste system and untouchability. It was, therefore, necessary to attack the evil customs of the followers of one religion separately from those of the
followers of the other religion. Moreover, as many leaders of
modern India realised, it was also difficult to separate social
reforms from religious reforms and each step to reform a particular religion had to/be undertaken within that religion. That
was why social reforms were often related to religious reforms
in modern India and leaders like Raja Rammohan Roy, Dayanand Saraswathi and Syed Ahmad Khan and movements like the
Brahmo Samaj and Arya Samaj were concerned with both the
social and religious questions of the day. But the fact that social
reform among the Hindus and Muslims were undertaken separately had the unfortunate effect of creating separate organisations
and further strengthening their separatist tendencies. This is
particularly true of the effect of religious reform movements.

## SIGNIFICANCE OF THE RELIGIOUS MOVEMENTS

The Brahmo Samaj, founded by Raja Rammohan Roy in
1825, was the first important organisation which concerned itself
with religious reforms in modern India. It opposed hereditary
priesthood and the caste system. By publishing Bengali
translations of some of the source literature of the Hindus
and making them available to the public, Raja Rammohan
Roy exposed the myth that they were the secret preserve
of the priestly class. He made many innovations in the matter
of conducting an agitation. He did not appeal to mysticism or
revelation but to reason and by the process of argument tried
to demolish the dogmatic structure of religious tradition. The
priests and the orthodox people reacted to his writings with
their own publications and writings. Further controversy was
created when Rammohan Roy published another tract in reply.
All these were healthy and new developments in that they introduced the concept of discussion in public, through the means of
published writings in a field such as religion, where they were
absent in the immediate past. The idea of forming associations,

such as Brahmo Samaj, for the purpose of religious reform was also something new. All these developments in social and religious fields were conducive to the growth of political movements later.

The Prarthana Samaj established in 1867 in Bombay was often referred to as the Brahmo Samaj of Bombay, because it stood for similar, if not identical, reforms.

There were other religious movements, which were very different in nature because they were revivalist in form, if not in content. The Arya Samaj, which was founded in Bombay in 1875, and reorganised in Lahore later was an example. Its founder was Swami Dayanand Saraswathi (1824-83). Another was the Ramakrishna Mission, the religious organisation connected with Ramakrishna (1834-86) and his disciple Swami Vivekananda (1863-1902). Although these two movements made great concessions to Hindu traditions they also took many steps which were conducive to the reform and reconstruction of Indian society on new lines. For instance the Arya Samaj fought against the caste system, as it was practised, questioned the superiority of hereditary priests and tried to raise the status of women. The Ramakrishna Mission preached the unity of all religions and its followers gave no blind allegiance to any scriptures. The tolerance towards other religions and the spirit of enquiry were spread by the followers of the Ramakrishna Mission.

While these intellectual and reform movements were shaking Hindu society to its foundations, Indian followers of Islam were also having similar experience. Syed Ahmad Khan (1877-98) was the outstanding Muslim leader of the nineteenth century who took a strong stand in favour of Indian Muslims accepting western culture and reconstructing their social and religious life in accordance with it. Another was Syed Ameer Ali (1849-1928) who maintained that Islam was commensurate with modern ideas and that its teaching released the very spirit which promoted these ideas. The Ahmediya movement, organised by Mirza Ghulam Azad, was of a different category because it was apparently a movement of protest against Christianity. But it also stood for some reforms directed against many superstitions and corruptions.

REVIVALIST CHARACTER OF THE REFORM MOVEMENTS

We have so far discussed the influence of the idea of nationalism and enlightenment on the social and religious movements.
Another aspect of these movements is often referred to as 'revivalism'. It cannot be rigidly maintained that, as far as the
social and religious movements were concerned, all the 'modernist' elements appeared first and the 'revivalist' elements did so
later; nor can it be said that a particular movement is exclusively
revivalist' and another is exclusively 'modernist'. At best what
one can say is that the revivalist attitude played a great part in
the thinking of the leaders of some religious movements and
the organisations they founded.

The Arya Samaj was one such movement. It insisted on the
infallibility of the Vedas, on *karma* and rebirth, the sanctity of
the cow, the efficiency of the *homa* and the importance of *sans-
karas*. Both as an intellectual movement and as a religious
organisation it embodied a revivalist and purely Hindu movement, as opposed to the thoroughly rational and cosmopolitan
character of the Brahmo Samaj. Such a movement naturally
antagonised the non-Hindu in general and the Muslims in particular, especially when it started to reconvert those Hindus, who
had embraced other religions, back to Hinduism.

The Theosophical Society, started in New York in 1875, was
another religious movement which was often associated with
Hindu revivalism. Its headquarters was later transferred to
Madras. Although its supporters claimed that theosophy was
the body of truths which formed the basis of all religions, it
gradually became identified with Hinduism and Buddhism. Like
the Arya Samaj, the Theosophical Society contributed to the
growth of Indian nationalism by raising the pride of educated
Indians in India's past and religious heritage.

The Ramakrishna Mission also performed a similar function.
Swami Vivekananda repeatedly said that the traditions of the
country should be taken into account while making attempts to
reform the society. He proudly asserted: 'If there is any land
on this earth that can lay claims to be the blessed *Punya Bhumi*,
to be the land to which all souls on this earth must come to
account for *karma*, the land to which every soul that is wending

its way Godward must come to attain its last home... it is
India.'42

There were parallel movements among the Indian Muslims.
Ameer Ali's book *Spirit of Islam,* published in 1891, was symbolic
of the revivalist trend among the Indian Muslims. These Muslim
revivalists, like their Hindu counterparts among the Arya
Samajists, viewed other religious systems with contempt. They
also defended certain orthodox customs, such as the practice of
*purdah* among Muslim women.

The main differences between the two approaches—one 'reformist' and the other 'revivalist'—was in the authority or
authorities from which the two types of leaders received their
inspiration. 'The former are bent on relying more upon reason
and the experience of European society, while the latter are
disposed to primarily look at their *shastras* and the past history,
and the traditions of their people and the ancient institutions
of the land which were in vogue when the nation was in the
zenith of its glory.'43

On an ideological plane the functions fulfilled by these revivalist movements in the political field was to give self-confidence to the rising national sentiment and to strengthen the
political awakening in the country. They also set in motion
some form of counter-reformation by making many exaggerated
claims for Indian and Islamic traditions and by trying to
belittle western science and civilisation. In a country like India,
where the population was chiefly divided into Hindus and
Muslims, revivalism had many political repercussions. While
Hindus went back to their religious and historical past to regain
their self-confidence the Muslims went back to early Islam and
the past history of Arabia; this led not only to a conflict between
the Indians and westerners whose cultural and religious 'inva-
son' they wanted to resist, but also to the schism between the
Hindus and the Muslims each of whom relied on then separate
sources of spiritual and intellectual power.

To sum up the political impact of the revivalist movements:
they gave self-confidence to the Indian national movement, but

42 Swami Vivekananda, *The Complete Works of Swami Vivekananda,*
III, 105.
43 Lajpat Rai, *The Man in his Word* (Madras, 1907) 128.

bred, in the process religious obscurantism and narrow sectarianism.

## COMPARISON BETWEEN RELIGIOUS MOVEMENTS AND POLITICAL TRENDS

When we turn from the social and religious movements to the political ones we see some parallels between them. There was the early phase of the Indian National Congress, led by the 'Liberals' and the 'Moderates'—as they were variously described—who owed allegiance to western political ideas, comparable to the Brahmo Samaj which wanted the reconstruction of Indian society on modern and western lines. This was followed by the extremist' political agitation by the beginning of the 20th century, which apparently stood for the rejection of western ideas and embodied within itself a certain degree of Hindu revivalism; this had its counterpart in religious movements like the Arya Samaj, which shared these characteristics. There was another similarity between the social and religious movements and the political movements. The early phase of the Indian National Congress—the first major political organisation of the country—like the first wave of social and religious movements of modern India, was an advance in the realm of ideas; but it could not influence a large number of people because of its narrow social base. The 'extremist' political leaders, who challenged the supremacy of the early leaders, were, in many respects, comparable to the leaders of the revivalist religious movements like the Arya Samaj; both of them, with the support they received from a large number of people, became very effective in fulfilling their limited tasks of social reconstruction and political regeneration.

This was an important feature of the social and political conditions of India at the beginning of the twentieth century; to be very effective as a reform movement or as a political agitation, its leaders had to take into account the traditions and even the prejudices of the people and make concessions to them. This meant turning back from some of the highly advanced views of the times. It also resulted in working within the framework of organisations with a direct appeal to members of one faith; this, in turn, strengthened separatist tendencies and organisations and created hostility between the two major communities.

# CHAPTER II

# LIBERALISM—FOR PROGRESS AND MODERATION

IN the last chapter we noted that liberalism was the most popular doctrine in Great Britain when her power expanded in India. Early leaders of the Indian national movement were naturally influenced by it and they tried to propagate liberal concepts among the people. As the acceptance of liberalism implied an attack on many Indian social institutions and customs which militated against social equality and stifled individual liberty this function of popularising liberal concepts was a progressive step in India in the nineteenth century and at the beginning of the twentieth. In the political field also the early leaders of the Indian national movement opened a new and useful chapter by acting in the spirit of liberal traditions and demanding civil rights and representative institutions. Their advocacy of economic nationalism, though not in line with orthodox liberalism, was in the interests of the new social classes which were coming into prominence.

Another aspect of liberalism was a moderate approach towards conducting political agitation. The efficacy of this approach was questioned by many Indian leaders, who emerged as a powerful political force at the beginning of the twentieth century. Since then, the earlier leaders and their followers were often referred to as the 'Moderates' and those, who challenged their leadership, as the 'Extremists.'

The Moderate leaders themselves thought that their philosophy was the combination of liberalism and moderation. One of them, Gopal Krishna Gokhale, quoted with approval the following exposition of Moderate creed by his master, M. G. Ranade:

Liberalism and moderation will be the watchwords of our association. The spirit of liberalism implies a freedom from race and creed prejudices and a steady devotion to all that seeks to do justice between man and man, giving to the rulers the loyalty due to the law that they are bound to administer, but securing at the same time to the people the equality which is their right under the law. Moderation implies the conditions of never vainly aspiring after the impossible or after too re-mote ideals, but striving each day to take the next step in the order of natural growth that lies nearest to our hands in a spirit of compromise and fairness.[1]

From 1885, the year of its inception, up to 1905 the Indian National Congress was dominated by leaders who subscribed to these ideas. From 1905 onwards their leadership was challeng-ed by the Extremists. In 1907 a split took place in the Congress and the Extremists broke away from it and carried on their political activities outside the organisation. In 1916 there was a reunion of the two groups and the Extremists again entered the Congress. By that time, however, the leadership of the Moderates was challenged from a new quarter, the political forces led by Gandhi, who had begun to emerge as an all-India figure. As Gandhi and his followers eclipsed almost all other political leaders, the influence of the Moderates began to decline and they broke away from the Congress and formed their own party. Although the leaders of this new party occasionally made important contributions to many of the political debates and negotiations which took place later, the Moderates ceased to be a major political force after 1918. But they did play a prominent part in the Indian political scene between 1905-18.

The history of the Indian National Congress is well known, but not that of the regional political associations which preced-ed it. In 1837 the Bengal Zamindari Association (later known as the Bengal Landholders' Society) was founded. Its primary aim was to resist encroachments on the rights of landlords. But it claimed 'to be based on liberal principles. In 1843 the Bengal British India Society was formed with the avowed object of helping the gradual advancement of the public welfare by peace-ful means. These two societies were amalgamated into one body, the British India Association, which was formed in 1851. Its

---

1 T. V. Parvate, *Gopal Krishna Gokhale* (Ahmedabad, 1959) 463.

members belonged to the landed aristocracy and their primary demands were the relaxation of the pressure of the revenue system, relief from monopolies, protection of the life and property of the people from . molestation and improvement of judicial administration. In 1876 another organisation, the Indian Association, was founded and in it the representatives of the middle classes found some place. While these organisations were taking shape in Calcutta, similar bodies made their appearance in Bombay. The 'Bombay Association' was established in 1852 and it asked for an enlightened system of government.

The eighteen-seventies witnessed the next stage in the political awakening of India: the discussions on the creation of a national organisation. The Sarvajanik Sabha of Poona appealed to all those who were invited to the Delhi Durbar of 1871 to utilise the opportunity to discuss national problems. The All-India Editors Conference held at Calcutta in 1878 also reflected the spirit of nationalism. By 1878 many Indian leaders were talking about national organisations and national problems. One of the most prominent among these was Surendranath Banerjea who later wrote about these developments:

> I took up the movement for the creation of a National Fund. A general meeting was held on 17 July 1883, attended by over ten thousand people, at which it was resolved to raise a national fund to secure the political advancement of the country by means of constitutional agitation in India and in England.... The moral transformation which was to usher in the Congress movement had thus already its birth in the bosom of the Indian National Conference which met in Calcutta, and to which representatives from all parts of India were invited.[2]

In the same period conferences were held in Madras, Calcutta and Bombay to discuss the question of establishing an all-India organisation. The conference held at Madras was convened by the Theosophical Society and it had, in the opinion of Surendranath Banerjea, a socio-religious character, while the Bombay conference was a 'socio-political' one. The Calcutta conference was purely political.

In 1885 was formed the Indian National Congress which has dominated the Indian political scene all through the twentieth

2. Surendranath Banerjea, *A Nation in Making* (London, 1925) 85.

century. As we have seen, the necessary background for the formation of such a body was created by the introduction of western political, educational and administrative institutions in the country. The work of the regional political organisations also favoured the establishment of an all-India body. The initiative for forming such a Congress came from A. O. Hume, a Scotsman who was sympathetic to the aspirations of educated Indians. Lord Dufferin, who was the Viceroy, welcomed the decision to form the Congress and encouraged it to discuss political matters.

The most prominent among the early leaders of the Congress were Dadabhai Naoroji (1825-1917), Surendranath Banerjea (1848-1926) and Gopal Krishna Gokhale (1866-1915). Few others like Pherozeshah Mehta and Rash Behari Ghose also distinguished themselves by their 'Moderate' politics and their opposition to the political campaigns of the 'Extremists'.

## INDIAN UNITY: THE FIRST CONCERN

One of the most important prerequisites for the growth and development of a national movement in a country like India was the acceptance of the concept of Indian unity by people who belonged to different parts of the country. Naturally early leaders were concerned with spreading this concept. As early as in 1876, Surendranath Banerjea focussed the attention of his countrymen to the life of Mazzini, the architect of Italian unity. He said:

I feel that Mazzini's is a life which my countrymen ought to be in possession of, for that life is full of lessons of the deepest importance to all. The Italians were degraded, downtrodden and oppressed. Under the influence of Mazzini's teachings, they achieved their unity and their nationality, and now they are on the highroad to the climax of national greatness.[3]

Banerjea added:

Gentlemen, Mazzini lived and died for Italian unity. He rightly judged that Italy would never be great, unless the different Italian peoples were united together by the bonds of a common nationality and common institutions. Might we

3 R. C. Palit, ed., *Surendranath Banerjea's Speeches* (Calcutta, 1880) 2-3.

not see in this much to guide and to instruct us? Is India's
greatness possible unless we are thoroughly welded together
into a compact mass?....And then the whole of India comes
to be bound in this treble chain of love, sympathy and esteem,
the day of Indian greatness would not be distant.[4]

Other leaders, particularly Dadabhai Naoroji, emphasised the
importance of bridging the gulf which existed between the followers of different faiths and welding India into a nation. As the
result of the propaganda carried on by them the educated
Indians did develop a vague sense of national unity. It is significant that Gokhale could claim in 1905:

> The minds of the people have been familiarised with the idea
> of a united India working for her salvation; a national public
> opinion has been created; close bonds of sympathy now knit
> together the different provinces; caste and creed separations
> hamper less and less the pursuit of common aims; the dignity
> of a consciousness of national existence has spread over the
> whole land.[5]

## DEMAND FOR A MODERN STATE, SOCIETY AND ECONOMY

Another important contribution of the early leaders of the
Congress was their propagation of the ideas of enlightenment
and scientific approach toward life. Many of the Indian social
institutions of the pre-British period were collectivist and subordinated the interests of the individual to those of the caste, the
family and the village panchayat. The Moderates, who accepted
the ideas of European enlightenment and Liberalism, attacked
privileges conferred upon the few as unjust and proclaimed the
principles of individual liberty and social equality. Unlike the
Extremists and Gandhi they never defended any of the social
institutions of the Hindus connected with caste system or maintained that the reforms in regard to them could only be taken up
after the political objectives were attained. Gandhi, of course, was
a social reformer in his own way.[6] But, unlike Gandhi, the
Moderates based their case for the reconstruction of Hindu
society not on any idyllic past as the 'Ramrajya' but on modern
theories of state and society which they imbibed from the writi-

4 *Ibid.*, 21.
5 Gopal Krishna Gokhale, *Speeches* (Madras, 1920) 697.
6 Details of the views of the Extremists and Gandhi are discussed in
subsequent chapters.

CC 3

ings of western scholars and philosophers. In their speeches and writings one finds innumerable quotations from western writers.

Far from reviving the past, the Moderates were interested in anticipating the future. Advocating the adoption of the Civil Marriage Bill, Gokhale said on 26 February 1912:

> It is quite true, as we have seen from opinions expressed both in this Council and outside, that the Bill represents ideas which are in advance of the views of the bulk of the Hindu and Muhammadan communities today; but I am quite sure that with the spread of higher education among Indian women, with late marriages coming more and more into vogue —and late marriages must lead to choice marriages, i.e., to free choice by the marrying parties— with these things coming, with the dignity of individual freedom realised better and better, and last, but not least, with the steady fusion of different creeds and different races, which is bound to take place under the stress of our growing nationality.... I say, under all these influence, the day cannot be far distant when the measure like the one before us will find its way to statute-book.[7]

It was significant that Gokhale not only welcomed such social reforms as civil marriages, but emphasised the role of the state in introducing them.

Gokhale connected the question of raising the moral and social conditions of the low-caste Hindus to national self-interest.

> How can we possibly realise our national aspirations, how can our country ever hope to take her place among the nations of the world, if we allow large number of our countrymen to remain sunk in ignorance, barbarism, and degradation? Unless these men are gradually raised to a higher level, morally and intellectually, how can they possibly understand our thoughts or share our hopes or cooperate with us in our efforts? Can you not realise that so far as the work of national elevation is concerned, the energy, which these classes might be expected to represent is simply unavailable to us?[8]

Presiding at the annual session of the Indian National Congress in 1897 C. Sankaran Nair summed up the views of the Moderates on these questions as follows:

> We want in brief to eliminate, if necessary, from our system all that stands in the way of progress. We desire to absorb and

7 Gokhale, n. 5, 471-2.
8 Ibid., 901.

assimilate into our own what appears good to us in western civilisation. This is impossible under a government which would uphold a particular social system or a particular form of religion to the exclusion of others as some of the ancient governments of India did. To break down the isolation of the Hindu religion, to remove the barriers which now prevent free social intercourse and unity of action, to extend the blessings of education to the lower classes, to improve the position of women to one of equality to men, we require the continuance of a strictly secular government in thorough sympathy with liberal thought and progress.[9]

In regard to the economic questions of the day the scientific approach of the Moderates was even more apparent. Criticising those aspects of Gandhi's programme which stressed cottage industries to the detriment of large-scale industries, Surendranath Banerjea wrote:

An industrial movement linked with a political controversy may receive a monetary impulse which may send it far forward, but in the long run it suffers by such association. An industry must be conducted on business lines; and business considerations must, in the long run, guide and dominate its course and progress. Capital, organisation and expert knowledge—these constitute the basic foundations of an industrial enterprise. A patriotic impulse will certainly help it; but only for a time, and will cease to be operative when normal conditions are restored.[10]

The Moderates envisaged the Swadeshi movement not as a part of a many-sided movement aimed at the boycott of all western goods and institutions but one which would modernise or westernise the economic life of the country. Explaining this view Rash Behari Ghose said: 'The Swadeshi movement is only a prelude to our determination to enter into the great brotherhood of the trading nations of the West, without, if possible, the eternal struggle between capital and labour, into which Japan has already been admitted.'[11]

9 *Indian National Congress containing an account of its origin and growth, full text of all the Presidential Addresses, a Reprint of all the Congress Resolutions, extracts from all the welcome addresses, notable utterances on the movement* (Madras, 1917) Pt. 1, 367.

10 Banerjea, n. 2, 200.

11 *The Honourable Dr. Rash Behari Ghosh: His Life-sketch and Speeches* (Madras, n.d.) 24.

Dadabhai Naoroji was another champion of the view that India should enter the international community of commercial and industrial nations as a full-fledged member.

It was Dadabhai's conviction that Indians should study the business methods of the British. Interested in the cotton trade, he became a member of the Manchester Cotton Supply Association; and while himself benefitting from the available opportunities to study the organisation of the cotton trade in that district, he also read before the members of the Association instructive papers on the supply of the Indian Cotton. Likewise, he repeatedly impressed the Bombay millowners and cotton merchants that they could not successfully compete with Lancashire in the London or Liverpool market, or in the Bombay market, until they had carefully studied the methods and devices of the Lancashire merchants and manufacturers to secure India's raw material at the lowest price and to sell manufactured articles to the best advantage.[12]

With a society and economy reconstructed on the basis of the ideas of enlightenment and liberalism prevalent in the West in the eighteenth and nineteenth centuries, the Moderates hoped that India would be capable of gradually occupying a position of equality with other nations of the world.

## THE CONCEPT OF RACIAL EQUALITY

When the Indian leaders realised that some foreigners were not prepared to accept Indians as their equals, they vigorously protested. They not only propagated that the concept of equality among the different sections of the people of India but maintaind that Indians are equal to any other group of people. In February 1866, John Crawford, the President of the Ethnological Society of London, produced a paper which sought to establish the intellectual and moral superiority of European races over Asiatics. His view, based on a superficial study of races according to the divergencies of their colour, facial angles and other features, was shared by many Europeans at that time. After making some study of the subject Dadabhai Naoroji read a rejoinder to it in the next month.

12 R. P. Masani, *Dadabhai Naoroji: The Grand Old Man of India* (London, 1939) 80-1.

Many of the Moderate leaders were distressed at the reports that many Indians who were sent as labourers to work in other countries were leading a miserable life. On 4 March 1912 Gokhale moved a resolution in the Imperial Legislative Council recommending the prohibition of the recruitment of Indian indentured labour and said:

It is true that the system is not actual slavery, but it is also true that it is not far from it. The contract is not a free contract. You have here the right of private arrest, just as they had in the case of slavery. Moreover, the labourer is bound to his employer for five years and he cannot withdraw from the contract during that period. And there are those harsh punishments for trivial faults. Therefore, though the system cannot be called actual slavery, it is really not far removed from it.[13]

As these statements indicate, the early leaders of the Indian national movement were trying to do two things simultaneously; on the one hand, they wanted their Indian followers to take the steps necessary to modernise their society and economy and on the other they wanted the rest of the world to acknowledge Indians as equals to any group of people. They also realised that the success of the first would facilitate their second task.

## THE SPECIFIC POLITICAL DEMANDS

The specific political demands which the early leaders of the Congress placed before the government and their attempt to educate the Indian public on the basis of these demands were in line with their general approach. Broadly speaking, these demands were the extension of civil and political rights of the people, increasing the number of Indians in the administrative services, the strengthening of parliamentary democracy by the expansion of legislative councils and the protection of Indian industries by tariff walls. In his presidential address to the annual session of the Indian National Congress held in 1905 Gokhale, who was one of their most outstanding leaders, grouped the main reforms advocated by them as follows:

(1) Those which aim at securing for our people a larger and larger share in the administration and control of our affairs; these include a reform of our legislative councils,

13 Gokhale, n. 5, 541.

the appointment of Indians to the Secretary of State's
Council and the Executive Council in India, and a steady
substitution of the Indian for the European agency in the
public service of the country;

(2) those which seek to improve the methods of administration, such as the separation of judicial from executive
functions, police reform, and so forth;

(3) those which propose a readjustment of financial arrangements with the object of securing a reduction of the
burdens of the taxpayers and a more efficient application
of our resources; under this head come a reduction of
military charges; the moderating of land-assessments and
so forth; and

(4) those which urge the adoption of measures calculated to
improve the condition of the mass of the people; these
include a vigorous extension of primary education, facilities of industrial and technical instruction, grants for
improved sanitation, and a real attempt to deal with the
alarming indebtedness of the peasantry.[14]

INDIANISATION OF THE SERVICES

Among these many subjects, one which interested the early
Congress leaders most was the Indianisation of the services. On
this question one of their resolutions, adopted in the annual
session of the Congress in 1905, stated:

That this Congress is of opinion that the true remedy for
many existing financial and administrative evils lies in the
wider employment of Indians in the higher branches of the
country's service; and while concurring with previous Con-
gresses in urging that immediate effect should be given to the
Resolutions of the House of Commons of 2nd June, 1893, in
favour of holding the competitive examinations for the Civil
Services simultaneously in England and in India, this Congress places on record its firm conviction that the only satisfactory solution of this question is to be found in the
reorganisation of the Indian Civil Service, which should be
reconstituted on a decentralised basis, its judicial functions
in the meantime being partly transferred to persons who have
been trained in the profession of law.[15]

14 Indian National Congress, n. 9, 821.
15 Ibid., Pt. II, 115-6.

## EXPANSION OF LEGISLATIVE COUNCILS

Expansion of legislative councils was another important issue which came up again and again before the Indian National Congress. In 1905 the annual session of the Congress adopted the resolution:

That in the opinion of this Congress the time has arrived for a further expansion and reform of the supreme and provincial legislative councils, so that they may become more truly representative of the people, and the non-official members thereof may have a real voice in the government of the country. The Congress recommends an increase in the number of the non-official and elected members and the grant to them of the right of dividing the councils in finanical matters coming before them—the head of the government concerned possessing the power of veto.[16]

This resolution shows the cautious attitude of its framers and the limited nature of the demands of the Moderate leaders in 1905.

By 1916 the Indian leaders began to speak about the new spirit that has arisen in the country. Ambica Charan Mazumdar, the President of the Congress during that year, said:

John Stuart Mill in his book on Representative Government lays down three conditions for self-government which are now universally accepted by all writers on political philosophy. These conditions are: first, that the people for whom the form of government is intended should be willing to accept it; second, that they must be willing and able to do what is necessary to keep it standing; and third, that they must be willing and able to do what it requires of them to enable it to fulfil its purposes. To these three tests I will add a fourth, by way of a rider directly to meet the argument of our critics,—have the people given satisfactory evidence of their capacity for self-government.[17]

Mazumdar maintained that the people of India fulfilled all these conditions and deserved the right to govern themselves. Many of the constitutional reforms suggested by the Indian leaders in this period were based on this view. The annual session of the Congress held in 1916 declared:

16 *Ibid.*, 114.
17 *Ibid.*, Pt. I, 1262.

(a) That having regard to the fact that the great communities of India are the inheritors of ancient civilisations
and have shown great capacity for government and administration and to the progress in education and public
spirit made by them during a century of British rule, and
further having regard to the fact that the present system
of government does not satisfy the legitimate aspirations
of the people and has become unsuited to the existing
conditions and requirements, this Congress is of opinion
that the time has come when His Majesty the King-
Emperor should be pleased to issue a proclamation an-
nouncing that it is the aim and intention of British policy
to confer self-government on India at an early date.

(b) That this Congress demands that a definite step should
be taken towards self-government by granting the reform
contained in the scheme prepaied by the All-India
Congress Committee in concert with the Reform Committee appointed by the All-India Muslim League.[18]

In a scheme of reforms jointly advocated by the All-India
Muslim League and the Indian National Congress in 1916 the
need for giving a larger representation to the elected members
in the legislative councils was emphasised. Some of its provisions
were: ' (1) Provincial legislative councils shall consist of four-
fifths elected and of one-fifth nominated members. (2) Their
strength shall be not less than 125 members in the major provinces, and from 50 to 75 in the minor provinces. (3) The
members of councils should be elected directly by the people
on as broad a franchise as possible.'[19] Referring to the powers
of the Legislative Council the proposed scheme suggested:

That the Provincial Council should have full authority to
deal with all matters affecting the internal administration of
the province including the powers to raise loans, to impose
and alter taxation, and to vote on the budget. All items of
expenditure, and all proposals concerning ways and means
for raising the necessary revenue, should be embodied in
Bills and submitted to the Provincial Council for adoption.[20]

Provisions in the scheme concerning the Imperial Legislative
Council were also based on the same liberal and democratic

18  Ibid., Pt. II, 180-1.
19  Ibid., App. B. xvii.
20  Ibid., xviii.

principles. One of the limitations on the Imperial Legislative
Council by the sponsors of the scheme was: 'The Imperial Legislative Council shall have no power to interfere with the Government of India's direction of the military affairs and the foreign
and political relations of India, including the declaration of war,
the making of peace and the entering into treaties.'[21]   On all
internal matters the scheme, as well as the speeches of their
sponsors emphasised the powers of the elected representatives of
the people. The purpose of all their demands concerning constitutional reforms was to train people in parliamentary democracy.
Even when they thought that the political situation in the
country was not ripe for the representatives of the people to
take over power in some spheres they insisted that they must
have the right of asking questions on them to the Executive and
the right of discussing them and giving expression to their views.

## CIVIL LIBERTY

Freedom of the press was another important item of the
liberal programme of the Congress. Even in the nineteenth
century many Indian leaders resisted the government's attempts
to curtail the freedom of the press. Rammohan Roy tried to
arouse his countrymen to a sense of seriousness of the government's measures to regulate and control the press.[22] In 1879 a
large public meeting was held in Calcutta to protest against
the Vernacular Press Act.[23] While commenting on the Press Bill
in the Imperial Legislative Council, Gokhale said on 8 February
1910:

> Force may afford temporary relief, but it never can prove a
> permanent remedy to such a state of things as we have in
> this county. It is only in the cooperation of all classes and
> the steady pursuit of a policy of wise conciliation on the part
> of government that the best hopes of thoughtful men on both
> sides for the future of this land must lie.[24]

Earlier, while opposing the Indian Official Secrets Act of 1899

21  *Ibid.*, xx.
22  Kalidas Nag, and Debajyoti Burman, ed., *The English Works of
Raja Ram Mohan Roy* (Calcutta, 1947) Pt. IV, 1-8.
23  Banerjea, n. 2, 62.
24  Gokhale, n. 5, 341

Gokhale expressed the strong views held by him and by his colleagues on the question of the freedom of the press:

> The vigilance of the press is the only check that operates from outside, feebly, it is true, but continuously, upon the conduct of the government, which is subject to no popular control....The press is, in one sense, like the government, a custodian of public interests, and any attempt to hamper its freedom by repressive legislation is bound to affect these interests prejudicially, and cannot fail in the end to react upon the position of the government itself....I recognise that the responsibility for the good administration of the country rests primarily on the shoulders of the government. But it is difficult to allow that this responsibility can be satisfactorily discharged, unless the government was supported in its legislative and executive measures by some sort of public opinion.[25]

In 1916 the Indian National Congress adopted the following resolution:

> This Congress places on record its strong conviction that the Press Act of 1910 has proved a menace to the liberty of the Indian Press and has hampered the legitimate expression of healthy public opinion which is so essential to good administration, and in view of the wide and arbitrary powers conferred by the Act upon the executive this Congress strongly urges the government to repeal it.[26]

The Seditious Meetings Bill introduced by the government in the Imperial Legislative Council was another step which resulted in the curtailment of civil liberties. Opposing it in the Council, Gokhale said: 'The Act admittedly confers dangerously wide powers on the Executive, which, if used at all, are almost certain to be abused, and which must in pratice paralyse all activity in the country.'[27]

EXTENSION OF THE RULE OF LAW

A series of other demands by the Indian National Congress and its leaders referred to the extension of rule of law in the country. The issues involved were: (1) reorganisation of the judicial system with special emphasis on the separation of the

25  *Ibid.*, 222-3.
26  Indian National Congress, n. 9, Pt. II, 179.
27  Gokhale, n. 5, 313.

judiciary from the executive and (2) the repeal of the laws of preventive detention.

The demand for the separation of the judiciary from the executive was a constant theme of the speeches of many Indian leaders and many Congress resolutions in the last decade of the nineteenth century. In 1902 P. C. Ray edited a fairly comprehensive book on this subject.[28] It was a compilation of authoritative opinion and statements of both sides of the question with notes of some of the most flagrant cases illustrative of the evils and dangers of the union of the functions and resolutions of Indian National Congress on the subject. The following resolution passed at the annual session of the Congress in 1893 was typical of the many resolutions adopted by that organisation under the leadership of the Moderates.

> That this Congress having now for many successive years vainly appealed to the Government of India to remove one of the gravest stigmas on British rule in India, one fraught with incalculable oppression to all classes of the community throughout the country, now hopeless of any other redress, humbly entreats the Secretary of State for India to order the immediate appointment, in each province, of a committee (one half at least, of whose members shall be non-official natives of India qualified by education and experience in the working of various courts to deal with the question) to prepare such a scheme for the complete separation of all judicial and executive functions in their own provinces with as little additional cost to the state as may be practicable and the submission of such schemes, with the comments of several Indian governments thereon to himself, at some early date which he may be pleased to fix.[29]

Another Congress demand was, that the judicial service, in all parts of the country, should be recruited from the legal profession more largely than at present, as the system of appointing civilians without special legal training to high judicial offices does not lead to satisfactory administration of justice in the mofussil.'[30]

These two demands of the Moderates—the separation of the

28 P. C. Ray, ed., *The Separation of Judicial and Executive Functions in British India* (Calcutta, 1902).
29 *Ibid.*, 352.
30 Indian National Congress, n. 9, Pt. II, 117-8.

judiciary from the executive and the recruitment of the judges from the legal profession—were connected with the fundamental questions of human liberty and the rule of the law. When the executive and the judicial functions were unified in one person, those who were connected with the prosecutor, if not the prosecutors themselves, often became the judges also. The result was that justice was often denied to the accused. Appointment of civil servants, who had no legal training, to the Bench also had the same result. The Moderate leaders, a good number of whom were lawyers, exposed the evils of the system in many of their public utterances.

Another one of the constant demands of the Congress in this period was that high courts should be established in such provinces as the Punjab, where they did not exist, and that the system of the trial by jury should be extended to many fields and that in all trials by jury Indians should have the right to claim that not less than half the judges should be Indians.

As the aim of all these demands was to ensure the rule of law in India, many of the speeches and books on these subjects tried to show how such practices as the combination of the judiciary and the executive hindered the working of the due processes of law.

## LIBERTY—THE FUNDAMENTAL PRINCIPLE

All these demands of the leaders and the organisations such as the Congress and the Muslim League and their objections to the arbitrary acts and legislation were based on liberal and democratic ideas to which they owed their allegiance. They had no faith in benevolent despotism. Commenting on the attitude of Lord Curzon, Gokhale said: 'Lord Curzon's highest ideal of statesmanship is efficiency of administration. He does not believe in what Mr Gladstone used to call the principle of liberty as a factor of human progress. He has no sympathy with popular aspirations....'[31] There was no doubt that Gokhale and his colleagues shared Gladstone's views and not those of Lord Curzon. In many of their speeches and writings they repeatedly quoted from the writings and speeches of British statesmen and philosophers who owed their allegiance to liberalism.

31 Gokhale, n. 5, 682.

## POLITICAL IMPLICATIONS OF THE ECONOMIC DEMANDS

In this study we are not concerned with the details of the economic demands of the Moderates and their economic philosophy as such, but only with their political significance. One important feature of their economic philosophy, as distinguished from their political philosophy, is that while in regard to the latter they seemed to have accepted the ideas embodied in the concept of liberalism in the West, in regard to the former they took into consideration the unique features of the Indian economic situation and, while consciously applying the western concepts in the economic field, they made the necessary alterations to them. In other words, they were, relatively speaking, more original in this field.

The chief economic spokesmen of the Moderates were Dadabhai Naoroji (1825-1917), Mahadev Govind Ranade (1842-1901), Gopal Krishna Gokhale (1866-1915) and Romesh Chandra Dutt (1848-1904).[32] As Ranade and Dutt belonged to a period not covered in the study, we shall concentrate here primarily on the views of Dadabhai Naoroji and Gokhale. Others like Surendranath Banerjea and G. Subramanya Aiyar also expressed themselves on economic questions and some of their views are worth noting.

The main issues with which the Moderate leaders of the Congress were concerned with were: (1) industrialisation of the country; (2) the role of state in economic dvelopment; (3) creation of tariff walls for the protection of Indian industries and (4) the principles on which taxation and financial administration should be based.

The interest of the Congress party in the industrialisation of the country was revealed by the following report of the work of one of its committees in 1902:

The delegates to the last Congress has been asked by the Committee of the Industrial Exhibition under the auspices of the last Congress, to furnish answers to the following questions: (1) What are the articles maufactured in your district? Have they been declining or making steady progress? (2) How many handlooms are to be found in your

32 A fairly comprehensive study of their views is undertaken by P. K. Gopalakrishnan in *Development of Economic Ideas in India* (New Delhi, 1959).

district? (3) What kind of cloths are turned out by them? From where are the threads in use procured? If it is coloured in the district, is dye used of indigenous manufacturers? (4) State the chief difficulties that confront the manufacture and sale of useful articles in your districts? Are such articles manufactured locally? (5) What do you think are the best feasible means by which indigenous arts and manufactures can successfully compete with foreign arts and manufactures?[33]

Industrial exhibitions very soon became a regular feature of the programme of the annual sessions of the Indian National Congress. As G. Subramania Aiyer, one of the prominent Congress leaders observed in 1905:

In the initial years of the Congress, there was no intention of taking up the work of an industrial propaganda, but now the industrial exhibitions and the Swadeshi movement are based on the Congress and derive their sustaining force from the feeling of national unity which the Congress has created.[34]

Even in the nineteenth century, Mahadev Govind Ranade had demanded that the state should guide the economic development of the country and protect the indigenous industries from foreign competition. Later these demands were taken up by other leaders.

Another important aspect of the economic thinking of the Moderates was that they, unlike the Liberals of England, stood for the protection of Indian industries. Addressing the Congress session of 1902 Surendranath Banerjea said:

If we have a potential voice in the government of our country, there would be no question as to what policy we should follow. We would unhesitatingly adopt a policy of protection. That was indeed the policy of England before her industries attained their maturity....If the country is to be saved, we must leave the beaten track of the services and the professions, and be the pioneers and organisers of a vast industrial movement, which will secure to us the possession of that wealth which nature has ordained for us, and which so secured, will lead to the final and satisfactory solution of the industrial problems.[35]

33 'Congress and Industrial Development,' *Modern Review* (March 1902) 158.
34 G. Subramania Aiyer, 'The Indian National Congress,' *Indian Review* (December 1905) 830.
35 *Indian Review* (February 1903) 117.

Dadabhai Naoroji also stood for giving protection to Indian industries. At the same time he found it necessary to reconcile it with his loyalty to the concepts of liberalism such as free trade. On one occasion he said:

I take this opportunity of saying a few words about the recent telegram that Lord Salisbury had instructed the Indian government to abolish the duties on cottons.... The real object, says today's *Times of India*, is to 'nip in the bud' the rising factories in India—the ostensible reason assigned is free trade.... I like free trade, but.... free trade between England and India in a matter like this is something like a race between a starving, exhausting invalid and a strong man with a horse to ride on.... Young colonies, says Mill, may need protection. India needs it in a far larger degree, independent of the needs of revenue, which alone have compelled the retention of the present duties.[36]

Other economic matters with which the Moderates were concerned, were the principles of taxation connected with fiscal autonomy, 'no taxation without representation,' and proper distribution of the incidence of taxation.

In a speech delivered on 27 March 1879 Surendranath Banerjea opposed the abolition of duties or customs on the ground that it was against the spirit of fiscal autonomy of India and that it affected the revenues of the country. He said:

Was it necessary to repeal them in the interests of free trade? I am an advocate of free trade and so I believe are the rest of my countrymen. But I emphatically deny that they had ever been levied for the purpose of protection. They had been levied before the Bombay mills had come into existence and they have been continued ever since. But suppose it were admitted that these duties are now protective in their nature, I contend that the question whether these duties should be abolished or not, must be decided not merely on economical but also on administrative grounds.... The abstract principles of free trade may call for their sacrifice, but a great government like that of this country should not be influenced by such considerations alone. The financial position of the country has to be borne in mind. I ask: are the finances of the country in such a condition as to admit of the sacrifice of these duties?[37]

36 Dadabhai Naoroji, *Poverty and Un-British Rule in India* (London, 1901) 61-2.
37 Palit, n. 3, 203.

Gokhale, who was a member of the Imperial Legislative Council, tried to secure government cooperation in granting the much needed financial and administrative reforms for India. His annual speeches on the Imperial budget were always listened to with great respect both by the ministers of finance and by the other members of the Council. In one of his speeches he raised the general principle known as 'No taxation without Representation.' Opposing the government's decision to meet all sorts of extraordinary charges out of current revenues, Gokhale said:

> How comes it that India is doing in regard to these extraordinary charges that which even the richest nations of Europe have not considered it advisable to attempt? The obvious answer is that in those countries it is the popular assemblies that control taxation and expenditure; in India the taxpayer has no constitutional voice in the shaping of these things. If we had any votes to give, and the government of the country had been carried on by an alternation of power between two parties, both alike anxious to conciliate us and bid for our support, the Hon'ble Member would assuredly have told a different tale. But I venture to submit, my Lord, that the considerations which the people of western countries receive in consequence of their voting power should be available to us, in matters of finance at any rate, through an 'intelligent anticipation'— to use a phrase of your Lordship's—of our reasonable wishes on the part of government.[38]

The Moderate leaders also demanded that the burden of taxation should be equitably distributed over the shoulders of all classes of people and the expenditure of the government should be curtailed as far as possible without impairing the efficiency.

As in the political sphere, in the economic sphere too, the early leaders of the Indian national movement were the exponents of nationalism. In his book *Poverty and Un-British Rule in India*, Dadabhai Naoroji gove a documented account of the drain of wealth from India to England and contended that this drain was the chief cause of India's poverty, misery and all material evils. He explained what he meant by this drain of wealth:

> This drain consists of two elements—first, that arising from the remittances by European officials of their savings, and for their expenditure in England for their various wants both

38  Gokhale, n. 5, 6-7.

there and in India; from pensions and salaries paid in England;
and from government expenditure in England and India.
And the second, that arising from similar remittances by non-
official Europeans. As the drain prevents India from making
any capital, the British by bringing back the capital which
they have drained from India itself, secure almost a monopoly
of all trade and important industries, and thereby further ex-
ploit and drain India, the source of evil being the official
drain.[39]

Dadabhai suggested the remedy to these evils:

The obvious remedy is to allow India to keep what it produces,
and to help it as much as it lies in the power of the British
nation to reduce her burden of the interest on the public
debt; with a reasonable provision for the means absolutely
necessary for the maintenance of the British rule. And for
such means British must pay its proper share for its own interests. For this purpose it is necessary on the one hand to
limit, within a certain amount, the total of every kind of expenditure (pay, pensions, and every possible kind of allowance)
for the European portion of all the services both in England
and India, directly or indirectly connected with or under
the control of the government (including, therefore, guaran-
teed railways or other works, manufactures, local funds, etc.),
and to guarantee the public debt; and, on the other hand,
for the important political object of maintaining the British
rule, to reserve by law, for Europeans alone, such places of
power of control only as may be absolutely necessary for the
purpose, with a fair proportion of the Army, within the limited
amount of expenditure for the European portion of all the
services. These European services being as much for the benefit
and interests of Britain as for those of India, Britain must pay
her proper share for their expenditure.[40]

In many of his speeches and writings Dadabhai emphasised
the importance of material production. He not only tried to
secularise politics—itself a great contribution in his times—but
brought home to the Indian people that unless the country produced more, there would be no prosperity for the people. According to him, 'The whole foundation of all administration,
financial and general, and of the actual condition of the people,
rests upon this one fact—the produce of the country, the ultimate
result of all capital, labour and land.'[41]

39 Naoroji, n. 36, 38.
40 *Ibid.*, 142.
41 *Ibid.*, 3-4.

CC 4

Both Dadabhai and Ranade were the spokesmen of the bourgeoisie which were gradually arising in India. As champions of
the industrialisation of the country, they realised that classical
economic thought of the West should not mechanically be applied to India. But, although they were aware of the socialist
and communist ideas of Europe, they were not influenced by
them.

## SPIRIT OF MODERATION

No one will doubt that the political and economic demands
of the early leaders of the Congress and of those, who were referred to as the Moderates after the emergence of the Extremists
in the Indian political field, were of a progressive character.
But after 1905 there was a controversy about the merits of their
methods of agitation. These were based on the assumptions that
the connection with the British was in the interest of India and
that the political agitation for civil rights and self-government
must be conducted only through constitutional means. Many
statements of these leaders reveal this approach. For instance,
Surendranath Banerjea said as early as 1878:

> The mission of England in the East is to elevate the people
> of India, to emancipate them from the chains of ignorance,
> error and superstition, to lead them onward to a higher career
> of social, intellectual and political life—that, I conceive, under
> the orderings of Providence, to be the grand and predestined
> mission which England has to accomplish in the East.[42]

Rash Behari Ghose, another Moderate leader, expressed th
following view:

> I can never believe that England will ever retrace her steps
> or forget her duty to India, where she came not as a conqueror;
> those who speak of the conquest of India by a mere handful
> of Englishmen cannot have read history, which does not record
> any authentic miracles, where she came not, I repeat, as a
> conqueror, but as a deliverer with the ready acquiescence of
> the people to 'heal and not to settle,' to substitute order and
> good government for disorder and anarchy, to fit stone to
> stone again, and restore that edifice which has been slowly and
> painfully built by the wisest and best of Indian sovereigns,
> that task has now been accomplished, whitewinged peace now

42 Palit, n. 3, 85.

broods over the whole land; and it only remains for England now to fit it gradually for that autonomy which she has granted to her colonies.[43]

According to Gokhale, one of the principles of the Servants of India Society, which he founded, was that 'Its members frankly accept the British connection as ordained, in the inscrutable dispensation of Providence, for India's good. Self-government within the Empire...is their goal. This goal, they recognise, cannot be attained without years of earnest and patient effort and sacrifices worthy of the cause.'[44]

The Extremists challenged the leadership of the Moderates in the Surat Congress in 1907 and questioned many of their assumptions. Later when Bhupendra Nath Basu asked Sir Pherozeshah Mehta, another Moderate leader, to submit his view with regard to the proposed union of the Moderates and the Extremists, Sir Pherozeshah Mehta replied:

The events which took place in Nagpur and Surat and circumstances under which the Congress broke up in Surat make it now absolutely essential that the unwritten law on which the Congress was based from the very commencement, namely, that it was to be a legal and constitutional movement carried on by our organisation which loyally accepted British rule, should be now put in express words, at once clear and unambiguous, unassailable by any such dialectical chicanery as was practised in the last Congress on the Boycott resolution when the words agreed to as meaning one thing were attempted to be explained into another and a very different thing.[45]

As far back as 1902, even before the Extremists began to challenge the leadership of the Moderates, Surendranath Banerjea observed: 'We recognise that the journey towards the goal must necessarily be slow, and that the blessed consummation can be attained only after prolonged preparation and laborious apprenticeship. But a beginning has to be made.'[46] The same idea was elaborated by him later as follows:

The ideal must be subordinated to the practical, governed by the environments of the situation, which must be slowly,

43 Speeches and Writings of Dr. Sir Rashbehari Ghose (Madras, 1921) 29.

44 Gokhale, n. 5, 915.

45 J. R. B. Jeejeebhoy, ed., Some Unpublished and Later Speeches and Writings of the Hon. Sir Pherozeshah Mehta (Bombay, 1918) 215.

46 Banerjea, n. 2, 314.

steadily developed and improved towards the attainment of the ideal. In nature as well as in the moral world there is no such thing as a cataclysm. Evolution is the supreme law of life and affairs. Our environments, such as they are, must be improved and developed, stage by stage, point by point, till the ideal of the present generation becomes the actual of the next.[47]

It is interesting to recall that even when the Swadeshi movement was becoming popular and some Moderate Bengali leaders, like Banerjea, were associating with it, they were afraid that it may lead to a certain resentment on the part of their British friends. For instance, Surendranath Banerjea felt:

The only objection that was felt and seriously discussed was, how it would affect our English friends. Would they approve of it? Would they sympathise with it? Might they not regard it as an open avowal of ill will? For, as I have already observed, there were many Englishmen in Calcutta who strongly disapproved of the Partition, and of the form and the manner in which it was carried out. They were helping us with their advice and the weight of their moral support. We were anxious that we should do nothing to alienate them, and that we should continue to receive their sympathy, which proved so helpful. Further, our appeal lay to the British public against the decision of the Government of India.[48]

In 1918, when the annual session of the Congress met to consider the proposed constitutional reforms, the Moderates abstained from it and Surendranath Banerjea explains their position as follows:

We felt that these hasty and extreme views would dominate the deliberations of the Congress, and that we should not lend them the weight of our support by our presence. We accordingly held a conference of the Moderate party in Bombay on November 1, 1918. I was elected President. It was the first of the Moderate conferences which are now held from year to year. Some of our friends, the Rt. Hon. Mr. Shastri and the Hon. Sir Narsingha Sarma among others, continued to attend the Congress, in the hope of making their influence felt. But it was a vain hope. The Congress had become more Extremist than ever, and they have since discontinued their attendance. We have parted company—it is difficult to say for how long.[49]

47  *Ibid.*, 320.
48  *Ibid.*, 191.
49  *Ibid.*, 305.

There were many reasons for the Moderates' eagerness to co-operate with the government when these reforms were proposed. Firstly, they thought that this was certainly an advance towards progressive evolution of self-government in India, and secondly, they were afraid that in the absence of the willingness of a politically conscious group to work out the proposed reforms, the government would withdraw them. Such a negative attitude, they feared, would retard the political progress of the country. In their opinion the best way of advancing the nation's interests was to cooperate with the British government as best as they could and, at the same time, agitate in a peaceful manner for civil rights and constitutional reforms.

## IMPACT OF LIBERALISM: AN ASSESSMENT

The total ideological impact of the activities of these leaders and of the organisations they controlled was in favour of liberal-ism—but it was liberalism with a difference. They rejected such concepts of European liberalism as free trade and advocated the state playing an important part in the economic development of the country. This apparent inconsistency in their thinking arose, among other things, from their class character and the level of the economic development of the country. Unlike the liberalism of Europe, the political philosophy of the leaders of the first phase of the Indian national movement was not based on solid foundations. They were trying to apply, often mechanically, the ideas they learned through the English language and the history of the western people. As one of the authors put it:

In the urban atmosphere, where birth and caste status were no longer decisive and where personal prestige was increasingly important, intellectual eminence and wealth were the only means of improving one's place in society. These had far-reaching social consequences, as literary, scientific and artistic education in urban areas came to be dominated by the intellec-tual classes. The intellectuals made little attempt to establish downward contacts, judging from the backwardness of a large percentage of the population. Thus, a new social rift opened, no less wide than the economic rift which was the result of capitalism. Legislative work, efficiency in administration, the need for preservation of law and order, challenged the best talent of the country; and the opening of the lucrative possi-bilities in the army and public works enabled the intelligent

and the educated classes to participate in most of these public
activities, which were denied to a large part of their unfortunate brethren. This gave the intellectual classes an immense
feeling of their own superiority which was personal rather than
corporate. This new class did not consist exclusively of the
Brahmin caste; characteristic and decisive for the intellectual
elite was the diversity of its social origins; for Parsees, Christians, Vaishyas, Kshatriyas and even the lower orders of the
Hindu society were represented in it.[50]

In regard to some matters these leaders displayed a capacity
to grasp the unique problems of India and suggest solutions to
them. Many of their utterances were symbolic of the aspirations
of the politically conscious Indians of their day. These aspirations
were primarily the industrialisation of the country and freeing
India from the economic domination of Great Britain. They
realised that the state had to play an important role in the economic development of countries like India. Their approach towards this question was pragmatic rather than ideological. Although some of them had a vague sense of social justice and the
concept of equitable distribution of income among all the sections of the people, they were not in any sense socialists. Their
economic demands, as their political demands, were based on
the interests of the rising new social classes represented by the
new middle class and the capitalists.

In the political sphere these interests demanded the Indianisation of the services, expansion of legislative councils and laying
the foundations for self-government in India. Such political and
administrative reforms would have given great opportunities to
the educated people to express themselves in the administrative
and legislative fields. The judicial reforms demanded by the representatives of the new social classes would have conferred upon
them the civil rights, which were at that time enjoyed by the
British people at home. All these demands were based on the
liberal political concepts of the West. But, in the economic
sphere, the interests of the rising new classes demanded that
the government must give protection to indigenous industries
and that it should assist in various ways in the economic development of the country. These were in variance with liberal
political philosophy, but as they were in the interests of an

50  Krishna Rao, *The Growth of Indian Liberalism* (Mysore, 1951) 62-3.

underdeveloped country like India, they had no difficulty in re-
conciling these economic demands with their political demands.
The political philosophy of these leaders was partly based on
the political ideas they learned from the West and which they
found to be of advantage to India, and partly based on their
understanding of the Indian situation and their feeling that
some of the western ideas should be altered here and there to
suit the Indian conditions. The effect of their political activities
was to strengthen parliamentary democracy and rule of law in
India and make people conscious of the economic problems of
the country and their solutions.

# CHAPTER III

# EXTREMISM—THE PHILOSOPHY OF POLITICAL RADICALISM

EXPLAINING the origin of the use of the term 'Extremists' Bal Gangadhar Tilak, who was himself an Extremist, said:

> Two new words have recently come into existence with regard to our policies, and they are *Moderates* and *Extremists*. These words have a specific relation to time, and they, therefore, will change with time. The Extremists of today will be Moderates tomorrow, just as the Moderates of today were Extremists yesterday.[1]

Here we are using the word extremism to indicate the political philosophy of those who were considered as 'Extremists' at the beginning of the twentieth century in India. They were primarily B. G. Tilak, Lajpat Rai, Aurobindo Ghose, Bipin Chandra Pal and their followers. During 1916.18 Mrs Annie Besant and her associates in Indian Home Rule League were also considered as Extremists by the government and the Moderate leaders. Tilak was of the opinion that it was not by their purpose, but by their methods that his party had earned the name 'Extremists,' because according to him their purpose was the same as that of the Moderates; it was not concerned with abolishing the British rule completely, but with obtaining a large share of power for the people in the administration of the country. The Extremists thought that they must bring pressure on the bureaucracy to make it realise that all was not well. Tilak explains the position of his party as follows:

> The immediate question for us is how we are to bring pressure on bureaucracy, in which we have no effective representation,

1 B. G. Tilak, *Speeches* (Poona, 1908) 21.

but are debarred from all except subordinate positions. It is only in our answer to that question that we differ from the so-called Moderates. They still hope to influence public opinion in England by sending deputations, supporting a newspaper, and pleading the justice of our cause. Both parties, of course, have long ago given up all hope of influencing Anglo-Indian opinion on here.... We Extremists have determined on other methods.... Our motto is self-reliance, not mendicancy. Besides the Swadeshi movement, we work by boycott and passive resistance.[2]

Similar views were expressed by other leaders of the Extremist camp. For instance, Lajpat Rai criticised the role of the earlier leaders of the Congress in the following words:

The founders of the Indian National Congress began their movement under inspiration of government and under the shadow of the high offices they held or aspired to under that government, but the founders and inspirers of the National Movement started their propaganda by boycotting government and government patronage.... The former appealed to the British government and the British nation, the latter appealed to their own people and to their God.[3]

This was how Aurobindo Ghose envisaged the transition from the Moderates to the Extremists:

...even for the partial objects they were intended to secure, the measures for which we petitioned and clamoured in the last century were hopelessly ineffective. So was it with all the Congress nostrums; they were palliatives which could not even be counted upon to palliate; the radical evil, uncured, would only be driven from one seat in the body politic to take refuge in others where it would soon declare its presence by equally troublesome symptoms. The only true cure for a bad and oppressive financial system is to give the control over taxation to the people whose money pays for the needs of government. The only effective way of putting an end to executive tyranny is to make the people and not an irresponsible government the controller and paymaster of both executive and judiciary. The only possible method of stopping the drain is to establish a popular government which may be relied on to foster and protect Indian commerce and Indian industry conducted by Indian capital and employing Indian labour. This is the object which the new politics, the politics of the twentieth century,

2 Quoted by H. W. Nevinson, *The New Spirit in India* (London, 1908) 73-4.

3 Lajpat Rai, *Young India* (New York, 1916) 150.

places before the people of India in their resistance to the present system of government....

Bipin Chandra Pal, another Extremist leader, summed up his views on the social and political ideas of the Moderates in the following words:

The older generations drew their inspirations of freedom and progress from European, and especially British, history and literature. The old patriotism did not feed upon the actualities of Indian thought and life, but upon the idealities of Europe and America. Freedom, except in the movements of religious and social revolt where it meant personal freedom only, was a vague idea. The conception of freedom has its natural growth in the sense of bondage, and its vitality is determined by the strength of this sense. There was a keen and growing sense of social and sacredotal restrictions in the English-educated classes, who were inspired with the ideals of liberty, equality, and fraternity, imbibed from the gospel of the French Revolution, through its English presentations; and consequently there was a real desire for social emancipation—a desire for freedom from the restrictions of caste and custom. But there was hardly any deep and real sense of political bondage in the country then. There was scarcely any sense of political wrongs. On the contrary, there was a general impression that the British have established peace where there was turmoil, and a settled government where there was anarchy. Nor was there yet any perception of the ruinous economic conflict between Great Britain and India. Consequently, the desire for political freedom was very weak; and it did not go beyond getting higher appointments in the administration, and some share in the shaping of the laws of the land. The old patriotism, therefore, simply represented an awakening of the educated classes to a consciousness of their inferior position in the modern world, and a revival of the memories of the past glories of their race.[5]

According to Pal the political ideas of the Extremists were based on entirely different assumptions. He said:

There is another attitude—that, with the decadence of the faith in the foreign government, with the decadence of our faith in the foreign administration which has come to us, we have learned to look nearer home. Our eyes have been turned away from the Government House, away from the Houses of

4 Aurobindo Ghose, *The Doctrine of Passive Resistance* (Pondicherry, 1948, 2nd edition, 1952) 15-6.

5 B. C. Pal, *The Spirit of Indian Nationalism* (London, 1910) 29-30.

Parliament, from Simla and Calcutta, and our faces have turned now to the starving, the naked, the patient and long suffering 300 millions of our people, and in it we see a new potency, because we view them now with an eye of love which we never had felt before, and in the teeming, toiling, starving and naked populations of India, we find possibilities, potentialities germs that have given rise to this New Movement. That is the cornerstone of this movement, namely, faith in the people, faith in the genius of this nation through ages by historic evolution, faith in the eternal destiny of the Indian people. With the decadence of our faith in the foreign government, and in the foreign nation, has grown up this higher, this dearer, this deeper, this more vital and more divine faith in Indian humanity.[6]

Although these statements of these leaders explain the term 'Extremists,' it must not be taken for granted that it had always a rigid and consistent meaning. Various other definitions were given to it. For instance, the editor of an Indian journal divided the Extremists into the following three sections:

The first section think that they must have nothing to do with British rule but must develop all their resources according to their own unaided endeavours, in spite of the British. ...The second section think that the continuance of the British rule is incompatible with our natural progress, and that we should prepare ourselves for the expulsion of the British from the country, and help ourselves to replace it as fast and as best as we can. The third section are of the opinion that the British must be made to clear out of India at once and leave us to our fate, no matter what...[7]

This is about their aim. They are divided into various groups on the basis of their methods also. The Extremists can roughly be divided into three classes: '(1) the revolutionaries; (2) those who sympathise with and secretly help revolutionaries but do not admit for fear of the law; and (3) visionaries impatient of foreign domination but opposed to violent methods.'[8] The characterisation of the third group as visionaries was not acceptable to them because they thought that they were political realists.

In this study we are making only a brief reference to the terrorists and other adventurists mentioned in the first two groups

6 Bipin Chandra Pal, *Swadeshi and Swaraj* (Calcutta, 1954) 137-8
7 *The Indian World* (March-April 1907) 350-5.
8 B. L. Mitter, *Extremists and Moderates: A Study* (Calcutta, 1918) 1.

because their contribution to the political philosophy of the
national movement was limited. The last group who were opposed to violent methods, or at least were not themselves engaged
in violent methods, played a great part in the moulding of the
political thinking of the people. With their programme of organising the masses to bring pressure on government, they
dominated the Indian national movement in the first two decades
of the twentieth century. The salient features of their political
agitation were based on these fundamental assumptions: (1) to
conduct a political campaign on the hope that an appeal to the
British public would redress India's grievances was unrealistic;
(2) these grievances were not just confined to the Indianisation
of civil services, the reduction of Indian military expenditure
and such specific legislation as the Arms Act and the executive
measures as the partition of Bengal; they were related to the
broader questions of Indians getting a larger share in the administration of the country and putting an end to Britain's exploitation of India; (3) the political agitation for the redress of these
grievances should be conducted from the angle of fulfilling the
nationalist aspirations of the people. And for this purpose popular enthusiasm should be aroused for a general cause such as
Swaraj; (4) the technique of agitation would be based on the
following ideas: (a) pride in India's past glories. Reference were
to be made to the earlier periods in history and to such heroes
as Shivaji. (b) Religious instincts of the people: The country
should be represented as a goddess and functions such as the
Durga Puja (worship of a Hindu goddess) should be used to
instil enthusiasm for political agitation. (c) Reorganisation of
education on national lines. (d) On an economic level the boycott of British and other foreign goods and the promotion of
Swadeshi (indigenous) goods. (e) In the political field non-
cooperation with the British government in India, and if necessary, passive resistance to it. (f) Increasing emphasis not only on
Indian traditions, but on the development of Indian langauges
and making extensive use of them for conducting political
agitations with the aim of drawing as large a number of people
as possible to the national movement.

During the beginning of the twentieth century the political
leaders of the Extremist school were not interested in consciously

developing a political philosophy concerning the structure of the state and government and individual's relations with the government; they were absorbed only in gaining some immediate political objectives and searching for the strategy and tactics of conducting political agitations to that end. Nevertheless their activities and their philosophy of conducting the political agitation did leave a mark on some of the basic aspects of the Indian national movement including its political philosophy.

It should be noted that there was no complete unanimity of views even among the prominent leaders of the Extremists and also that one and the same individual showed occasional signs of revising his earlier views. Expressions such as 'the political philosophy of the Extremists' has therefore to be used with great caution. However, it does indicate some salient features of political thought prevalent in India during the political agitations conducted by such leaders as Tilak, Pal, Lajpat Rai and Aurobindo Ghose.

In this connection it will be useful to examine some of the new features in the Indian political situation and in the international field at the beginning of the twentieth century which led to the rise of these Extremists as a powerful factor in Indian politics.

## THE MOMENTUM OF THE EARLIER MOVEMENT

The emergence of an extremist wing in Indian politics was to some extent the logical development of the earlier phase of the Indian national movement which was confind to constitutional agitation and moderate demands. As Dadabhai Naoroji told an Englishman as early in as in 1895·

Whether your past system was a righteous one for India may be a matter of argument, but face to face with an awakened population such as India now has, and will have more and more every year, the present system of government is an absurd and dangerous anachronism. Russia shows you what will happen in India unless Indians are given more interest in the government. There will be secret societies. Do not misunderstand me....There is immense gratitude in India to England. The present generation feels the benefit it has derived from education....But succeeding generations will not feel that. They will start where men in India today leave off. They will have no personal memory of old India. However improved the conditions in India in which they find themselves, they will accept them as a matter of course. They will demand more, and if they do not get it, they will rebel.[9]

Dadabhai Naoroji was not the only leader who realised that the social forces set in motion by the earlier events were gathering new momentum. The same view was expressed by Motilal Nehru in a letter to Dadabhai Naoroji sent on the eve of the annual session of the Indian National Congress held in 1905. He said:

The Indian people want a practical scheme from you, so that the Congress programme may be an all-year-round affair and keep the entire nation interested in it. Now it is an organisation of the upper five, the lower millions knowing nothing and caring nothing for it. Some such direction should, therefore, be given to it as to make it really a national thing and an object of attraction to the highest and the lowest.[10]

The developments in the Indian economic field and the social and religious movement in the country were also creating a new situation. As we noted in the earlier chapter many Indian writers like Dadabhai Naoroji and R. C. Dutt took up the economic aspect of the British rule in India and commented on the impoverishment of the country, which, in their opinion, was the result of the heavy military expenditure and 'home charges'. Towards the end of the nineteenth century some parts of India experienced prolonged and disastrous famines also. Owing to all these factors there was a widespread discontent in this country.

The representatives of the educated middle class, who were denied opportunities to rise to high positions in the political and administrative life of the country, were the most articulate spokesmen of this discontentment. In the same period some prominent Indians started thinking on the lines of starting new industries in the country. They were inclined to support a vigorous political programme which included the promotion of indigenous industries and the boycott of foreign goods.[11]

9 R. P. Masani, *Dadabhai Naoroji* (London 1939). Dadabhai Naoroji's interview with *The Humanitarian* quoted on pages 358-9.

10 Quoted by Masani, *ibid.*, 497.

11 An Indian scholar describes the situation as follows:

'The earlier years of British rule—the period up to the middle of the nineteenth century—were marked by a spirit of cooperation between the

## BRITAIN'S POLICY BECOMES MORE RIGID

Under the circumstances, even if the British administration in India had functioned in the same manner as they did in an earlier period, the aspirations and demands of some of the Indian leaders would have come into conflict with them. But at the close of the nineteenth century and the beginning of the twentieth the British administrators were far from maintaining the same attitude towards Indian aspirations as they did earlier.

In the first chapter we noted the developments in the British economic and political fields towards the close of the nineteenth century and how they led to the concept of 'New Imperialism in relation to British policy abroad and a weakening of liberal trends at home. These were reflected in the British administrators' attitude towards India. Referring to this matter Surendranath Banerjea, who was himself considered as a Moderate in Indian politics, wrote:

> The present unrest in India may be set down to the following cause: (1) The utter disregard of Indian public opinion by the government, of which the most notable illustration was afforded by the partition of Bengal. (2) The creation of racial animosities in at least two of the great provinces in India—the Punjab and East Bengal—by the introduction of racial bias into the administration. (3) The wide divergence between profession and practice on the part of the government and the nonfulfilment of solemn pledges such as are given in the Queen's Proclamation and the consequent failure to associate the people in the government of the country and to accord to them a recognised status in the administrations. (4) The contemptuous treatment of Indians by Europeans. (5) The

British rulers and the neo-rich-landlords, traders and moneylenders. But this class was to seek openings in commerce, industry, and the civil service; but here it found itself faced with stiff opposition from the middle classes of Britain that constituted the main power behind British rule in India. The national movement in India was an expression of the conflict between the middle classes of the two countries, one aspiring for wealth and influence, the other already in possession of them.

The new class was imbued with the profit motive like its counterpart in Europe, but in the pursuit of that aim it was balked by the British monopoly in trade and business, and by the lack of means and conditions of industrial development. It was largely an urban class with urban interests. It developed a thirst for western education, a hankering for government service and a keenness for the learned professions.'—Tara Chand, *History of the Freedom Movement in India* (Delhi, 1961) I, 352.

hostile attitude of an influential section of the Anglo-Indian Press (whose views are listened to by the government with respect) in regard to Indian aspirations and the violent and contemptuous language which often marks its utterances. (6) It may be added that the subsequent repressive measures have greatly intensified the unrest.[12]

This was how a Moderate leader, who was a friend of the British, felt about the government's policy. The reaction of the Extremist leaders was even more intense and their opposition to the government more uncompromising.

The decision to partition Bengal into two provinces, which was announced on 7 July 1905, was one of the most unpopular steps taken by the government. The decision itself was made primarily for administrative reasons as the discussions among government officials on the question dating back to 1901 indicate. But ever since the Bengali leaders came to know about the scheme of partition of their province they organised agitation against it. Many meetings were held and representations were made to the government to show the opposition of a section of the people to this scheme. When government finally decided to partition the province, there was a widespread impression in the country, Bengal in particular, that this government was not at all responsive to public opinion.

Lord Curzon, the Governor-General, who pushed through the scheme of partition against all opposition, was unpopular with the educated classes of the Indian people for many other reasons also. For instance, his following comments on the 'Asiatics' aroused widespread protest in India:

> I hope I am making no false or arrogant claim when I say that the highest ideal of truth is to a large extent a western conception. I do not thereby mean to claim that Europeans are universally or even generally truthful, still less do I mean that Asiatics deliberately or habitually deviate from the truth. The one proposition would be absurd, and the other insulting. But undoubtedly truth took a high place in the moral codes of the West before it had been similarly honoured in the East.[13]

12  Surendranath Banerjea, *Speeches and Writings of Hon. Surendranath Banerjea* (Madras, n.d.) 380.
13  University of Calcutta, *Convocation Addresses 1889-1906* (Calcutta, 1914), III, 981.

This action of the government and the pronouncement of the Governor-General aroused widespread resentment in the country. Referring to the state of public opinion regarding the decision to partition Bengal, Surendranath Banerjea wrote later:

> The announcement fell like a bombshell upon an astonished public.... We felt that we had been insulted, humiliated and tricked. We felt that the whole of our future was at stake, and that it was a deliberate blow aimed at the growing solidarity and self-consciousness of the Bengalee-speaking population. Originally intended to meet administrative requirements, we felt that it had drawn to itself a political flavour and complexion, and, if allowed to be passed, it would be fatal to our political progress and to that close union between Hindus and Mohammadans upon which the prospects of Indian advancement so largely depended.[14]

Although this was at first considered as a local matter which was of interest only to Bengal, it developed into an all-India question. In his presidential address to the Indian National Congress held at Banaras in 1905 Gokhale said·

> The question that is uppermost in the minds of us all at this moment is the Partition of Bengal. A cruel wrong has been inflicted on our Bengalee brethren, and the whole country has been stirred to its deepest depths in sorrow and resentment, as had never been the case before.[15]

The meeting of the Indian National Congress also passed a resolution protesting against the Partition and appealing to the Government of India and to the Secretary of State to reverse or modify the decision. The agitation which followed the Partition was an unprecedented one in the history of modern India and very often the Bengal Partition was rightly referred to as a landmark in the history of the Indian national movement.

## INTERNATIONAL FACTORS HELP INDIAN EXTREMISM

When all these factors in the political, economic and social fields within India were favouring political extremism in the country, some events outside the country also had the same

14 Surendranath Banerjea, A Nation in Making (Madras 1925) 187-8.
15 The Indian National Congress, containing an account of its origin and growth, full text of the Presidential Addresses, Reprints of all the Congress Resolutions, extracts from the Welcome Addresses (Madras, 1917) 795-0

effect. As Lajpat Rai, one of the leaders of the Extremist school, himself reported:

> There can be no doubt that Indian nationalism is receiving a great deal of support from world forces operating outside of India. On the political side it has been inspired and strengthened by the forces of European nationalism—the struggles and successes of the English proletariat, the suffering and the eventual triumph of the French revolutionists, the efforts and victories of the Italians, the continued struggle of Russians, Poles, Finns, Hungarians, and others. The Indian nationalist is an ardent student of the history of Modern Europe, of England, France, Germany, Netherlands, Italy, Russia, Austria, and last but not least of Turkey and the Balkan states. The Nationalist Calendar of great men followed by young India contains such names as those of Washington, Cavour, Mazzini, Bismarck, Kossuth, Emmet, Parnell...[16]

Lajpat Rai himself was one of those Indian leaders who took an interest in the events outside the country. He wrote books and articles on India with foreigners as readers in mind and with the purpose of getting at least moral support from them for India's demands. He also tried to enlighten Indians on foreign events. He wrote monographs on Mazzini and Garibaldi.

Apart from the events mentioned by Lajpat Rai, the defeat of Italians at the hands of the Abyssinians in 1896, the incidents of the Boer War (1899-1902), the revolutionary movements of China and Persia, Japan's victory over Russia (1905) and China's boycott of American goods also inspired Indian nationalists for active political action. Among these events Japan's victory over Russia made the most profound impression. The following editorial comments which appeared in an Indian journal was typical of the Indian reaction:

> The fall of Port Arthur opens a new chapter in the history of the brilliant career of this wonderful and marvellous country which, within a single generation, has risen from a backward to a most forward place in the scale of the world.... Almost for the first time in the history of the world an Asiatic power, hitherto somewhat despised and not taken into account, has humbled a huge European power, by no means a mean representative of all that is haughty and arrogant among the nations of the West.... The great feature which strikes the

16 Lajpat Rai, n. 3, 221.

reader as the secret of this wonderful progress is the spirit
of self-sacrificing patriotism which pervades the whole nation
from the Emperor down to the lowest subject.[17]

The editor of the same journal quotes with approval what
Swami Vivekananda wrote to one of his friends from Japan:

The Japanese seems to have fully awakened themselves to the
necessity of the present times. They have now a thoroughly
organised army equipped with guns which one of their officers
have invented and which are said to be second to none. Then
they are continuously increasing their navy.... Come, be men!
Come out of your narrow holes and have a look abroad. See
how nations are on the march. Do you love man? Do you
love your country? Then come, let us struggle for higher and
better things, look not back, no, not even if you see the dearest
cry.[18]

These new developments in India and in the international field
gave a new strength to the desire of many politically conscious
people in India to agitate for freedom from foreign domination
in an uncompromising manner. It resulted in the emergence of
the 'Extremists' as a major political force in the country in the
first decade of the twentieth century.

BOYCOTT OF FOREIGN GOODS AND THE SWADESHI MOVEMENT

One important item of the programme of the Extremist
political leaders was the Swadeshi movement. There were two
aspects to it; the economic boycott of foreign, and particularly
British, goods and the promotion of indigenous industries. Like
many other features in their programme, the boycott of the foreign
goods also had deep roots, although it took a crystallised shape
only after the partition of Bengal had created widespread dissatisfaction with the government. It is difficult to trace the
origin of the use of economic boycott as a political weapon in
the anti-partition agitation. Surendranath Banerjea, who was
connected with the boycott movement in Bengal during 1905-07,
notes in his autobiography:

From whose fertile brain did it spring—when did it first
see the light? Both these questions it would be difficult to

17  *The Indian Review* (January 1905) 1-2.
18  *Ibid.*, 8.

answer with anything like accuracy. When the public has been roused by any stirring event, its hidden springs touched, and its slumbering forces set in motion by some great calamity or by the passionate desire to work out a cherished ideal, promising to unfold a new chapter in a nation's history, the moral atmosphere becomes fruitful under the pressure of new ideas; for the mind of the whole community is at work and makes its contribution to the sum total of national thought....

It was in this state of the public mind that the idea of a boycott of British goods was publicly started—by whom I cannot say—by several, I think, at one and the same time. It first found expression at a public meeting in the district of Patna, and it was repeated at public meetings held in other moffusil towns....[19]

On 13 July 1905 *Sanjivini,* a weekly organ, asked the people to renounce the foreign goods as much as possible and to spread the ideology of 'Boycott.' The most well-known development regarding boycott was the meeting held at Calcutta on 7 August 1905 which passed the following resolution:

... this meeting fully sympathises with the Resolution adopted at many meetings held in the mofussil, to abstain from the purchase of British 'manufacturers so long as the partition Resolution is not withdrawn as a protest against the indifference of the British public in regard to Indian affairs and the consequent disregard of Indian public opinion by the present government.[20]

The twentysecond session of the Congress held at Calcutta in 1906 gave limited support to the boycott. Its resolution stated:

Having regard to the fact that the people of this country have little or no voice in its administration, and that their representations to the government do not receive due consideration, this Congress is of opinion that the Boycott Movement inaugurated in Bengal by way of protest against the Partition of that province was and is legitimate.[21]

There was no unanimity of opinion about the political significance of economic boycott. Many 'Moderates' considered it only

19    Banerjea, n. 14, 190-1.
20    Haridas Mukherjee and Prof. Uma Mukherjee, *India's Fight for Freedom* (Calcutta, 1958) 45-6.
21    D. Chakrabarty and C. Bhattacharya, comp., *Congress in Evolution*: *A Collection of Congress Resolutions from 1885-1934* (Calcutta, 1940) 11.

as a temporary measure intended to express the indignation of the Bengalis against the partition of their province, but one which should be given up when that limited objective was fulfilled. A few thought that the boycott of foreign goods would be helpful to the industrial development of the country. Some of the leaders welcomed the steps taken to promote the production of indigenous (Swadeshi) goods, but opposed the concept of boycott. Many, however, conceived the boycott as a political weapon for the furtherance of freedom from the alien rulers of the country. Explaining this view G. Subramanya Iyer said:

Though boycott may be adopted as a part of the industrial development, it is difficult to separate it from its political result.... There is no meaning in Swadeshism 'endeavouring to develop home industries in home market,' as Lord Minto said; nor is the so-called 'honest Swadeshi dissociated from political aspirations.' conceivable. Every Swadeshi, and for that matter, every boycotter is a helper in the cause of nationality. For, Swadeshism, in its fullest significance, is political as well as economical.[22]

Tilak also agreed with this view. Opposing the view of the British administrators that the Swadeshi campaign must be divorced from politics, Tilak said:

If the Indian government dissociates itself from the commercial aspirations of the British nation, then it will be time for Swadeshi workers to consider the question of dissociating their movement from politics. But so long as politics and commerce are blended together, in this policy of the Government of India, it will be a blunder to dissociate Swadeshi from politics. In fact Swadeshism is a large term which includes politics and to be a true Swadeshi one must look on all lines—whether political or industrial or economical—which converge our people towards the status of a civilised nation.[23]

Another advocate of this view was Bipin Chandra Pal who said:

... this Swadeshism or boycott is not a mere economic movement. No economic movement is purely economic. Politics and economics are indissolubly bound up together in every country, as it is in India.... Swadeshism must associate itself with politics and when Swadeshism associate itself with

22  *Indian Review* (March, 1907) 175.
23  Tilak's *Speeches* (Madras, 1918) 73.

politics, it becomes boycott, and this boycott is a movement of passive resistance. It is a movement of the determination of the people not only to save the industries of the nation but also to create those forces in the community which by passive methods work out the problem of Swaraj.[24]

According to Aurobindo Ghose the ultimate aim of the boycott should be to paralyse the alien administration of the country. He wrote:

We are dissatisfied... with the foreign exploitation of the country, the continual bleeding of its resources, the chronic famine and rapid impoverishment which result, the refusal of the government to protect the people and their industries. Accordingly, we refuse to help the process of exploitation and impoverishment in our capacity as consumers.... By an organised and relentless boycott of British goods, we propose to render the further exploitation of the country impossible.[25]

To Aurobindo Ghose the boycott of economic goods was a part of comprehensive boycott of everything British.

There were also others like Bipin Chandra Pal who also thought on similar lines. In Bengal and elsewhere, occasional attempts were made to boycott government courts and settle disputes through non-official agencies. But they succeeded only in rare cases and that too for a short period. Not so the economic boycott. It had solid foundations on the economic needs of the country and the new social classes arising from the industrial development that was gradually taking place in India at the beginning of the twentieth century. There was a widespread realisation of the fact that, along with political problems, economic problems of the country should also be tackled. Subramanya Iyer emphasised the interrelation between the political work and the industrial development in the following words:

Under the healthy and everwidening influence of the Congress and the national sentiment of the people, they are discovering fresh avenues of national work in the fulfilment of their national future. In the initial years of the Congress, there was no intention of taking up the work of an industrial propaganda, but now the industrial exhibitions and the Swadeshi movement are based on the Congress and derive their sustaining

24 *Speeches of Bipin Chandra Pal* (Madras, 1907) 105-6.
25 Ghose, n. 4, 36-7.

force from the feeling of national unity, which the Congress has created.[26]

In this connection the following comments made by the same leader, while reviewing Hobson's *Imperialism,* is worthy of note:

This is a very interesting and instructive book which should largely be read by students of Indian politics.... [But] the present rulers of the world show no disposition to abandon the policy of exploitation of the world in the interest of plutocracy and adventurers; and India, from her own experience, will readily echo Mr Hobson's verdict regarding the greedy selfishness, cruelty and immorality of imperialism.[27]

This understanding of the basic economic conflicts between the forces of Indian nationalism and the British government in India was the economic basis of the political agitation led by the Extremist political leaders. Many of the books of Ranade, R. C. Dutt, Dadabhai Naoroji and the speeches of G. K. Gokhale had emphasised the destruction of Indian industries resulting from Britain's economic and political penetration into India. Compared to these leaders, referred to as the 'Moderates,' the Extremists were less emphatic on the economic aspects of British rule in India. Apparently, they were more concerned with the religious, spiritual and political questions. But, in practice, they fought the British administrators on economic grounds also and the support they received was also partly due to their espousal of economic questions. They promoted, along with political nationalism, economic nationalism. This creed was inherent in their programmes even when it was not explicitly stated. And it had greater force than the 'religious' and 'spiritual' creeds which were given great prominence in their utterances.

REORGANISING EDUCATION ON NATIONAL LINES

Another important feature of the programme of the leaders of the Extremist school was 'National Education.' Various definitions were given to it. According to Bipin Chandra Pal, 'National Education is education conducted along national lines, controlled by the representatives of the nation, and so controlled

26   *Indian Review* (December, 1905) 830.
27   G. Subramanya Iyer, review of the book *Imperialism*: A *study* by
T. A. Hobson, *Indian Review* (March 1906) 192.

and conducted that it should have for its object the realisation of national destiny'.[28] Aurobindo Ghose's view on the
subject was as follows:

> National Education cannot be defined briefly in one or two
> sentences, but we may describe it tentatively as the education
> which starting with the past and making full use of the pre-
> sent builds up a great nation.... We must therefore save
> for India all that she has stored up of knowledge, character
> and noble thought in her immemorial past. We must acquire
> for her the best knowledge that Europe can give her and
> assimilate it to her own peculiar type of national tempera-
> ment.[29]

Occasionally this demand for national education strayed into
certain irrational channels and expressed itself in a desire to
return to a glorious past. This view was very popular in Bengal
during 1905-10, but it was neither confined to that province
nor to that period. G. S. Arundale wrote as late as in 1916:

> From the modern standpoint, I incline to think that the most
> remarkable feature of the code,[30] so far as it relates to educa-
> tion, is its applicability at the present time. Indeed, I would
> go so far as to say that Manu's educational scheme is the ideal
> scheme for modern conditions, and is only prevented from
> being given actual currency by the fact that we have some
> distance yet to go in the matter of educational readjustment
> before we can hope even roughly to approximate to the
> system propounded by Manu hundreds of thousands years
> ago.[31]

Many other exponents of national education did not accept
this extreme view of going back to the past or rejecting the
modern concepts. Lajpat Rai, one of the leaders of the Extremist school, had a balanced approach towards this whole
question. He said:

> We have to remove the causes and destroy the influences that
> created the atmosphere of despondency and pessimism into

28  Pal, n. 6, 252.
29  Aurobindo Ghose in *Bande Mataram Weekly* (March 1908). The
full article appears as Appendix IV in Prof. Haridas Mukherjee and Uma
Mukherjee, *The Origins of the National Education Movement* (Calcutta,
1957) 421.
30  Manu's Code. Written by an ancient Hindu legal scholar—it is
considered as a source of Hindu law and social conventions.
31  G. S. Arundale, *National Education* (Madras, 1916) 1.

which this country was sunk immediately before the birth of the new nationalist movement. For that purpose, we have to construct the history of our past, and to establish by documentary evidence of the best kind that there is nothing in our heredity which inherently unfits us for the great role to which we are aspiring.... It is not necessary for us for that purpose to claim that our civilization was in any respect superior to modern civilization, nor that our ancestors enjoyed the monopoly of spiritual insight or of divine wisdom.[32]

Tilak, another supporter of national education, was very pragmatic in his approach towards this question. He enumerated its objectives as follows:

Of the many things that we will do there (in these schools of national education) the religious education will first and foremost engage our attention. Secular education only is not enough to build up a character....

The second thing that we will do, will be to lighten the load of the study of the foreign languages.... We spend twenty or twentyfive years for the education which we can easily obtain in seven or eight years if we get through the medium of our vernaculars.... The industrial education will be the third thing.... Education in politics will be the fourth thing.[33]

The Indian National Congress also supported the demand for national education. In its twentysecond session held at Calcutta, 1906, the following resolution was adopted:

In the opinion of this Congress the time has arrived for the people all over the country earnestly to take up the question of national education for both boys and girls and organise a system of education—literary, scientific and technical—suited to the requirements of the country, on national lines and under national control.[34]

The National Council of Education established in 1906 at Calcutta was one of the foremost institutions founded by the advocates of national education.

The fundamental object of the N.C.E.'s scheme of studies was the 'quickening of the national life of the people' for the

32    Lajpat Rai, *The Problem of National Education in India* (London, 1920) 70-1.
33    Tilak, n. 23, 122-5.
34    Chakrabarty and Bhattacharya, comp., n. 21, 133.

realisation of the national destiny. On its liberal side, the
scheme as a whole sought to train students intellectually and
morally so as to mould their character according to the highest
national ideals; and on its technical side to train them so as
to qualify them for developing the natural resources of the
country and increasing its material wealth. A very important
feature was that it sought to make education easy by imparting it through the medium of the learner's vernacular.... A
second feature was that arrangements were made for technical
education in all classes up to the fifth standard of the
secondary stage along with literary and scientific education on
a compulsory basis, while provisions were made for specialisa-
tion in the collegiate course.... The third feature was the
systematic provision for the study of physical, natural or
positive sciences along with liberal arts, culture and human-
ism. The fourth feature was its provision for moral and
religious as well as physical education subject to certain conditions.... A fifth and a most characteristic feature was provision for researches into ancient Indian history, philosophy,
economics, politics, arts and sciences as well other aspects of
culture.[35]

According to Satish Chandra Mukherjee, who published a
'scheme of National Collegiate Education for the proposed
National University for Bengal' in January 1906, the objective
of national education was not merely acquisition of learning,
but the quickening of the national life of the people and the
development of a certain spirit, ideal, temper which should in
the first instance be national as well as modern in its character.'[36]

As these quotations indicate, the concept of national education
was neither clearly nor uniformly defined by its supporters; but
it had received a great deal of emotional support from a large
section of political agitators at the beginning of the twentieth
century. However, it also had its critics. The Indian Review, a
leading monthly journal of that period, wrote in one of its
editorials:

It is really difficult to see what the people really mean by a
National University or a National Council of Education or
education on national lines. Is It the Indian or the Bengalee
nation for whose benefit the National University is to be
established? Can a university be conceived in India, or for
that matter in Bengal, that would not eschew moral and

35   Mukherjee and Mukherjee, n. 20, 152-3.
36   Dawn Magazine, quoted by Mukherjee and Mukherjee, n. 29, 43

religious training nor would ignore social environment and yet meet with the educational requirements of the Indian Christian, the Indian Mussalman and the Hindu of the thousand and one castes and sectors of this land? Can a *National* University to run in India or in Bengal according to the narrow ideals of either the Aligarh Muhamadan College or the Banaras Central Hindu College or the D.A.V. College at Lahore? Or is it possible to revive in the twentieth century the ideals of the Universities of Nalanda, Banaras, Mithila, Nuddea and Vikrampore of the pre-Christian or the pre-Moslem era.[37]

These were some of the views on the concept of national education as propagated and practised in India. In this study we are not concerned with the details of the organisation of the institutions of national education and their functioning but only with their philosophical and other legacies in the political field. Some of the most important among these institutions were the Arya College at Lahore, the Hindu College at Banaras and the National Council of Education at Calcutta. There were innumerable other institutions which were less known, but were established with same or similar purpose. All these were not established under the auspices of one central organisation or in a particular year. They grew and developed in different parts of the country at different periods under the inspiration of one leader or association. Although the Hindu College and the Arya College owed their origin to the desire of their founders to have educational institutions on national lines and under Indian control, they were not directly connected with any one place or any political movement. Not so the National Council of Education established in Calcutta in 1906. It was directly connected with the boycott and swadeshi movements and the anti-Partition agitation of Bengal of 1906-8. In one sense it was a part and parcel of the political movement led by the 'Extremist' political leaders like Bipin Chandra Pal, B. G. Tilak and Lala Lajpat Rai.

Although it was the political movements of 1905-6 which gave a concrete shape to the demand for national education in Bengal, it should be noted that the demand itself was of earlier origin and arose from more fundamental causes than the parti-

37   *The Indian Review* (November, 1905) 284.

tion of Bengal. Gooroo Das Banerjee, the first Indian vice-chancellor of a university, drew attention to the numerous deficiencies of the educational system prevailing in that period in many of his university convocation addresses. Rabindra Nath Tagore also agreed with this view and pleaded as early as 1893 for the acceptance of Bengali as the medium of instruction. Satischandra Mukherji expressed similar views in many of the articles contributed by him in the *Dawn Magazine* during 1897-98.[38]

Influenced by the ideas of these leaders, the National Council of Education ignored the official university curricula and tried to give a special kind of training to its students. But this led to a conflict with the government and in the long run it was responsible for its failure. The National Council of Education was primarily the expression of a political movement and it did not take into account the educational needs of the country. As soon as the enthusiasm for political struggle subsided, popular support for the Council's work in the educational sphere also dwindled. Both the government and the general public refused to recognise the educational qualifications of those who were trained by these institutions. During 1916-17 no one showed any interest to join the Bengal National College as students and it automatically ceased to function.

Lajpat Rai, who was one of the leaders of the Extremist school, became later a strong critic of the attempts to reoganise education on narrow national lines based on Indian traditions and indigenous languages. His attitude was indicative of the temper of the people and the growing realisation on their part that the attempt to live in the past was futile and foolish and that the educational system should take into account the progress in different branches of knowledge in different parts of the world. This was how Lajpat Rai gave expression to this view:

This advanced knowledge and its resultant wisdom is at present embodied in foreign languages. Every year, every month, nay every day in the year, it is making further progress. No one who does not want to fall behind others can

38  A detailed account of the history of the demand for national education is given by Mukherjee and Mukherjee, n. 29, 5-11.

afford to neglect these sciences, which can only be studied effectively for at least a number of years in these foreign languages.... No nation, however ideal in its desires and ambitions, however spiritually inclined in its standards and values of life, can live a life of isolation even if it desires to do so. Intercourse with other nations for purposes of trade and commerce is no longer optional.[39]

Lajpat Rai also maintained that studying a complicated, difficult and ancient language like Sanskrit was a flagrant misuse of energy that was bound to harm the general efficiency of the nation. He was also of the opinion that India's ancient methods of education were also out of date and antiquated.

Apart from these factors, one of the reasons for the failure of the movement for the spread of national education was the opposition from the government. Some of these institutions took full cognizance of the economic needs of the country as a whole and tried to give some technical and scientific training to the students. But the country's economy was not developing rapidly and there were few avenues for employment outside the government services. So the majority of the young men were looking for an education which would qualify them for a job under the government or in an institution approved by the government. This itself made education which was not approved by the government unattractive.

Another difficulty facing these national institutions was that in the absence of the government patronage, they did not have a continuous income. In a flush of enthusiasm many individuals donated vast sums of money to some of the institutions. But neither the enthusiasm nor the contributions of the non-officials was sustained continuously. Under these circumstances the experiments at national education were bound to fail.

The institutions which survived and continued to flourish were those which compromised with their 'national' character like the Arya College at Lahore and the Hindu College at Banaras. Each preferred to provide its own kind of national education. But in actual practice, though not in theory, these institutions functioned more or less in the same manner as the government institutions did. They might have differed in some

39  Lajpat Rai, n. 32, 43-4.

detail from the latter and also in encouraging the study of the vernaculars and the 'sacred' languages; but their primary purpose was to coach students for the university examinations. In two of the leading colleges in the United Provinces, some of the prominent members of the staff were often Europeans. The results achieved in the university examinations were the measure of the success and popularity of these institutions and not their contribution to the study of Hindi, Urdu, Sanskrit and Arabic.

These institutions did promote some political ideas. Unfortunately they were not wholly national in character, but, like the Ganesh and Shivaji festivals, were sectarian in outlook. Looking back on their activities, Lajpat Rai wrote in 1920:

The Muhammedan College at Aligarh, the Arya College at Lahore, the Hindu College at Banaras, all embodied the 'national' ideals of their founders, limited and sectarian as they were at the time. Each professed to provide its own kind of national education. The educational facilities provided by these institutions were open to persons of all creeds, denominations and religions, but the nationalism aimed at was undisgustedly denominational. Each institution created an atmosphere of its own—national to a certain extent, so far as the general cult of love of the country was concerned, but otherwise openly sectarian. The education imparted in these institutions, as distinguished from the ordinary state-owned schools and colleges, was 'national' only in so far as it helped the creation of the denominational atmosphere aimed by its promulgators [40]

We are not concerned here with the details of the demand for the spread of the national education or with the vagaries of the fortunes of the institutions connected with it, but only with its total political effects. Some of the most prominent among them were: (1) This movement and these educational institutions partly succeeded in arousing national pride and by reminding the younger generation of the achievements of their ancestors in the religious and other fields. (2) By emphasising the role of Indian languages as the medium of instruction in educational institutions, the new movement enriched these languages and to some extent spread education to a large section of the people and narrowed down the intellectual and

40   *Ibid.*, 17.

cultural gap between different groups in that section of the people. (3) But as each of the institutions glorified only the past achievements of the predecessors of each group and the interpretation of history which each one of them gave were from the narrow angle of the founders of each one of these institutions, they did not promote national solidarity but only encouraged sectarianism and communalism. (4) As the demand for national education was not entirely based on revivalism, but one which arose from the feeling that government-sponsored institutions did not care for the industrial needs of the country, it also tried to spread industrial and scientific education.[41] (5) The share of the institutions, which stood for national education, in the educational setup of the country was so small that they did not make a great contribution in any special field. As we noted earlier, those among them which survived did so only because they fulfilled more or less the same functions as other institutions.

## PASSIVE RESISTANCE AND NON-COOPERATION

Some of the leaders of the Extremist school thought that in addition to the spread of national education and economic boycott some other effective means should be employed by the people of India to wrest the control of the national life from the grip of an alien bureaucracy. Aurobindo Ghose, who was the ablest exponent of this view, stated:

The mere effort at self-development unaided by some kind of resistance, will not materially help us towards our goal. Merely by developing national schools and colleges we shall not induce or force the bureaucracy to give up to us the control of education. Merely by attempting to expand some of our trades and industries, we shall not drive out the British exploiter or take from the British Government its sovereign power.... Still less shall we be able by that harmless means

41 'The sponsors and organizers of the National Council of Education did not try, as some well-known scholars want to have us beileve, to reorganize the educational life of the nation on "decaying and corupt metaphysics" nor "on the basis of the most antiquated religion and religious supersition." ... If they were loud in their cry for the preservation of what was best in the historic traditions of the race, they were equally passionate in their zeal for the wide diffusion of modern scientific knowledge among their countrymen.' Mukherjee and Mukhrjee, n. 29. 65.

to get for ourselves the control of taxation and expenditure. Nor shall we, merely by establishing our own arbitration courts, oblige the alien control to give up the elaborate and lucrative system of Civil and Criminal Judicature.[42]

The effective means suggested by Aurobindo Ghose were:

The first principle of passive resistance,... is to make administration under present conditions impossible by an organised refusal to do anything which shall help either British commerce in the exploitation of the country or British officialdom in the administration of it—unless and until the conditions are changed in the manner and to the extent demanded by the people.[43]

Aurobindo Ghose even approved the social boycott of those Indians who refused to cooperate with the Indian nationalists.

He did not always stop with the advocacy of 'passive' resistance, because, according to him, there was a limit to passive resistance and he contended that the people could go beyond that limit:

So long as the action of the executive is peaceful and within the rules of the fight, the passive resister scrupulously maintains his attitude of passivity, but he is not bound to do so a moment beyond.... The moment coercion....is attempted, passive resistance ceases and active resistance becomes a duty. If the instruments of the executive choose to disperse our meeting by breaking the heads of those present, the right of self-defence entitles us not merely to defend our heads but to retaliate on those of the head-breakers.... The new politics, therefore, while it favours passive resistance, does not include meek submission to illegal outrage under that term; it has no intention of overstressing the passivity at the expense of the resistance.[44]

Other political leaders did not go so far as Aurobindo Ghose in expounding the importance of passive resistance to the civil authority; nor did they consistently maintain that resistance to the government must be continuously practised. But the idea of passive resistance was not absent from their minds also. For instance, Tilak said in 1907:

42  Ghose, n. 4, 23-4.
43  *Ibid.*, 35-6.
44  *Ibid.*, 62-4.

What the New Party wants you to do is to realise the fact that your future rests entirely in your own hands. If you mean to be free, you can be free; if you do not mean to be free, you will fall and be for ever fallen. So many of you need not like arms; but if you have not the power of active resistance, have you not the power of self-denial and self-abstinence in such a way as not to assist this foreign Government to rule over you? This is boycott, and this is what is meant when we say, boycott is a political weapon.... We shall not assist them in fighting beyond the frontiers or outside India with Indian blood and money. We shall not assist them in carrying on the administration of justice. We shall have our own courts, and when time comes we shall not pay taxes. Can you do that by your united efforts? If you can, you are free from tomorrow.[45]

Bipin Chandra Pal also defended passive resistance. Addressing a public meeting in Madras he said:

Passive resistance is recognised as legitimate in England. It is legitimate in theory even in India and if it is made illegal by new legislation these laws will infringe on the primary rights of personal freedom and will tread on dangerous grounds. Therefore, it seems to me, Sir, that by means of this boycott, we shall be able to negative the work that will have to be done for the attainment of Swaraj. That is negative work. The positive work will also have to be done. But this negative work may create a determination in the people to attain Swaraj. It may create the strength in the people to sacrifice their interest, immediate interest for the good of the country. Boycott may do all these things, but without positive training, no self-government will come to the boycotter. It will have to be done through the organization of our village life, organization of our talukas and districts. Let our programme include the setting up of a machinery for popular administration, running parallel to, but independent of, the existing administration of the government.[46]

When these leaders were thus expounding the theme of passive resistance to and non-cooperation with the government they were, perhaps, only thinking of the tactics and strategy to be employed in the struggle against the alien government, and not on the fundamental political questions concerning the duties and rights of citizens under any political setup. But the

45    Tilak, n. 23, 117-8.
46    Pal, n. 6, 246-7.

prolonged discussions on the question of passive resistance and
its continuous use as a political weapon during the national
movement have considerably influenced the political thinking
and behaviour in modern India and even in free India, civil
resistance to authority is extensively practised by those who
have any grievance against the government.

## EMPHASIS ON COLLECTIVE FREEDOM OF THE NATION

Another important aspect of the political thinking of this
period was the emphasis on the collective freedom as separate
from, if not opposed to, the freedom of the individual. In this
respect the political philosophy of the Extremists stood in contrast with that of the Moderates, who always emphasised the
civil and other rights of the individual. The latter accepted the
political concepts of liberalism, even when they went against
its economic ideas and advocated protectionist tariffs.

Although in a vague sense, many of the Extremist leaders
seemed to have inclined towards idealism as a doctrine, there
was no unified understanding between them on this aspect of
political philosophy, as they did not have on other aspects also.
This was how Bipin Chandra Pal put his views:

A nation is not a collection of individuals.... A nation is
an organism, it has organic life; and like all organisms a
nation has an end unto itself, which is different from the
ends that regulate the activities of other similar organisms,
other similar nations.[47]

Then again:

... a nation is an organism, the individuals are its organs.
Organs find the fulfilment of their ends, not in themselves
but in the collective life of the organism to which they be-
long. Kill the organism—the organs cease to be and to act.
Paralyze the organs, the organism also ceases to live and work.
An organism is logically prior to the organs. Organs evolve,
organs change, but the organism remains itself all the same.
Individuals are born, individuals die; but the nation liveth
for ever.[48]

Expressing a similar view Lajpat Rai said:

A social organism can be...considered efficient, only if, be-

47  *Ibid.,* 252.
48  *Ibid.,* 289.

yond requiring its members to sacrifice what to them seems to tend to their individual good, happiness or prosperity; if the same clashes, or is inconsistent with the good of the whole, it also takes sufficient care of the interests of the generations yet unborn as to guarantee the continuance of that state of efficiency in the future. The social system of a nation is perfect or imperfect, complete or incomplete, natural or unnatural, progressive or retrogressive, according as it does or does not fulfil the requirements set forth above.[49]

It is difficult to trace an utterance of Tilak in which he has taken a similar stand. But he was not very enthusiastic of promoting the political tenets of liberalism. More than once he pointed out to the existence of the native (princely) states as an evidence of the capacity of the Indians to govern themselves and on that basis he demanded that self-government should be extended to British India, although individual citizens enjoyed considerably greater civil liberties and political rights in British India than in native states. Tilak was emphasising the indigenous character of the internal administration under the princes as opposed to its alien character in British India. While making a reference to his book, *Gita Rahesya,* he once indirectly made the following statement about his affinity with Green:

I have shown in this book how the Hindu religious philosophy helps to solve the moral issues.... To a certain extent my line of argument runs parallel to the line of thinking followed by Green in his book on Ethics.[50]

Although this is not a statement which clearly indicates that Tilak belongs to Green's school of thinking, it shows his leanings. Tilak's indifference to social reforms also showed his lack of enthusiasm for liberal principles.

One aspect of the political attitude of the Extremist leaders like Tilak and Lajpat Rai, which was not well understood, was their views on the terrorism practised by many political adventurists in India during the first decade of the twentieth century. Leaders like Tilak, Pal and Lajpat Rai did not encourage terrorism as such; Aurobindo Ghose occasionally organised and helped violent action on the part of a group of

49 Lala Lajpat Rai, *The Man in His Word* (Madras, 1907) 71-2.
50 Quoted by D. V. Tahmankar, *Lokmanya Tilak* (London, 1950) 204.

individuals. But even Ghose conceived the struggle against the
rulers primarily as a political fight to be conducted by the
masses of the people.

The confusion about the attitude of the Extremists arose
from the fact that many of the terrorists were inspired by those
writings and speeches of the former which emphasised the
resistance to the British. Moreover, even when leaders like
Lajpat Rai and Tilak criticised the activities of the terrorists,
they expressed admiration for their courage and sincerity. Commenting on the activities of the terrorists Lajpat Rai said:

> I cannot bring myself to believe in the sanity of the pro-
> gramme of the Revolutionaries.... I have tried to
> remonstrate with them and to show to them the weakness
> and the hopelessness of their methods.[51]

But he also added:

> I do not mean to justify them but I have not the soul to
> condemn them as ordinary murderers or cutthroats. They may
> be misguided or foolish or insane; yet in the eyes of a large
> number of their countrymen they would ever live as martyrs
> for the cause of their liberty.[52]

Tilak expressed his admiration for the Bengali terrorists:

> There is considerable difference between the murders of 1897
> and the bomb outrage of Bengal. Considering the matter
> from the point of view of daring and skilled execution, the
> Chapekar brothers take a higher rank than members of the
> bomb party in Bengal. Considering the ends and means, the
> Bengalis must be given the greater commendation.  Their
> (the Bombay terrorists') aim was especially directed towards
> the oppression consequent upon the plague, that is to say,
> towards the particular act. The Bengal bomb party had of
> course their eyes upon a more extensive plan brought into by
> the partition of Bengal.[53]

### THE PHILOSOPHY OF REVOLUTIONARY TERRORISM

This extensive plan had as its objective the complete independence of India. But it is very difficult to define the political

51  Lajpat Rai, *Reflections on the Political Situation in India* (Lahore? 1915?) 47-8
52  *Ibid.*, 55.
53  Quoted in the *Report of the Sedition Committee* (Calcutta, 1918) 5.

philosophy of the terrorists because, apart from this broad objective of achieving the freedom of the country, one group of terrorists did not have very much in common with another group.

The most important among them was the group in Bengal. About their aims the Sedition Committee Report says:

... the intentions of the revolutionaries were eventually to subvert by violent means British rule in India, and meanwhile to assassinate Government officials, to obtain such help as might be obtainable from the Indian army, and to finance their enterprises by plundering their fellow-countrymen.[54]

They functioned through secret societies. The members of these societies were given anti-imperialist indoctrination by their leaders.

Many of the activities of this band of terrorists were based on the assumption that political freedom could be achieved by a small group of people vowed to celibacy and austere living and devoted to a revolutionary cause. They believed in such principle as absolute surrender to the 'Divine Will,' and Divine Will in this case was to work for the freedom of the country. As a student of their history notes:

The philosophical and the moral fountain-head for the revolutionaries was thus the Gita and its doctrine of selfless fight against evil.... The religious bias remained very strong in Bengal's revolutionary terrorist groups at least till the end of the First World War (1918), and the Hindu bias in their nationalism persisted even later.[55]

In some other parts of India also there were terrorism and revolutionary activities. The government arrested many of those connected with them and held trials in what are known as the conspiracy cases of Nasik and Gwalior.

Some of the revolutionaries went abroad and tried to work for Indian independence from foreign countries. The India House in London led by Krishna Varma and the journal *Indian Sociologist* published by him from Paris were some of the well-known associations and organs founded by them. Another was

54  *Ibid.*, 25.
55  Gopal Haldar 'Revolutionary Terrorism' in Atual Chandra Gupta ed., *Studies in the Bengal Renaissance* (Jadavpur, 1958) 234-5.

the Ghadr organisation formed in America under the leadership of Hardayal. The Ghadr organisation had members in the USA, Canada, Mexico, Japan, China the Honduras, Hongkong and in many other parts of the world where there were Indian immigrants. A rebellion organised by them in 1915 petered out within a few months. Unlike other terrorists and revolutionary movements the Ghadr organisation was secular in character although the majority of its supporters belonged to one religion, Sikhism.

The task conceived by these Indian revolutionaries who worked abroad is summed up as follows:

> First, the revolutionaries did not belong to a single unified party, but were divided into a number of secret groups, generally working independently. Second, they did not subscribe to any common ideology but expressed the common nationalist aspiration for full freedom and a common faith in armed revolution. Third, the common features of their 'terrorism' were organisation of secret societies, anti-imperialist indoctrination of their members, physical and moral training, ...collection of funds by dacoities, assassination by bombs and firearms of enemies and traitors. Fourth, by no means were all who belonged to these revolutionary secret societies reconciled to all such activities.... Almost all took to these as necessary steps in the process of revolution, in the preparation for guerilla campaigns, defection of Indian forces, and finally, for armed insurrection on a wide and national scale. A good number valued the method as calling for maximum sacrifice by minimum men.... The democratic content was relatively weak in their political consciousness and of course it was alien to their methods of organisation which were intended to be military and secret.[56]

None of the conspiracies and rebellions organised by these exponents of armed action inside India and abroad achieved their objective of ending British rule in this country. The government could, in the long run, suppress all revolts and unearth all conspiracies. Some of the organisers and leaders connected with them went abroad and lived as exiles; among others the majority were arrested and convicted to long terms of imprisonment or to death penalty. As a result of the failure of these 'terrorists' and 'revolutionaries' to achieve their objectives and

56   *Ibid.*, 226.

because of the fact that their propaganda and literature never penetrated into the massess, their share in the moulding of the political philosophy of the national movement was limited. When, later, M. K. Gandhi—the most important leader of the national movement—openly opposed the British government and worked among the masses, the programme of the terrorists based on conspiratorial action was completely eclipsed by the campaigns led by him. The work of the Indian revolutionaries in other countries also met with the same fate. But the political tradition of revolutionary terrorism was not entirely forgotten. Under favourable circumstances they tried to assert themselves. The Indian National Army formed abroad during the Second World War under Subhas Chandra Bose was to some extent inspired and supported by the Indian revolutionaries who worked abroad. Some of the 'terrorists' who were released from jail after the expiry of long terms of imprisonment, joined various political parties and movements of the country. A larger number of them felt fully at home in the Indian Communist Party, which, in the nineteen-twenties, was more or less a conspiratorial organisation.

## HOME RULE LEAGUE GIVES A NEW SLOGAN

Another political movement which had a close affinity with the activities of the Extremists was organised by the All-India Home Rule League. It was founded by Mrs Annie Besant in September 1916. Mrs Besant was not the first to establish a Home Rule League in India. Tilak started one in Poona in April of the same year. But it did not make as much an impact as the organisation established by Mrs Besant. The work of Tilak's League was more or less confined to Western and Central India, while the All-India Home Rule League tried to spread in all other parts of the country.

In the public life of India Mrs Annie Besant was at first known as a prominent leader of the Theosophical Society. Ever since she took a keen interest in Theosophy, she considered India to be her home. Before she came to India Mrs Besant led an active life in Great Britain where she was closely connected with the Fabians. When she entered the political field of India in 1916 she immediately made a mark by her ceaseless activity

and capacity for organisation. The work of the Home Rule
League was conducted on the lines of the Irish nationalists and
English suffragettes.

The Home Rule movement did not give a new political doctrine to the country; but it did supply a new slogan to the
national movement. The aim of Mrs Annie Besant and the
movement she led—self-government within the British empire—
was modest, but her advocacy was militant. Commenting on her
activities Dinshaw Wacha, one of the Moderate leaders, wrote
to Dadabhai Naoroji:

> We do not approve of the methods of Mrs Besant who late
> in the day has come forward to support the Congress move-
> ment.... We are alarmed at the way in which she is going
> about on her own responsibility, supported by the Extremists
> ...[it] is a distinct menace to the progress of the country.[57]

It was perhaps Annie Besant's capacity for organisation which
frightened the Moderates and annoyed the government. One
of her admirers wrote in 1918:

> I am not one of those who are unaware of the services done
> by the Congress and by the Congress leaders, but consider
> what has been done in the last few years—the wave of activity,
> galvanic activity that has run through the country and arous-
> ed the self-respect, aspirations and ideal of the people. To
> whom is all this due? It is due to Mrs Besant who, scorning
> leisure and ease and travails and turmoils and position, has
> transcended the difficulties of race that is not ours, of a breed-
> ing that is not ours, of a culture that has become hers.[58]

This tribute to Mrs Besant is fully justified and is indicative
of her achievements in regard to organising Home Rule
Leagues all over the country.

Mrs Besant and many of her followers explained the meaning
of the term, 'Home Rule,' and raised the political consciousness
of a large section of the educated people of the country. Mrs
Annie Besant gave the following reasons for demanding self-
government for the Indians:

1. British rule has destroyed her Village and Council Gov-

57    Masani, n. 9, 531.
58    C. P. Ramaswami Iyer, *Annie Besant—Builder of New India*
(Madras, 1942) 48.

ernment, and has put in its place a hybrid system o Boards and Councils which are impotent for good....

2. British rule, after eighty years of its education, is educating 3.4 [per cent] of the population, and bases her [sic] denial of liberty on the 'microscopical minority' of the educated, due to her [sic] own policy. Japan, under eastern rule, has educated her whole population in 40 years....

3. British rule has destroyed India's finest arts and industries in order to favour the importation of cheap foreign goods....[59]

The term, 'Home Rule was explained as follows:

Home Rule means the Government of the People by the People. Home Rule means the right of the people to send their Representatives to make laws for the People, and to levy taxes on the People. Subjection to laws not made by the Representatives of the People is Tyranny....[60]

The leader of the Home Rule League movement was unequivocal both in the condemnation of the British rule and in the demand for self-government for the people of the country; but she never envisaged a break between Britain and India. Explaining the use of the words 'Home Rule' she said:

It chanced that a year ago I used the words 'Home Rule' instead of Self-Government. The first is shorter: Self-Government is four syllables and Home Rule only two. For a popular cry a short name is better than long one. Moreover, it was a more explicit phrase, because Self-Government might mean independence, and so, to show you did not mean a break between Great Britain and India, it was necessary to add 'within the Empire,' and so you have a great mouthful 'Self-Government within the Empire on colonial lines.' I prefer to call it Home Rule. The advantage is that it is a cry for Freedom without separation.[61]

Other champions of the Home Rule also stated that they did not want Britain to quit India. For instance, Ramananda Chatterjee wrote: '... the present Indian demand is for Home Rule, not Independence.'[62]

59  Annie Besant, India: A Nation (Madras, 1923) 51.2
60  Ramaswami Iyer, n. 58, 270.
61  Annie Besant, Home Rule and the Empire (Madras, 1917) 9-10.
62  Ramananda Chatterjee, Towards Home Rule Part I (Calcutta, 1917) 3.

Although the basic objectives of the Home Rule Leaguers were not radical, the nature of their agitation and organisation and the methods of their functioning gave the impression that they belonged to the Extremist school in Indian politics. Unlike the terrorists, and like the 'extremists' of other persuasions, the organisers of the Home Rule League made their influence felt on the Indian national movement on a large scale.

### 'EXTREMISM'—AN ASSESSMENT

While trying to make an assessment of the work of the Extremists, one must bear in mind that their political philosophy was not a consistent whole. It was never logically worked out as a systematic political thought. As a result, it varied from individual to individual and from one period to another. For instance, Tilak and Lajpat Rai never conceived of swaraj as complete independence from the British, as Ghose and B. C. Pal did. They would have been satisfied with a large measure of self-government. Passive resistance and boycott of everything British did not appear as important items in the progamme of Tilak and Lajpat Rai.

Such differences existed not only between the views of different Extremist leaders, but between the views held by one leader at different times. For instance, Tilak, at the end of his political career, showed greater signs of cooperation with the British administration than he did before that period, and Bipin Chandra Pal, the champion of complete independence during 1906-8 began to advocate India participating in an Imperial Federation later. Aurobindo Ghose moved away from political radicalism and aggressive nationalism to the ideal of 'Human Unity,' in which 'cosmopolitanism' and 'world-union' were stressed. But in this chapter we were concerned only with the political views of these leaders during the period when they were referred to as the Extremists—this was during 1905-8 when, consequent on the agitation following the partition of Bengal, these leaders came out as the champions of swaraj, economic boycott of foreign goods, promotion of indigenous industries and national education. In this period the political thought of all these leaders had many features in common.

The most important among these is that they gave new meaning to the concept of the 'Indian Nation'. They invented and spread such terms as Mother India and swaraj.[63] The term 'swaraj' meant different things to different leaders; but there was no doubt that to all of them it meant some degree of independence from the foreign control. Although it was not the Extremists who first spread the message of patriotism and demanded self-government, they could take credit of the fact that they popularised these concepts among a large section of the people of different parts of the country. Nationalism was thus the first political creed of the Extremists.

Another important task accomplished by them was that they instilled courage and self-confidence among the politically conscious section of the people of the country. After their entry into the field the Indian nationalist movement outgrew the earlier phase in which the leaders of the country were engaged in petitioning the foreign government for the redress of their grievances. In the next phase the champions of Indian nationalism asked for their rights and not for favours from the government. 'Self development' was very often the term used to indicate a political programme based on the inherent strength of the people and not on any help received from the alien masters. In this period there was a widespread realisation of the fact that there were some basic conflict between the interests of the Indian people and those of their British masters. In the political campaign of the leaders there was, therefore, an emphasis on bringing pressure on the rulers and not on arguing with them, it was also realised that this pressure could be exerted not by a small section of the people but by the organised work of the masses.

The arousal of the enthusiasm of the masses for political action thus became another important feature of the political activities of the Extremists. They, therefore, gave a democratic direction to the nationalist movement both by bringing a large number of people into political action and also by trying to break the monopoly of the leadership of a few within the Congress party. Aurobindo Ghose was emphasising this aspect of the

63 The term swaraj was used by Dadabhai Naoroji in his presidential address at the Congress session at Calcutta in 1905, and Dadabhai was not an Extremist, but it was was the Extremists who popularised it.

conflict between the old leadership and the Extremists when he wrote:

> As happens inevitably in such popular contests, personal questions and differences of minor importance intervened to perplex and embitter the strife, but the real questions in debate were those which involved the whole future development of the spirit and form of self-government in this country. Were that spirit and form to be democratic or oligarchic? Were they to be constitutional in procedure or governed by arbitrary and individual choice and discretion? Was the movement to be progressive and national or conservative and parochial in its aims, policy and spirit? These were the real issues. The Nationalist party stood for democracy, constitutionalism and progress. The Moderate party, governed by an exaggerated respect for old and esteemed leaders, helped, without clearly understanding that they did, those who stood for oligarchy, arbitrary procedure and an almost reactionary conservatism.[64]

There is an exaggeration in Aurobindo Ghose's claim in favour of the Extremists; but he is right in so far as he points attention to the new direction they gave to the Congress.

Although the participation of the masses in the political action and the uncompromising opposition to the arbitrary action of the alien government were healthy developments, there were other aspects of the political movements led by the Extremists which had disastrous results. One was connected with the participation of the masses in the political agitation itself. Unlike the Moderates, the Extremists took into account the traditions of the masses of the people and appealed to them in their attempt to arouse them for political action. But some of these traditions to which they made an appeal were religious ones and this intermingling of religion with politics had some disastrous consequences.[65]

Another aspect of the political philosophy of at least one Extremist leader (Aurobindo Ghose) was that he gave a theological explanation to history and politics. This was a repudiation of the ideas of enlightenment, reason and liberalism, which were to some extent accepted by the Moderate leaders. There was an inherent mysticism and non-scientific, if not

64 Sri Aurobindo, *Speeches* (Pondicherry, 1952) 145-6.
65 This is discussed at length in the next chapter.

unscientific, approach in the political philosophy of Aurobindo Ghose. This promoted a certain degree of obscurantism in the political thinking.

The programme of boycott associated with the Extremists also had two sides: while in the economic field it fulfilled a positive function of fostering indigenous industries, in the field of education, in the name of national education, it encouraged a certain degree of sectarianism because different institutions glorified the heritage of different communities and thus conveyed the impression to members of one community that it was superior to others. But as the institutions covered by the demand of 'national education' were few and far between, their total impact on the education of the people at large was limited.

As the economic boycott was more widespread, the Extremists succeeded in promoting economic nationalism as well as political nationalism.

Passive resistance to authority was another one of the concepts of the Extremists. Perhaps, they wanted it to be used only against an alien ruler who refused to yield to other kinds of agitation. But the passive resistance to authority, which was later extensively used by Gandhi, had come to stay as not an uncommon political practice in India.

The Extremists, as a group, did not subscribe to any collectivist philosophy as such. But many of their utterances indicated that they were less interested in defending the civil liberties of individual citizens than in fighting for the collective freedom of the nation. In the militant nature of the struggle they launched, the individual was often asked to sacrifice his interests for the nation. There was thus an implicit collectivist element in the political thinking of the Extremists.

It is difficult to sum up in one sentence the political philosophy of such a group of leaders as the Extremists who were primarily concerned with evolving a strategy and some tactics for conducting a struggle for freedom from the British rule. The form of the political campaigns conducted by them and the methods used by them to make their cause popular gave the impression that they were social reactionaries and religious revivalists. But the most important contribution they made to the Indian nationalist movement was to make it a popular movement devoted to the cause of promoting nationalism—and an uncompromising opposition to the arbitrary character of the alien government in the country. By emphasising the inherent right of the people to be free from foreign control and by realising and acting on the assumption that the means of the struggle for freedom depended on its popular support, the Extremist leaders set in motion those political forces at work which were, in the ultimate analysis, helpful to the cause of freedom and democracy in the country.

In the next chapter we will discuss, among other things, the interrelation between religion and politics in the campaigns organised by the Extremist leaders and try to examine how it has affected their political thinking.

# CHAPTER IV

# INTERRELATION BETWEEN RELIGION AND POLITICS

VERY few students of modern Indian politics will deny that religion was a major factor in the political thinking of a large number of people during the national movement. The utterances of many political leaders and the establishment of organisations like the All-India Muslim League and their functioning emphasise the interrelation between religion and politics in the country. In different phases of the national movement it took different shapes. In some periods religious issues and political slogans couched in religious terms came to the forefront and at other times they were dormant; but, at least, during 1905-21 religion was rarely absent in the political thinking of a large number of the people. This applies to both the Hindus and the Muslims of the country.

We will begin this chapter with the analysis of role religion played in the political thinking of the Extremist leaders and the majority of their followers who were Hindus. We will next note the political thinking of many Indian Muslims with reference to the role religion played in it. The chapter will conclude with an examination of the religious issues brought forward by M. K. Gandhi in connection with the political movements he led and supported towards the end of this period.

There are two aspects to this interrelation between religion and the political movements associated with the Extremists; one is what is termed as the spiritualisation of politics associated with Aurobindo Ghose and the other was the attempt of the leaders like Tilak to arouse enthusiasm for the political movement by appealing to the religious instinct and traditions of the vast majority of the people. While the first tried to give a theocratic explanation to social and political events and pictured India as a mother who should be worshipped, the second was primarily concerned with using religious festivals for arousing enthusiasm for political movements and for organising political agitation on the model of the then existing religious festivals. These two types of mixing religion with politics did not run on parallel lines, but were often fused in one and the same political movement led by the Extremists. Leaders like Lajpat Rai and Bipin Chandra Pal did not share all the views of Aurobindo and Tilak; but some of their political activities were coloured by their religious outlook and their association with some social and religious reform movements. Broadly speaking, one can conclude that religion in one form or other did play a prominent part in the political movements connected with the Extremist leaders.

## RELIGION—A SOURCE OF COURAGE

Hindu religious scriptures were a source of inspiration and courage to many of these leaders. It is not an accident that many of them made their own commentaries on *Bhagavad Gita*. Tilak's *Gitarahasya* attracted much attention not only among those who were interested in religion but among the political and social workers. He thought that the message of the *Gita* was primarily the call to action. In his own words: 'I differ from almost all commentators when I say that the *Gita* enjoins action even after the perfection in *Gnana* and *Bhakti* is attained and the Diety is reached through these medium.'[1]

On another occasion he said:

The study of the *Gita*, *Ramayana* and *Mahabharatha* produce the same ideals throughout the country. Are not these— common allegiance to the *Vedas*, the *Gita* and the *Ramayana* —our common heritage? If we lay stress on it forgetting all the minor differences that exist between different sects, then by the grace of Providnce we shall ere long be able to conso- lidate all the different sects into a mighty Hindu nation. This ought to be the ambition of every Hindu.[2]

1  Bal Gangadhar Tilak, *His Writings and Speeches* (Madras, 1918, 2nd ed., 1919) 234.
2  Bal Gangadhar Tilak, *Speeches Delivered During 1889-1918* Madras, 1918) 66-7.

Lajpat Rai, another prominent leader, also wrote a short book entitled *The Message of the Bhagavad Gita*.[3] The importance of this book lies not so much in its content—the author does not say anything new—but in the fact that here is another instance of a leader trying to find solace in religious scripture when he is facing hardships owing to his political convictions and in the fact that he tries to instil courage in others by appealing to an ancient Hindu religious text.

## NATIONALISM AS RELIGION

Aurobindo Ghose was the powerful exponent of the view that nationalism was a religion. His own words were:

Nationalism is not a mere political programme; Nationalism is a religion that has come from God. Nationalism is a creed which you shall have to live.... If you are going to be a Nationalist, if you are going to assent to this religion of Nationalism, you must do it in the religious spirit. You must remember that you are the instruments of God.[4]

Aurobindo Ghose did not stop with this statement that nationalism must be approached in a religious spirit but further developed the view that in the Indian context it must be connected with Hinduism:

I say no longer that nationalism is a creed, a religion, a faith; I say that it is the Sanathana Dharma which for us is nationalism. This Hindu nation was born with the Sanathana Dharma; with it it moves and with it it grows. When the Sanathana Dharma declines, then the Nation declines and if the Sanathana Dharma is capable of perishing, with the Sanathana Dharma it would perish.[5]

According to Bipin Chandra Pal also, the Indian national movement was essentially a spiritual movement and to regard it as either a mere economic or political movement is to misunderstand it altogether.

The philosophy that stands behind it is the philosophy of the

3   Lajpat Rai, *The Message of the Bhagavat Gita* (Allahabad, 1908).
4   Sri Aurobindo, *Speeches* (Pondicherry, 1952) 6.   The speech referred to was delivered in 1908.
5   Sri Aurobindo, *Uttarpara Speech* (Calcutta, 1943) 20. Speech was delivered in 1909.

Absolute, the philosophy of Brahman, as applied to the interpretation of Man's social and civic life. It looks upon man as the spirit of God incarnated, and views social and civic institutions as instruments and vehicle for the progressive revelation and realization of God and through man.[6]

Referring specifically to the influence of Hindu religious traditions on Indian nationalism, Pal observed:

Behind this mighty transfiguration of the old religious ideas and symbols of the country stands, however, a new philosophy of life. Strictly speaking, it is not a new philosophy either, but rather a somewhat new application of the dominant philosophical speculations of the race. Behind the new nationalism in India stands the old Vedantism of the Hindus. The ancient Indian philosophy, divided into many schools, has one general idea running through it from end to end. It is the idea of the essential unity of man and God. According to this philosophy, Substance is one though expressed through many forms. Reality is one though appearances were multitudinous.... Neo-Vedantism, which forms the very soul and essence of what may be called Neo-Hinduism, has been seeking to realise the old spiritual ideals of the race, not through monkish negations or medieval abstractions, but by the idealisation and spiritualisation of the concrete contents and actual relations of life. It demands, consequently, a social, an economic and a political reconstruction, such as will be helpful to the highest spiritual life of every individual member of the community. The spiritual note of the present nationalist movement in India is entirely derived from this revived Vedantic thought.[7]

C. R. Das, while defending Aurobindo Ghose in the Alipore Bomb Case, explained the latter's concept of nationality.

The doctorine of Vedantism is that man is not dissociated from God; that is to say, if you want to realise your self you must look for the God within you. It is within your heart and within your soul that you will find that God dwells, and as no man can attain to his own salvation without reaching to that God that is within you, so also is the case of nations.... No nation can attain this unless it realises the highest and noblest and the best of that nation. As in the case of individuals you cannot reach your God with extraneous aid, but you must make an effort—that supreme effort—

6   Bipin Chandra Pal, *Swadesh and Swaraj* (Calcutta, 1954) 1.
7   B. C. Pal, *The Spirit of Indian Nationalism* (London, 1910) 33-40.

yourself before you can realise the God within you; so also with nation. It is by itself that a nation must grow; a nation must attain its salvation by its unaided effort. No foreigner can give you that salvation. It is within your own hands to revive that spirit of nationality. That is the doctrine of nationality which Aurobindo has preached.[8]

Although Tilak's concept of the role of religion in politics was different from that of Ghose and Pal, he occasionally referred to Vedantic ideas and Dharma in relation to political work. Elaborating the view that Home Rule was his right he said:

I said that it was our right to have Home Rule but that is a historical and a European way of putting it; I go further and say that it is our 'Dharma'; you cannot separate Home Rule from us, as you cannot separate the quality of 'heat' from fire.[9]

INDIA—A MOTHER GODDESS

Another feature of the nature of the political agitation in this period was the glorification of India as a mother goddess. This was connected with the Hindu practice of praying to the idols of many gods and goddesses. Bipin Chandra Pal explains the evolution of the concept of Mother India.

The so-called idolatry of Hinduism is also passing through a mighty transfiguration. The process started really with Bunkim Chandra, who interpreted the most popular of the Hindu goddesses as symbolic of the different stages of national evolution.... This interpretation of the old images of gods and goddesses has imparted a new meaning to the current ceremonialism of the country, and multitudes, while worshipping either *Jayadhatri*, or *Kali*, or *Durga*, accost them with devotion and enthusiasm, with the inspiring cry of 'Bande Mataram'. All these are the popular objects of worship of the Indian Hindus, especially in Bengal. And the transfiguration of these symbols is at once the cause and evidence of the depth and strength of the present movement. This wonderful transfiguration of the old gods and goddesses is carrying the

8  V. P. Varma, *Political Philosophy of Sri Aurobindo* (Bombay, 1960) 444. Extracts from C. R. Das's arguments at the trial are given as Appendix II in this book.

9  Tilak, n. 1, 230.

message of new nationalism to women and the masses of the country.[10]

As Pal observes, the adoption of these religious symbols made the message of nationalism popular with the masses; but unfortunately it was only with the Hindu masses. Such an important minority as the Muslims were not only not moved by them. but were repelled by these symbols. This reaction of the Muslims was particularly manifest when many leaders, for political purposes, made use of the Hindu religious functions like the Durga Pujas and Ganesh festivals.

Bipin Chandra Pal tried to justify the attempts of the leaders to make political propaganda during the Durga Puja as follows:

> Durga stands today to immense members of the Bengali people, not merely as a Pauranic Deity or as a mythological figures, but as the visible representative of the Eternal Spirit of their race.... It is impossible to conceive a better or more inspiring symbol of the Race-Spirit than this, and it is not all strange that thousands of Bengali Hindus should stand before it today and cry Bande-Mataram.[11]

## CONCEPT OF HINDUS AS A SEPARATE POLITICAL ENTITY

Those aspects of the political agitation of the Extremists which were connected with Mother Worship, Durga Puja and Shivaji festivals were no doubt connected with a certain degree of Hindu revivalism; but as they were primarily directed against the foreign political domination over India, they only indirectly affected Hindu-Muslim relations. It did not take the form of mutual antagonism, but only in the Muslims not participating on a large scale in such festivals and *Pujas* which were not in line with their religious traditions and practices. But there were some other features of the political thought and activities of the Extremists which directly affected Hindu-Muslim relations.

Some typical ones are those of Lajpat Rai of the Punjab. Unlike Aurobindo Ghose he did not give any theological explanation to Indian history; nor was he, unlike Tilak, unenthusiastic of social reforms under the then existing circumstances. But as many other political leaders of the Punjab he

10  Pal, n. 7, 36-8.
11  *Ibid.*, n. 6, 105.

was very much eager to protect what he considered to be the Hindu interests. On one occasion he said:

> As at present situated the absence of such an organisation (Hindu political or semi-political organisation) places the Hindu at distinct disadvantage, and takes away from them, the chances of a united action or of a united expression of opinion upon matters, which affect the unity, prosperity, the well-being and generally the interests of Hindus all over India.... In my opinion it should be the business of such a Hindu Congress or conference to support and take, as far as possible, such steps which might conduce to their unity and strength as a religious nationality, as for instance, the language question, the question of characters, the advisability of having common textbooks, the teaching of Sanskrit language and literature all over India, the taking of steps which might lead to the protection of Hindu orphans from the hands of proselytising agencies of other denominations and if necessary to record a protest against those confidential circulars of the Government, which aim at the favouring of other communities to the loss of the Hindus.[12]

These observations of Lajpat Rai were of a defensive character because they arose from a fear that there was a discrimination against the Hindus by the government and their number were being reduced by conversion to other religions. But Lajpat Rai, far from confining to such a defensive attitudes, advocated the promotion of Hindu nationalism. For instance he said:

> In my humble opinion it is sufficient for the growth of nationality, if the different parts that claim the shelter of its ways have a sense of unity, which is sufficient to make them combine against a common enemy and a common danger. Run on a few basal principles in religion, on the community of a sacred language, and on the community of interests, the Hindus ought to foster the growth of a national sentiment which should be sufficiently strong to enable them to work for the common good in the different ways and according to the lights vouchsafed to each.[13]

Lajpat Rai was not alone in expressing such views. Commenting on Shivaji, in whose name a festival was organised

12  Lala Lajpat Rai, *The Man in his Word* (Madras, 1907) 258.
13  *Ibid.*, 63.

under the guidance of Tilak, Bipin Chandra Pal stated:

To us, he is the great Hindu nation-builder. He is, to us, the only incarnation, so to say, of the civic ideals and possibilities of the great Hindu people. Not as Bengalees, therefore, but as Hindus, really, we commemorate him today. As we pointed out year before last, when the Shivaji celebrations were first started in Calcutta, the rise of the great Mahratta confederacy proved for all time to come the political potentialities of the Hindu people.[14]

Tilak himself did not give much importance to the fact that Shivaji was Hindu. He explained the significance of Shivaji festival in these words:

Hero-worship is a thing deeply implanted in human nature and our political aspirations need all the strength which the worship of Swadeshi hero is likely to inspire into our minds. For this purpose, Shivaji is the only hero to be found in Indian history of modern times. He was born at a time when the whole nation required relief from misrule. By his self-sacrifice and courage, he proved to the world that India was not a country forsaken by Providence. It is true that the Mahomedans and Hindus were then divided and Shivaji who respected the religious scruples of the Mahomedans had to fight against the Mogul rule that had become unbearable to the people. But, it does not follow from this that now that the Mahomedans and the Hindus are equally shorn of the power they once possessed and governed by the same laws and rules, they should not agree to accept as a hero one who in his own days took a bold stand against the tyranny of his own time.... No one ever dreams that every incident in Shivaji's life is to be copied by anyone at present. It is the spirit which actuated Shivaji....that is held forth as the proper ideal.[15]

Although this was the aim of Tilak and although some Muslims did occasionally participate in the Shivaji festival, there was no doubt that Shivaji was in the eyes of many Indians --both Hindus and Muslims—a hero of the Hindus who fought against their Muslim enemies.

Apart from these actions of Tilak connected with the organisation of these festivals of a Hindu religious character, his

14    Pal, n. 6, 73.
15    This extract is from an article in the *Mahratta* dated 26 June 1906. Quoted by T. V. Parvate in *Bal Gangadhar Tilak* (Allahabad. 1958) 124.

resistance to the carrying out of some social reforms like the raising of the marriageable age of the girls was indicative of his essentially conservative nature. In 1890 the Bombay government sponsored a Bill which among other things (1) made the cohabitation by a husband and his wife under twelve years of age a penal offence, (2) gave the wife, who had been married in infancy, the right to dissolve the marriage, after attaining majority and (3) denied a husband, who had married his wife when she was an infant, the right to sue for the restitution of conjugal rights. Tilak opposed the Bill and worked energetically to organise the orthodox Hindus against it. Later, he explained his position as follows: 'It is a well-known fact that I differ from Mr Paranjpye and his party in matters social. I don't hold that a social reconstruction must be undertaken prior to political emancipation.'[16] Expressing an identical view Aurobindo Ghose said:

Political freedom is the life-breath of a nation; to attempt social reform, educational reform, industrial expansion, the moral improvement of the race without aiming first and foremost at political freedom, is the very height of ignorance and futility.[17]

Aurobindo Ghose also paid the following tribute to Tilak:

His [Tilak's] separation from the social reform leader, Agarkar, had opened the way for the peculiar role which he had played as a trusted and accredited leader of conservative and religious India in the path of democratic politics. It was this position which enabled him to effect the union of the new political spirit with the tradition and the sentiment of the historic past and of both with the ineradicable religious temperament of the people, of which these festivals (Ganapathi and Shivaji festivals) were the symbol. The Congress was for a long time occidental in mind, character and methods, confined to the English educated few, founded on the political rights and interests of the people read in the light of English history and European ideals, but with no rights either in the past of the country or in the inner spirit of the nation. Mr. Tilak was the first political leader to break through the routine of its somewhat academical methods, to

16 S. L. Karandikar in *Lokmanya Bal Gangadhar Tilak* (Poona, 1957) 601.
17 A. Ghose, *The Doctrine of Passive Resistance* (Pondicherry, 1952) 3.

bridge the gulf between the present and the past and to restore continuity to the political life of the nation. He developed a language and a spirit and he used methods which Indianised the movement and brought it to the masses.[18]

This was not only an Indianising process as Ghose maintained, but also a Hinduising process.

Tilak's earlier role in promoting Hindu solidarity was also in line with these actions. During the Hindu-Muslim riots in 1893 and 1894 he tried to defend the Hindu community. In 1893 he popularised the Ganesh festival and tried to make it a powerful agency for imparting instructions to the masses. Until then the worship of Ganesh, who was one of their gods, was confined to the household. One of Tilak's biographers explains Tilak's action on the ground that it was purely defensive:

... The building of Hindu solidarity seems to have been the immediate reason for the organisation of the Ganapathi festival. The Hindu-Muslim riots of 1893 in Bombay and Poona.... gave Tilak every reason to believe that the British Government was favouring the Muslims and directly or indirectly encouraging them to take up an aggressive attitude. He rightly argued, therefore, that the Hindus must take a firm stand against Muslim provocation, not because they are Muslims, but because they are allowing themselves to be used as agents of foreign rulers.[19]

There can be considerable difference of opinion on Tilak's motives in organising Ganesh and Shivaji festivals and in opposing social reforms, but there can be no doubt that some of the effects of all these developments were to introduce and to promote the notion that Hindus were a separate political entity, or a least a group of people who had separate political interests to protect. Unlike Tilak, Lajpat Rai, the Arya Samajist, and B. C. Pal, the Brahmo Samajist, were ardent social reformers. But, as we noted earlier, they also spoke of a Hindu nation and the protection of Hindu interests on a political level. The total effect of all these developments was to promote some kind of Hindu solidarity. It was no doubt primarily directed against the alien ruler; but when it was coupled with some other deve-

18  Tilak, n. 1, 5-6.
19  D. V. Tahmankar, *Lokmanya Tilak* (London, 1956) 62.

lopments it strengthened the schism between the Hindus and the Muslims.

## RELIGION AND THE POLITICAL IDEAS OF MUSLIMS

During 1885-1921 there was no one single cardinal political thought that dominated the Indian Muslims. There were divergence of views among them on the questions of cooperation and non-cooperation with the British government, participation along with other communities in the Indian National Congress, the establishment of a separate political organisation for protecting and promoting Muslim interests and supporting a Pan-Islamic movement to protect the interests of Muslims abroad. The role of religion in politics was also another matter of controversy. Apart from these cleavages of opinion among the Indian Muslims, a factor which makes the study of their political philosophy a difficult task is that no single trend dominated the whole period. For instance, while in one period there was a distrust of the Congress and a willingness to cooperate with the government, in another the Muslims showed great eagerness to ally with the Congress in their political campaigns against the British. Their attitude was also influenced by different factors. To begin with, a good number of Indian Muslims were averse to the study of English language. They also showed no eagerness to take up new ways of life opened by the introduction of Western political and administrative systems and the changes that were taking place in the economic field. It was the participation in these new educational, political, administrative and economic activities that led to the rise of new social classes among the Hindus. As the majority of the Muslims kept away from them, their share in the new social classes was small and not in proportion to their total number in the country. Later the Muslim leaders tried with some success to popularise Western type of education among the Muslims. But owing to their late start, there was always a gap between the vast majority of the Hindus and the minority of Muslims who were educated. As the political movements of India during the first two decades of the twentieth century were primarily influenced by these new social classes, the difference between the number of Muslims and the number of Hindus who were represented in them created a difference in the political approach of the Hindus and that of the Muslims in India.

There were also many historical reasons for the divergence of political views between the Hindus and Muslims. As we noted earlier, a historical figure like Shivaji was to many Hindus a political hero who fought for freedom; but to many Muslims he was the political opponent of the Muslim rule of India. Under some of the Muslim monarchs, with a few notable exceptions, Muslims enjoyed many political privileges which were denied to the Hindus and these privileges were often associated with their scholarship in Arabic, Persian and Urdu languages. The special tax imposed on the Hindus by some Muslim kings accentuated these differences. All these factors led to intermingling of politics and religion in the minds of Muslims and a good number of them into believing that they were not only a religious, but a political, entity. Even in the twentieth century, while making an attempt to glorify their past, many Indian Muslims referred back to the history of Arabia and to the history of India under Muslim rule. On the other hand the majority of Hindus went back to the glorious days of Indian history connected with the Guptas and the Mauryas.

This was not the only strand of thought among the Indian Muslims. There was another which stood for cooperation with the non-Muslims. Under the Mughal rule this trend found its best expression in Akbar, while the Muslim separatism found it in Aurangzeb. Under the British period also there were these two currents of thought among the Muslims.

Although the political attitude of the Indian Muslims can be broadly divided into these two categories—one standing for cooperation with the non-Muslims and another emphasising their separateness—we must note that these two cannot be kept in watertight compartments. They were not always mutually exclusive. Very often the idea of Muslim separateness was mingled with the desire to cooperate with non-Muslims and *vice versa*.

In the period under survey, 1885-1921, the Indian Muslims manifested all these varying shades of opinion. To begin with, they accepted the ideas of prominent Muslim leaders like Sir Syed Ahmad Khan and Ameer Ali which emphasised the Muslim separateness. They were also influenced by Badruddin Tyabji and R. M. Sayani, who were the presidents of the Indian National Congress and who stood for united political action on the part of all the people of India. Apart from these legacies many internal and international developments during 1905-21 influenced the political thinking of the Indian Muslims. Some of the major events in India were: the partition of Bengal in 1905, the creation of the Muslim League in 1906, the deputation of the Muslim leaders to the Viceroy in 1906, introduction of the system of separate electorates on the basis of religion in 1909, the annulment of the partition of Bengal in 1911, the Congress-League Pact of 1916 and the Khilafat Agitation of 1919-21. Some of the major international events which affected the Muslim thinking were: the war in the Balkans in 1912, Italian attack on Turkish positions in Tripoli, the Russian attack on Persia and the dismemberment of the Turkish empire after 1914-18 war and the new situation it created regarding the Caliphate.

Some of the most important leaders who made a mark on the political thinking and activities of the Muslims during 1905-21 were: the Aga Khan, Ameer Ali, Abul Kalam Azad, Muhammad Ali Jinnah, Mohasin-ul-Mulk, Muhammad Ali and Shams-ul-Ulema Allaf Shibli.

The main trends of political thinking of the Indian Muslims in this period were as follows:

(1) The Muslims must not involve themselves in political activities but should concentrate their energies on matters connected with their social backwardness, education and economic progress. This view, which had great support toward the end of the nineteenth century, was gradually losing its influence by the beginning of the twentieth century.

(2) The Muslims must join the rest of the people in their constitutional agitation for the extension of civil rights and political progress. Tyabji was one of the early spokesmen of this view. During 1910-17 Jinnah became its champion.

(3) Indifference towards, if not active opposition to, the Extremist political agitation led by leaders like Tilak, Pal, Lajpat Rai and Aurobindo. One of the immediate demands of the Extremists was to annul the partition of Bengal and

Muslims were not enthusiastic about it. They were also not inspired by the Hindu religious symbols used by the Extremist leaders.

(4) Demand for separate electorates for the Muslims— symbolised by the Muslim deputation to the Viceroy in 1906.

(5) Disillusionment with the British government because it annulled the partition of Bengal and also because it did not, in the view of some Indian Muslim leaders, protect Muslim interests abroad. This attitude encouraged close cooperation with the non-Muslims in the political sphere and led to the League-Congress Pact.

(6) Emergence of political radicalism among the Indian Muslims. Maulana Azad was the first representative of this trend. Later, during the Khilafat agitation, Maulana Muhammad Ali became the most dominant leader of these radical elements who stood for vigorous struggle against the British government.

Although each one of these strands of thoughts was different from the other, many of them emphasised that religion was connected with politics, or at least that Muslims had their own separate political interests to protect. This aspect was clearly evident in the demand for separate electorates and weightage. It was present, though not so openly, in the Muslim support to the non-cooperation movement and to other aspects of their participation in radical political movements. Very often it was the sympathy for the foreign Muslims who suffered at the hands of the Western governments that encouraged a section of the Indian Muslim to support the political agitation directed against the British government. The methods of some of the struggles against the government had also a religious colour in it.

There were of course exceptions. Azad's support to vigorous political agitation against the British government was not devoid of religious appeal; but it was not concerned with any separate Muslim interests. It conceived of an Indian nation as one unit. A leader who took an almost secular approach towards political problems was Jinnah, whose activities in this period were confined to constitutional agitation. He qualified even his support to the system of separate electorate by his assertion that it was a necessary evil, which should be welcomed only for a short period.

## MUSLIMS ASKED TO BE NON-POLITICAL

One of the first acts of Muslim separatism was the attempt of many Muslim leaders to keep away their co-religionists from the rudiments of a political agitation associated with the birth of the Indian National Congress. The Muslims were socially and educationally backward and they had suffered the worst under the repression following the 1857 uprising. Muslim leaders like Syed Ahmad Khan thought that the Muslim must concentrate on raising their educational level and on proving that they were the loyal subjects of the British Crown. In their opinion, participation in political activities would divert their attention from these important tasks. The Scientific Society which Sir Syed Ahmad Khan founded in Garipur in 1862 was indicative of this attitude. He advised the Muslims to keep away from the Indian National Congress because he thought that it was disrespectful to the authorities.

## FOREIGN RULE IN PREFERENCE TO MAJORITY RULE

Another view which received widespread support among the Indian Muslims was that representative institutions were not suited to India. Syed Ali Imam, addressing the All India Muslim League, said in 1908:

> What has kept the Mahomedans as a people away from the Indian National Congress? It was, I say, this very demand for the transfer of legislative and administrative control from the rulers to the ruled, in other words, that the ruling authority should vest in the party that commands a majority of votes in the Council chambers of the Indian Autonomy. It does not require much imagination to see that such a majority could be the Hindu majority.[20]

Many reasons were given to show that Muslims were loyal to the government. For instance, one of the pamphlets stated:

> It is not so well known as it should be that Muslim subjects of

20 Speech of Syed Ali Imam, Bar-at-Law, as President of the All India Muslim League Amritsar Session (Bankpur, Bengal, 1908) 19.

His Majesty are the most loyal supporters of the Crown and the Constitution. The chief reason for this is that we are forbidden by the Koran to take part in any rebellious or seditious movements.[21]

R. M. Sayani, one of the Muslim Presidents of the Congress, summing up 'the objections of the Mussulmans to the Congress' said:

That it is against their religion to join the Congress, as by joining the Congress they will be joining the Hindus who are not Mussulmans. 2. That it is against their religion to join the Congress, as by joining the Congress they will be joining a movement opposed to Government, a thing which is opposed to their religion, which directs obedience and loyalty to Government albeit Government may not be treating them properly. 3. That it is against their religion to learn the English language. 4. That the success of the Congress would weaken the British rule, and might eventually end in the overthrow of the British power and the substitution of Hindu rule. 5. That Government is against the Congress movement; that in addition to the duty of loyalty, the Mussulmans owe the duty of gratitude to Government for giving them a liberal education; therefore by joining the Congress, the Mussulmans would be guilty of the sin of ingratitude towards Government. 6. That the Congress does not adequately represent all the races of India. 7. That the motives of the persons constituting the Congress are not honest. 8. That the aims and objects of the Congress are not practical. 9. That the Congress is not important enough to deal satisfactorily with the subjects it takes up. 10. That the modes of Government prevailing in the West, namely, examination, representation, and election, are not adapted to India. 11. That such modes are not adapted to Mussulmans. 12. That the result of the application of Western methods to India would be to place all offices under Government in the power of the Hindus, and the Mussulmans would be completely ousted from Government employment. 13. That Government employment should be conferred not on the test of examinations, but by selection on the ground of race, position of the family and other social and local considerations. 15. That in as much as the Congress is a representative body, and in as much as the Hindus formed the majority of population, the Congress will necessarily be swamped by the Hindus, and the resolutions of the Congress will,

21 Sheik Memir-ud-din, *The Indian Muslim Attitude towards the British Government* (Cuttack, 1915) 22.

to all intents and purposes, be the resolutions of the Hindus and the Mussulman's voice will be drowned and therefore, if the Mussalmans join the Congress they will not only not be heard, but will be actually assisting in supporting Hindus to pass resolutions against the interests of the Mussulmans, and to give colour to such resolutions as the resolutions of Hindus and Mussulmans combined and thus aiding in passing resolutions against themselves and misleading Government into believing that the Mussulmans are in favour of such resolutions.[22]

Following were some of the assumptions on which these views were based: (1) the Muslims and the Hindus are two nations; (2) representative institutions were unsuited to India because its population was not a homogeneous one; (3) the Indian Muslims must be loyal to the British and must depend on them for safeguarding their interests; (4) they must concentrate on spreading education and on taking over steps to raise themselves socially; (5) they must not participate in the agitation for the grant of political power to the representatives of the people. It was not an accident that in 1886, only a year after the establishment of the Congress, Syed Ahmad Khan organised the Muslim Educational Conference and thus tried to divert the attention of the Muslims to such channels.

Syed Ahmad and other Muslim leaders also appealed to their followers to keep away from the Congress. This appeal had the desired result. At the second session of the Congress there were 33 Muslims out of 440 delegates; in 1905 there were only 17 Muslim delegates out of a total 756.

The widespread view among the educated Muslims was that they should not associate with the Congress in its early phase.

By the beginning of the twentieth century the separatist elements among the Indian Muslims realised that this decision not to participate in the political life and to oppose political progress of the country had become out of date. They began to feel that professions of loyalty to the British government would not automatically safeguard their separate interests. They

22 Razaul Karim, ed., *Muslims and the Congress: Being A Symposium of addresses of the Muslim Presidents of the Congress from 1885 to 1940* (Calcutta, 1941) 35-7.

felt that they must organise themselves separately and put forward their own demands to the government.

## THE SIMLA DEPUTATION AND THE IDEA OF
## SEPARATE ELECTORATES

The All India Muslim League was the outward expression of
this feeling. Many Muslim leaders emphasised their separate
entity and the need for a separate organisation. A landmark
in the political history of Indian Muslims in the twentieth
century was the Muslim Deputation which met the Viceroy on
1 October 1906. The Delegation consisted of 70 prominent
Muslims and was led by the Aga Khan. They asked, among other
things, for separate representation of Muslims in all levels
of government—district boards, municipalities and legislative
councils. Their memorandum stated:

> The position accorded to the Mahomedan community in any
> kind of representation, direct or indirect, and in all other
> ways affecting their status and influence, should be commen-
> surate not merely with numerical strength, but also with
> their practical importance and the value of their contribu-
> tion which they make to the defence of the empire, and we
> also hope that Your Excellency will, in this connection, be
> pleased to give due consideration to the position which they
> occupied in India, a little more than a hundred years ago,
> and of which tradition have naturally not faded from their
> minds.[23]

These demands made one thing clear: the Muslims were not
only concerned with their proportionate share in the administration, but with a weightage for them.

The Simla Deputation of the Muslim leaders was a matter
of great controversy. Many Indian leaders contended that it
was inspired by individual Englishmen if not by the British
government itself. Maulana Azad is reported to have said:

> I am a living witness to the fact that when as a result of the
> agitation of the people, certain reforms were about to be
> conceded in 1906, the late Nawab Mohsin-ul-Mulk was sent
> for, by telegram at Simla, from Bombay where he was then
> putting up with a friend. The result of the interview was that

23 All India Moslem League, *The Indian Mahomedans and the
Government* (London, 1909) 4.

the Aga Khan who was on his way to Europe had to return from Aden. An address was, then, drawn up by Syed Bilgrami of Hyderabad (Deccan) on behalf of the Muslims of India asking for separate electorates. All this was manoeuvred from Simla.[24]

Maulana Mohamed Ali also takes a similar view of the Simla Deputation. He said:

To follow the fashion of British journalists during the War, there is no harm *now* in saying that the Deputation's was a 'command' performance! It was clear that Government could no longer resist the demands of educated Indians, and, as usual, it was about to dole out to them a morsel that would keep them gagged for some years. Hitherto the Muslims had acted very much like the Irish prisoner in the dock who, in reply to the judge's inquiry whether he had any counsel to represent him in the trial, had frankly replied that he had certainly not engaged counsel, but that he had friends in the jury! But now the Muslims' friends in the jury had themselves privately urged that the accused should engage duly qualified counsel like all others.[25]

Another view on the Simla Deputation was that it sprang primarily from the Muslims themselves and the part played by individual Englishmen in it was relatively unimportant. A Muslim League document refers to incessant activity on the part of many Muslims before the interview with the Viceroy in 1906 and notes:

The Muhammedan Associations and Anjumans, and leading Muhammedans all over the country were consulted. The draft memorial was submitted and carefully scrutinized and discussed in every centre of Muhammadanism from Peshawar to Madras, and there was much correspondence and consideration before it assumed its final form. A Committee which included many leading Muhammedans assembled at Lucknow a week or two before to make the concluding arrangements.[26]

### THE ESTABLISHMENT OF THE MUSLIM LEAGUE

Another important function fulfilled by the Simla Deputation

---

24 Quoted in Ram Gopal, *Indian Muslims: A Political History 1858-1947* (Bombay, 1959) 97-8.
25 Afzal Iqbal, ed., *Select Writings and Speeches of Maulana Mohamed Ali* (Lahore, 1944) 254.
26 All India Muslim League, *The Rules and Regulations* (Allahabad, 1907) 144.

was that it indirectly led to the establishment of the Muslim League. Even before 1906 Muslim leaders like the Aga Khan and Ameer Ali had thought about the idea of establishing a separate political organisation for the Muslims, but they had not worked out a concrete scheme for its implementation. During a meeting of some prominent Muslims of the Punjab held at Lahore in February 1906, Fazl-i-Hussain coined the term the Muslim League.[27] But no further step was taken to establish a permanent organisation. Later, the Simla Deputation made an impact on the minds of many Muslim leaders. Mohsin-ul-Mulk, who was a prominent member of the Deputation, wrote to the Aga Khan:

> The deputation which went to Simla should be kept alive, and I suggest that a committee of Members of the deputation should be appointed to correspond with the Government for the realisation of the representations made. That is the work of an all India Association, and if you agree, I shall make detailed proposals.[28]

Other individuals were also thinking on the same lines. The Nawab of Dacca circulated among the various Muslim organisations his scheme of an All-India Muhammedan Confederacy with its dual object of safeguarding Muslim interests as well as the British Raj. This was how the Aga Khan explained the interrelation between the Simla Deputation and the Muslim League:

> For ourselves in 1906 we asked for the establishment of a principle, a principle which would have to be embodied in any legislation as a consequence of these proposals for reform. We asked for adequate and separate representation for Muslims both on local bodies and on the legislative councils, we asked that this representation be secured by a separate communal franchise and electoral roll. In short, we Muslims should have the right of electing our own representative on it.[29]

The Aga Khan adds:

> Our achievement in 1906 seemed important enough; and it was obvious to those of us most closely associated with it—

27  Azim Hussain, *Fazl-i-Hussain* (London, 1946).
28  *Ibid.*, 97.
29  The Aga Khan, *The Memoirs of Aga Khan* (London, 1954) 93.

especially Nawab Mohsin-ul-Mulk and myself—that, since we' had obtained separate electoral recognition, we must have the political organisation to make that separate representation effective. The All-India Muslim League was therefore founded at a meeting at Dacca after that year....[30]

The meeting which was convened in December 1906 to establish the Muslim League declared:

That this meeting, composed of Mussalmans from all parts of India, assembled at Dacca, decides that a political association styled the All-India Muslim League be formed for the furtherance of the following objects: (a) To promote among the Mussalmans of India feelings of loyalty to the British Government and to remove any misconceptions that may arise as to the intention of Government with regard to any of its members; (b) to protect and advance the political rights and interests of the Mussalmans of India and respectfully to represent their needs and aspirations to the government; (c) to prevent the rise among the Mussalmans of India of any feelings of hostility towards other communities, without prejudice to other objects of the League.[31]

The Muslim League, like the Indian national Congress, passed through different stages. Its attitude towards the British government, the Indian National Congress and towards the non-Muslims varied from one period to another. It is therefore difficult to locate one single principle as the most dominating theme of the Muslim League politics of 1907-21. In some respects this early phase of the Muslim League resembled the early phase of the Congress.

The first activities of the Muslim League were an almost word for-word repetition, along communal lines, of those of early Congress twenty years before. In a quite clerical atmosphere the men concerned, protesting their imperial loyalty, pointed out that they did not have quite enough influence nor enough jobs. At the first session 'the resolutions passed related to adequate Muslim representation in the new Councils, to Muslim places in the public service, and to Muslim loyalty.'[32]

Apart from the fact that the League resolutions referred to

30  *Ibid.*, 95.
31  *The Pioneer*, 2 January 1907.
32  W. C. Smith, *Modern Islam in India* (London, 1946) 171.

exclusively 'Muslim' representations, it created a gulf between
the Muslims and Hindus by putting forward those demands
which in Congress circles, had by that time been replaced by
the more militant demands associated with swaraj, swadeshi
and boycott. As late as 1912 the spirit of the Muslim League's
resolutions was as follows:

(1) The object of the League shall be to promote and main
tain among Indians feelings of loyalty towards the British
Crown. (2) To protect and advance the political and other
rights and interests of the Indian Mussalmans. (3) To promote
friendship and union between the Mussalmans and other
communities of India. (4) Without detriment to the fore-
going objects, the attainment of a system of self-government
suitable to India by bringing about through constitutional
means a steady reform of the existing system of administra
tion by promoting national unity and fostering public spirit
among the people of India; and by co-operating with other
communities for the said purpose.[33]

## MUSLIM REACTION TO HINDU REVIVALISM

There was no doubt that some aspects of the political agitation led by the Extremist political leaders did strengthen
the separatist tendencies among the Indian Muslims. Presiding
over the annual session of the All-India Muslim League in
1908, Syed Ali Imam said:

I ask the architects of Indian nationalism both in Calcutta
and Poona; do they expect the Mussalmans of India to accept Bande Mataram and Sivaji celebration? The Mahommedans may be weak in anything you please but they are not
weak in cherishing the traditions of their glorious past. I
pray the Congress leaders to put before the country such a
programme of political advancement as does not demand
sacrifice of the feelings of the Hindu or the Mahommedan,
the Parsee or the Christian.[34]

Muslims also reacted against the manifestations of Hindu
revivalism in some literary works. This was one of their comments on the subject:

33 *The Indian Review* (Madras, January 1913) 54.
34 *Speech of Mr. Syed Ali Imam, as President of the All India Muslim*
*League* (Bankpur, 1908) 28.

The pages of most of the Bengalee novels, especially those of Bankim Chandra—for whose literary merit even the Bengalee Mussalmans, of course, entertain a high admiration —are saturated with anti-Muslim bias so much so that non-Muslims cannot but be adversely impressed on reading the works of the greatest Bengali novelist of our generation. In most of Bankim's books, especially *Rajsinha,* deliberate offence is given to the Mussalmans; when a Mussalman goes through the book his blood simply boils.... The mischief that the literary lawlessness of Bankim Chandra has created in the country far outweighs that committed by some lawless people in Eastern Bengal and elsewhere. Many of the Bengali novels abound in the abuse of Mussalman monarchs, queens and princesses, whom the community rightly or wrongly hold in high esteem. Even Akbar has not been left alone by Damodar.[35]

## DISCONTENT IN THE THEOLOGICAL AND RELIGIOUS FORM

These grievances and the educational, social and economic backwardness were the main sources of strength of Muslim separatism. But it often expressed itself through theological and religious language and by so doing it added further strength to it. Focussing attention to the extra-territorial loyalty of the Indian Muslims, Dr. S. M. Iqbal wrote:

The membership of Islam as a community is not determined by birth, locality or naturalization; it consists in the identity of belief. The expression, Indian Muhammedan,' however convenient it may be, is a contradiction in terms; since Islam in its essence is above all conditions of time and space. Nationality with us is a pure ideal; it has no geographical basis. But in as much as the average man demands a material centre of nationality, the Muslim looks for it in the holy town of Mecca; so that the basis of Muslim nationality combines the real and the ideal, the concrete and the abstract.[36]

Similar views were expressed by others. At a meeting of the London branch of the All-India Muslim League Ameer Ali said:

35 Majumdar Rahman, *The Hindustan Review* (Allahabad), 18 (November 1908) 420.

36 Dr Sheikh Muhammad Iqbal, 'Islam as a Moral and Political Ideal,' *The Hindustan Review,* 20 (August, 1909) 168.

... (But) the Mahommedans have their own particular interests, interests which generally speaking, concern them alone and the administration. It is impossible for them to merge their communal existence in that of any other nationality or to strive for the attainment of their ideals under the aegis of any organisation other than their own, Diversity of religion and ethical standards make the absolute fusion of the races and peoples of India impracticable.[37]

The following resolution passed at the meeting of some Muslims in Allahabad was indicative of the opinion held by many Muslims in the country:

The Mahommedans of Allahabad look with much concern on the agitation of their Hindu countrymen to thwart the joint claims of Mussalmans.... The Mussalmans of Allahabad beg to point out most emphatically that the difference between Mussulmans and Hindus is no mere difference of articles of religious faith but difference between life, traditions, history and all social things; and in view of the state of feeling existing between both parties, nothing short of separate representation at all stages can secure the interests of the Mussulmans.[38]

One Muslim who supported the Swadeshi movement in principle, thus qualified his support to it:

Mussalmans cannot possibly join in militant Swadeshism, They have an international importance and a greater responsibility. They are bound by duty and religion to be loyal to the ruling authority. They have to win the sympathies and affections of the British people not only for themselves in India but also for the sake of their co-religionists abroad. So if their Hindu countrymen want them to join hands with them in Swadeshism, that Swadeshism must be run on peaceful and economic and not on political and militant lines.[39]

In a period when the political agitation led by the Extremist leaders was spreading political dissatisfaction, Islamic scriptures were often quoted by some Muslims to propagate loyalty to the government. The following extract from a speech of Iqbal is an example:

37 *Report of the Inaugural Meeting of the London Branch of the All India Muslim League with the President's Address* (London, 1908) 7.
38 All India Muslim League, n. 23, 36.

Listen to him and obey him, says the Prophet in a tradition mentioned by Bukhari, even if a Negro slave is appointed to rule over you.... In this country we are living under a Christian government. We must always keep before our eyes the example of those early Mohammedans who, when persecuted by their own countrymen, had to leave their homes to settle in the Christian state of Abyssinia. How they behaved in that state must be our guiding principle in this country where an overdose of Western ideas have taught people to criticise the existing government with a dangerous lack of historical perspective. Our relations with the Christians are determined for us by the Quran which says: 'And those will find nearer in friendship of the believers those who call themselves Christians; this is because among them are learned men and hermits, and because they are never vain.'[40]

## THE ALLEGED SUPERIORITY OF THE MUSLIMS

Another feature of the Muslim separatist movement in this period was that it was based on the alleged superiority of the Muslims to the Hindus. A resolution passed at the annual conference of the All-India Muslim League in 1908 stated:

That the All-India Muslim League regrets that the Secretary of State for India has not explicitly confirmed in his Despatch on the scheme of reform of Councils just pronounced, His Excellency the Viceroy's reply to the address presented by a deputation of Mussalmans in October 1906, that in consideration of the value of the contribution which Mussalmans make to the defence of the Empire and in view of the position which they occupied in India until recently, His Excellency was in entire accord with the members of the deputation who, in His Excellency's opinion, justified the claim that the position of the Mussalman should be estimated not merely on their numerical strength, but in respect to the political importance of their community and the service it has rendered to the Empire, and the League trusts that the important pronouncement will speedily be confirmed by the Secretary of State, and given practical recognition in fixing the proportion of seats in Councils to be filled in by purely Mahommedan electorates.[41]

39 M. K. Kidwai, 'Indian Muslims and Swadeshism, *The Hindustan Review* (October, 1908) 341.
40 Dr. S. Y. Hashimy, ed., *Muhammed Iqbal: Iqbal's Maiden English Lecture — Islam as an Ethical and a Political Ideal: delivered in 1908* (Lahore, 1955) 91-2.
41 All-India Muslim League, n. 23, 33.

There were four aspects to these separatist demands of the Muslim League: (1) the fear of the domination of the Hindus, who constituted the majority of the population; (2) the belief that Muslims were part and parcel of a community whose interests extend beyond the corners of this country; (3) their relations with the British authority in India were on a footing different from that of the rest of the population, because of theological considerations and because of their interest in the welfare of the Muslims outside the country with whom the British government were connected in various ways; and (4) the feeling that Muslims were entitled to some privileges in India because they were once enjoying them as the rulers of the country and also because they contributed more than their proportionate share to the defence of the British Empire.

These demands can be grouped into three categories: (1) those which were of a defensive nature and which arose from the fear of domination by Hindus who were in majority and who were educationally and economically the most advanced section of the people; (2) based on religion and religious affinity with many non-Indians—a non-secular approach to politics and (3) the alleged superiority of the Muslims arising from historical reasons—this was an aggressive idea.

There were two important features in the political situation arising from these developments: (1) one section of the Muslims and the British government in India found themselves in each other's company in their opposition to the political agitation organised by the Indian National Congress; (2) the different levels of development of the Hindus and of the Muslims in educational, social and economic fields were a political factor in modern India; (3) the legacy of the continuous preaching that religion and politics are interrelated and the constant appeals to religious scriptures in support of a political view.

The partition of Bengal, which was one of the immediate causes for a militant agitation against the British government, was also one of the first issues on which an influential section of the Muslims gave support to the government against the nationalists. After the Simla Deputation, some Muslims held a political meeting at Dacca on 30 December 1906 to consider the question of establishing the Muslim League. At that meeting a resolution was passed welcoming the partition of Bengal and deprecating the agitation against it. Later, after the creation of the Muslim League, its central committee expressed grave anxiety over the anti-partition movement and expressed the hope that the government would stand firm on its decision.[42] Their view was that the partition had saved the Muslims of East Bengal from degradation and ruin. Other Muslim organisations which welcomed the partition of Bengal were the Central National Muhammadan Association and the Muhammadan Literary Society. Commenting on the differences in the attitudes of the Hindus and Muslims towards the anti-partition agitation, the Sedition Committee stated:

> The agitation was Hindu and drew its strength from the *Bhadralok*. It was keenly resented by the Muhammedans. who form the majority of the inhabitants of Eastern Bengal; and thus throughout the year 1906-7, Hindu and Muhammedan relations became exceedingly strained in the province. The boycott and the consequent picketting of shops by students and schoolboys led inevitably to frequent disturbances. In both Bengals it was frequently asserted and sometimes believed that Government was getting the Muhammedans against the Hindus. Educated Hindu feeling reached a remarkable intensity of feeling.[43]

Thus we see that during 1905-12, a large section of the Indian Muslims stressed the difference between the Hindus and Muslims. At first those who belonged to this school of thought contended that Indian Muslims must keep away from the political activities conducted by the Indian National Congress, whose prominent leaders were non-Muslims, and that they should raise themselves socially through education and with the support of the British government to which they must be loyal. In this phase they also opposed the introduction of representative institutions in India on the grounds that they were not suited to a multi-religious society like that of India and that it would lead to Hindu domination over the Muslims. Later, when these Muslim 'separatists' began to realise that

42  *Aligarh Institute Gazette* (Aligarh) 19 August 1908, 9.
43  India, *Sedition Committee Report* (Calcutta, 1918) 14.

some kind of representative institutions would be introduced in this country, they demanded that Muslims must have separate electorate and weightage in the assemblies so that they could safeguard their interests. And they also hoped that the British authorities in the country would protect their interests, if they were threatened by the Hindus. In short, suspicion of the Hindu domination, and faith in the British government's willingness and capacity to help the Muslims, were the two main features of the political thinking of Muslim separatists during 1905-12.

## RELIGIOUS BASIS FOR MUSLIMS' COOPERATION
### WITH NON-MUSLIMS

We were so far examining how a religious bias in political thinking led many Indian Muslims to stand apart from the dominant national movement in the country. We also noted that they were in the company of the British government. Very often the same faith in Islam and what many Indian Muslims considered to be their separate interests encouraged them to cooperate with non-Muslims in the political field and participate in joint political campaigns against the rulers of the country.

As far as one section of the Indian Muslims were concerned, it was the changed circumstances that were responsible for their taking two different stands in two different periods. There was also a new factor. With the spread of education to new sections of Indian Muslims and their becoming aware of the conditions and developments in different parts of the country, new elements entered in their political thinking.

Among the Indian Muslims these were the currents of thought which favoured cooperation with the non-Muslims in the political sphere; (1) support to the constitutional agitation for the extension of civil rights and political progress; (2) organisation of the revolutionary movements demanding freedom for the country, conceiving it as a part of an international movement against colonialism, in which many Muslim countries of the Middle East were participating: (3) opposition to the British government arising from the feeling that they had not protected Muslim interests in India and abroad. In the struggle against the government to redress these Muslim grievances, Hindus were conceived as the allies of the Muslims.

## MUSLIMS AND LIBERAL POLITICAL IDEAS

The earliest among these currents of thoughts was Western liberalism, which exerted some influence among some sections of the Muslims as it did among the Hindus towards the end of the nineteenth century. The few Muslims who supported the Indian National Congress from its inception, represented this view. Presiding over the annual session of the Indian National Congress in 1913, Nawab Syed Mohammad said:

> In the eloquent address delivered by the late Badruddin Tyabjee as the President of the Third Congress held at Madras in 1887, he said: 'It has been urged in derogation of our character as a representative national gathering, that one great and important community—the Mussalman community— has kept aloof from the proc dings of the two last Congresses. Now, gentlemen, this is only partially true, and applies to one particular part of India, and is moreover due to certain especial local and temporary causes.' These temporary causes alluded to by Mr Tyabjee are now gradually disappearing with the progress of education and it is a happy sign of the advancing times that there is an increasing rapprochement between Hindus and Mussalmans—a rapprochement emphasis- ed this year by the fact that the All India Muslim League, during its session in Lucknow has adopted the following resolution, viz., the 'All India Muslim League places on record its firm belief that the future development and pro- gress of the people of India dtpend on the harmonious working and co-operation of the various communities and hopes that leaders of both sides will periodically meet together to find a modus operandi for joint and concerted action in questions of public good.'[44]

By 1913 the Muslim League moved away from its earlier moorings and began to advocate a system of self-government to India. Of course, these ideas were not absent in the League circles even in an earlier period. Addressing the London branch of the League, Ameer Ali said in 1908:

44 Razaul Karim, n. 22, 74-5.

The general interests of the nationalities of India are identical. The Muhammedans are equally, with the others, interested in broadening of the basis of sympathy between the official classes and the people, in the growth in India and in the colonies of better relations between Easterners and Westerners, in the development of representative institutions, in the improvements of various departments and administration.[45]

In 1913, the Muslim League accepted as its aim 'the attainment under the aegis of the British Crown, of a system of self-government suitable to India through constitutional means, by bringing about, amongst others, a steady reform of the existing system of administration, by promoting national unity, by fostering public spirit among the people of India and by cooperating with the other communities for the said purpose.[46]

This created an area of agreement between the politically conscious section of Hindus and that of the Muslims. There was still the outstanding dispute concerning the electorate— Muslims demanding separate electorate and the Hindus opposing it. In this period some Muslims showed a tendency to maintain that communal representation should be considered as a temporary measure, which should be dispensed with later.

The Congress held its annual session at Lucknow in December 1916 simultaneously with that of the Muslim League. Representatives of the two organisations agreed upon a scheme of reforms as a definite step towards self-government. The agreed scheme, which was known as the Lucknow Pact, accepted the principle that Muslims should have separate electorate in regard to elections to the legislative councils and that they should have weightage in those provinces where they were in a minority. According to this scheme, the Muslim position in various provincial legislative councils was as follows:

The Punjab 50%, the U.P. 30%, Bengal 40%, Bihar 25%, C.P. 15% Madras 15% and Bombay 33½%. The joint scheme also envisaged that no bill, nor any clause thereof, nor a resolution introduced by a non-official affecting one or the other community in any legislative council should be proceeded with, if three fourths of members of that community in the

45  *Report*, n. 37, 6-7.
46  Azim Hussain, n. 27, 99.

particular council would oppose the Bill or any clause thereof or the resolution.[47]

The importance of the Lucknow Pact can be realised from the fact that its main principles were later incorporated in the Government of India Act, 1919. It was largely the accomplishment of constitutionalists and indicated the area of agreement between the liberal wing in the League and that in the Congress. M. A. Jinnah was an important leader of the Muslim League in this period.

But those who did not owe any allegiance to liberalism and to constitutional methods gradually became more influential in both the communities.

## REVOLUTIONARY ZEAL OF AZAD

Some individual Muslims were exponents of political radicalism even in an earlier period. Abul Kalam Azad was one among them. Later he became the symbol of those Muslims who wanted to participate fully in Indian nationalist movement in its uncompromising fight against the alien rule. Religion had made tremendous impact on him and many of his appeals to his co-religionists to join the nationalist movement were not free from a religious approach. But unlike many other Muslim leaders who were dissatisfied with British government on sectarian and religious grounds, Azad joined the nationalist movement, primarily on political grounds.

Azad was distressed to find that some Hindus conidered Muslims to be the agents of the British. Referring to the terrorist and other revolutionary groups of Bengal in 1905-6, he wrote later:

In those days the revolutionary groups were recruited exclusively from the Hindu middle classes. In fact all the revolutionary groups were then actively anti-Muslim. They saw that the British Government was using the Muslims against India's political struggle and the Muslims were playing the Government's game. East Bengal had become a separate province and Bamfield Fuller, who was then Lieutenant-Governor, openly said that the Government looked upon the

47 The full text of the scheme of reforms jointly sponsored by the Congress and the League is given in D. Chakrabarthy, and C. Bhattacharya, comp., *Congress in Evolution* (Calcutta, 1935) 189-93.

Muslim community as its favourite wife. The revolutionaries felt that the Muslims were an obstacle to the attainment of Indian freedom and must, like other obstacles, be removed. One other factor was responsible for the revolutionaries' dislike of Muslims. The Government felt that the political awakening among the Hindus of Bengal was so great that no Hindu officer could be fully trusted in dealing with these revolutionary activities. They therefore imported a number of Muslim officers from the United Provinces for the manning of the Intelligence Branch of the Police. The result was the Hindus of Bengal began to feel that Muslims as such were against political freedom and against the Hindu community.[48]

In 1908, Azad visited some Arab countries and referring to his experience there he says:

Contact with these Arab and Turk revolutionaries confirmed my political beliefs. They expressed their surprise that Indian Musalmans were either indifferent to or against nationalist demands. They were of the view that Indian Muslims should have led the national struggle for freedom, and could not understand why Indian Musalmans were mere camp-followers of the British. I was more convinced than ever that Indian Muslims must cooperate in the work of political liberation of the country. Steps must be taken to ensure that they were not exploited by the British Government. I felt it necessary to create a new movement among Indian Musalmans and decided that on my return to India, I would take up political work with greater earnestness.[49]

On his return to India, Azad started an Urdu journal, *Al Hilal*. Its first number was published in June 1912 and very soon it achieved tremendous popularity. It gave a new note of intense nationalism and it created a revolutionary stir among its readers.[50]

Although Azad's fervent nationalism, or at least his political writings, were based on religion, he did not write or say anything which were antagonistic to non-Muslims. His writings gave the impression that his ultimate objective was to arouse enthusiasm among the Indian Muslims towards the nationalist cause. As his political record indicated, he did not waver from this purpose throughout his life.

48  Maulana Abul Kalam Azad, *India Wins Freedom* (Calcutta, 1959) 4-5.
49  *Ibid.*, 7.

## PAN-ISLAMIC SENTIMENTS AND THE KHILAFAT AGITATION

Another trend of thought which influenced Indian Muslims in this period was pan-Islamism. Although it started from an assumption, which was different from that of the political ideas preached by Azad, it ended by supporting the Indian national cause. Since 1912, a section of Indian Muslims began to express their increasing sense of dissatisfaction with the manner in which many Muslim countries were treated by the European powers. Since Britain was also responsible for the miseries of their co-religionists abroad, they turned anti-British. In a period when Indian nationalist forces were organising agitation against the British government in India for the national cause, these Muslims became their allies. The culmination of this trend was the widespread Khilafat agitation of 1920-21 which coincided with the non-cooperation movement launched by the Indian National Congress under Gandhi's leadership.

Tracing the interrelation between pan-Islamism and the origins of political radicalism among the Indian Muslims, Maulana Mohamad Ali, a prominent leader of the Khilafat movement says:

> The attitude of England towards the enemies of Turkey, Persia and Morocco had begun to alienate the sympathies of Indian Musalmans ever since 1911; and this estrangement could not but react on their relations with the British officials in India, who in spite of their detestation of the radical politicians in power at home could not help looking askance at Indians daring to criticize an English Government with a candour and courage unusual for a subject race. In 1913 I was precipitated into open conflict with the official world when they declared the forfeiture of a pamphlet I had received along with several other Indian Musalmans from Turkey, appealing to England for Christian succour against the Balkan Allies, whose Macedonian atrocities were therein depicted.[51]

50 See Appendix for the English translation of Maulana Abul Kalam Azad's article on 'The Aims and Objectives of the Party of God' published in one of the issues of *Al Hilal*.

51 Afzal Iqbal, ed., *My Life: A Fragment — An Autobiographical Sketch of Maulana Mohammed Ali* (Lahore, 1942) 39.

Elaborating the same theme elsewhere, Mohamad Ali added:

But it is with Pan-Islamism or the Revolt of Islam that we are at this moment concerned. Islamic Kingdoms today stand on the brink of a great precipice. Morocco, the extreme Western representative of Islam, is feared to sink to the position of a European dependency. Tripoli, the last section of the Muslim Empire in Africa, was expected by Italy to follow the same fate. In Asia too, Persia has been in imminent danger—though,...it has now passed away—of partition and annexation, and is still in some danger of becoming a European dependency. Turkey which was to have been sent back bag and baggage to Baghdad by Mr. Gladstone, may possibly lose even Asia Minor to Germany which seeks a place in the sun, and if Mr. Hogarth be true, Arabia itself is not immune form falling into the hands of Christendom. And in Europe anything may happen when the snows melt and the spring flowers bloom. Is it strange then that uneasiness should prevail throughout the Islamic world?[52]

In this respect the Indian Muslim's hostility to British government derived from their sympathy for Muslims abroad and their feeling that Britain did not help them. One action of the British government in India also increased this hostility and indirectly led them to join the Hindus in their struggle for freedom from alien domination. Curiously enough this was the annulment of the partition of Bengal, which was very popular among the Hindus. When the partition was annulled many Muslims began to feel that the old policy of loyalty to the government as advocated by Syed Ahmad Khan and the founders of the Muslim League would not pay.

Nothing could have more clearly convinced them that their dependence upon a foreign government for support against sister communities laid them perpetually open to such betrayals. They now realized that they could place no reliance on such support, whether at home or abroad, and it set them thinking that perhaps at a much smaller sacrifice of their interests they could purchase lasting peace and even secure the friendship of their neighbour and fellow-countrymen.[53]

When the atmosphere was thus conducive to the promotion of cordial relations between the two communities, younger

52 Iqbal, n. 25, 54-5.
53 Ibid., 262-3.

Indian Muslims, who were affected by the racial nationalism of the educated classes, began to assert themselves. Such intellectuals as Dr Ansari, Maulana Azad, Maulana Shibli and the Ali brothers came into prominence. As W. C. Smith, the author of the well-known book, *Modern Islam in India,* observes:

> Akbar's caustic epigrams and satires, Shibli's wistful and pungent *Trouble in the Balkans,* Iqbal's nostalgic ode to once-Arab Sicily and his powerful, puzze *Complaint* to God, these and much else in the same vein roused the middle-class Muslim discontent, and satisfyingly gave it expression.[54]

In this period, the following four journals also promoted political redicalism among the Indian Muslims: *Al Hilal* edited by Azad; *Zamindar* edited by Zafar Ali Khan and *Comrade* and *Hamdard* edited by Muhamad Ali.

These developments were favourable to the Muslims and the Hindus joining in a political struggle against the British authority in India and such a struggle took a crystalised shape in the Khilafat agitation led by the Ali brothers and the non-cooperation movement led by Gandhi during 1920-21. During the war the Indian Muslims' concern about the fate of Britain's Muslim enemies in Turkey did create a resentment in their minds, but it did not lead to any widespread political agitation. The government, however, imprisoned Muhamad Ali and Shaukat Ali during most part of the war period. Azad was arrested towards the end of 1916 and was released only on 31 December 1919. During the war the Prime Minister had said that the Allies had no intention of breaking up the Turkish Empire. After the war Muhamad Ali led a deputation to Britain and tried to convince the British government that in the final settlement of the international boundaries of the Muslim world, the sentiments of Indian Muslims should be taken into account. He did not succeed in his mission.

When subsequent developments indicated that the British government was in no mood to act in accordance with these views and sentiments expressed by Muhamad Ali and his colleagues, the 'Khilafat' agitation was organised in India.

The word 'Khilafat' is derived from the Arabic root 'khalf, to

54 Smith, n. 32, 196.

leave behind,' and the word *Khalifa* (from *Khalafa* past tense,
meaning he came after or succeeding another that had perish-
ed or died) means primarily a successor, and hence the
supreme or greatest ruler who supplies the place of him who
has been before him. Thus Khilafat constitutes in a man's
serving as an agent to or a representative of another after
him in certain matter or in a certain capacity or position. This
man is called Khalifa in Arabic philology, i.e., one who comes
after and fills another's place whether his agency be due to
death or removal of that other, or to his absence or to a
voluntary transfer of his authority and power.[55]

Many Indian Muslims held the following view regarding the
importance of their loyalty to their Khalifa:

A Muslim or non-Muslim ruler cannot command the loyalty
of the faithful (Muslim) living under him if that loyalty is at
variance with his loyalty to his Khalifa (Imam). The loyalty
to one's God and faith should always take precedence over
his loyalty to a purely secular ruler. Among the Mussalmans,
loyalty and obedience to the Khalifa means loyalty and
obedience to God: No ruler of the Muslims can legally and
legitimately, according to Islamic doctrines, expect their
obedience against the authority of their Khalifa. If a Muslim
or non-Muslim prince demand the obedience of his Mussalman
subjects he must live on terms of accord and harmony with
the commander of the Faithful—Khalifa and it was therefore
that in the history of the Islamic peoples the politico-religious
controversies which turned upon the right to the Khalifa are
by far the most important.[56]

No cause aroused as much enthusiasm among the Indian
Muslims as the Khilafat and when their political agitation concerning it was combined with the non-cooperation movement
led by Gandhi in 1921, India witnessed an unprecedented mass
political action against the established authority in the country.
Many rural people in North India thought that the term 'Khilafat' originated from the Urdu word 'Khilaf' which meant
'against' and that Khilafat agitation meant that they were sup-
posed to oppose the government.

A separate organisation was created to conduct the Khilafat
agitation. The first Khilafat conference was held at Delhi on
23 November 1919. The leaders of the Khilafat conference

55 M. H. Abbas, *All About the Khilafat* (Calcutta, 1923) 2-3.
56 *Ibid.*, 21-2.

decided to launch a non-cooperation movement if the injustices imposed upon Turkey were not removed by 1 August 1920.

By 1920, the deliberations in the meetings of the Muslim League also began to reflect the deep feelings of the Muslims over the Khilafat question. Its annual convention adopted the following resolution on 29 December 1919:

> This meeting of the All-India Muslim League shares with the entire Muslim world the wide belief that His Imperial Otto-man Majesty Sultan Waheed-ud-din is the recognised Khalifa of Islam and places on record its deep-seated and unshakeable devotion to the sacred person of His Imperial Majesty as a successor of the Prophet and the head of Islam. This meet-ing of the All-India Muslim League expresses its deep dis-appointment at the disregard shown by the British Govern-ment to the repeated representations made by Indian Mussal-mans through their representatives in England and India re-garding the question of Khilafat, holy places and Jazirat-ul-Arab and feels constrained to express that no settlement con-templating the dismemberment of Turkey would ever satisfy Indian Mussalmans but keep them in a state of perpetual dissatisfaction and discontent, for the grave consequences of which they shall not be responsible. Under the circumstances the Mussalmans would be fully justified in carrying on all possible methods of constitutional agitation open to them including a boycott of the British army if it is likely to be used outside India for Imperial and anti-Islamic purposes.[57]

Many Muslims also tried to get the cooperation of Hindus in their struggle against the government and tried to convey the impression that all sections of the people of India were in-terested in the Khilafat question. While, on the one hand, this was the line taken, on the other, there was an emphasis on the exclusively religious character of the Khilafat agitation. The All-India Khilafat Conference which met at Karachi in July 1921 stated:

> ...this meeting clearly proclaims that it is in every way religiously unlawful for a Mussalman at the present moment to continue in the British army and it is the duty of all the Mussalmans in general and the Ulema in particular to see that these religious commandments are brought home to every Mussalman in the Army.[58]

57 The Indian Review (January, 1920) 23.
58 The Indian Annual Register 1922 (Calcutta, 1925) 134.

The strength of the Khilafat movement was that for the first time in modern India it led to the Hindus and Muslims participating in a single mass movement directed against the alien authority in the country.

But it had many negative aspects. As the author of the book *Modern Islam in India* observes: 'It was a wrong ideology, romantic and out of touch with actualities.'[59] The following conversation between the British Prime Minister and Muhamad Ali indicates how out of date the latter was as far as the developments in Arabia are concerned:

The British Prime Minister asked Muhamad Ali:

'That means that you are opposed to the independence of Arabia?' Mr. Muhamed Ali: '... since we have got to provide sufficient territories and resources and naval and military sources for the Khalifa, the requirement of the utmost economy which has to rule and govern all our claims in these matters suggests that both these requirements may easily be satisfied if the Jazirat-ul-Arab remains, as before the war, under the direct sovereignty of the Khalifa. We have great hopes that if we have opportunities of meeting our co-religionists we shall bring about a reconciliation between them and the Turks'.[60]

Later events proved that these hopes of Muhamad Ali were not based on any knowledge of the situation in Arabia and Turkey. Neither the Arabs were enthusiastic of Turkish domination over them nor were the Turks very keen on holding on to their possessions in Arabia. The victorious powers of the World War were also not prepared to reorganise the political map of Arabia in accordance with the religious interests of the Indian Muslims. They felt that Turkey must face the consequences of her fighting the war against the Allies.

Another interpretation given to the Khilafat agitation is that, although it led to a united action on the part of Hindus and Muslims against the British government, it had the seeds of Muslim separatist movement in it. As Dr Khalid Bin Sayeed notes:

Muslims seemed to suggest to the Hindus through the Khilafat movement that they could become passionately interested

59 Smith, n. 32, 207.
60 M. H. Abbas, n. 55, 119-21.

` in the freedom of their country only if it ensured the safety and glory of Islam both in India and Muslim countries.[61]

The Moplah rebellion of 1921 clearly showed how slender were the foundations of the Hindu-Muslim unity created by the Khilafat. The Moplahs were the Muslims of Malabar district of the Madras Presidency. As a result of a series of clashes between the authorities and the Khilafat agitators, the Moplahs rose in revolt against the government. For more than two weeks they were in a position to maintain their complete authority in some parts of Malabar. The rebellion was later suppressed by the government. Many Moplahs felt that in the life and death struggle they were waging against the government, many Hindus did not stand firmly on their side, but with the government. The Moplahs were economically and socially very backward and many Hindus in that area belonged to the privileged sections of the community. The latter was naturally upset by the violent turn of events and many of them did help the government to maintain law and order. All these developments created great bitterness among the Muslims towards the Hindus. From the very beginning of the revolt- a fanatical section of the Moplahs had thought that they were conducting a religous war against the non-Muslims. Another section wanted to make use of the opportunity to dispossess the Hindu landlords who oppressed them. All these factors resulted in many outrages against Hindu religion, life and property. The reports of these happenings, often exaggerated ones, reached other parts of India and led to deterioration of relations between the Hindus and the Muslims in those areas. In 1922 a number of communal clashes took place and they gave a deadly blow to the Hindu-Muslim unity which was apparently created during the Khilafat agitation.

POLITICAL ATTITUDE OF THE MUSLIMS—

AN ASSESSMENT

From the ·preceding account of the various political activities of the Indian Muslims one can draw some general conclusions.

61 Dr. Khalid Bin Sayeed, *Pakistan: The Formative Phase* (Karachi, 1960) 62.

In many respects the political movement in which the Hindus took a prominent part and those in which the Muslims were active participants shared many common characteristics. For instance, the beginnings of the Muslim League with the help of individual Englishmen, if not under the direct patronage of the British government, had its parallel in the birth of the Indian National Congress in 1885 with the active assistance of Hume and passive support of Lord Dufferin. The intermingling of Hindu religion in politics manifested in the Extremist move ment during 1905-8 was followed by the active part played by Islam in the Khilafat agitation of 1921. If the first two were symbolic of the influence of liberalism on the people concerned and their desire to conduct political agitation in a constitutional manner the last two reflected the uncompromising opposition to the foreign government and to many of the ideas connected with it. In spite of the fact that each one of the two political currents had an almost similar influence on the Hindus and on the Muslims the political activities of the two communities did not meet in one stream because, even when they did not run on cross purposes, they did not run on the same levels. When the founders and the early leaders of the Indian National Congress were ready to accept some of the political doctrines of Western liberalism, the leaders of the Muslim community like Syed Ahmad Khan thought that his duty was to spread Western education and a sense of loyalty to the British government in India—a function which, as far as the Bengali Hindus were concerned, Raja Rammohan Roy tried to perform fifty years ago. By the time the Muslims were in a position to organise the Muslim League in 1907, on the model of the Indian National Congress which was created in 1885, a very important section of the politically conscious Hindus had moved to the swadeshi and boycott movements led by the Extremists. The Muslims underwent a similar experience only after fifteen years. This gap of years between the two communities in undergoing similar experiences was one of the important reasons for the existence of the political gulf between the two communities. This itself was the result of the different levels of development of the two communities in such fields as education and the economic life of the country.

This was the result of historical factors. While the Muslims, who were the erstwhile rulers of the best parts of the country, showed great resistance to the learning of the language of the new masters of the country who had deprived them of their power and influence, the Hindus who did not have any such grievance against the British, took to Western education and made use of the opportunities offered by it in the government and other walks of life. Under the Mughal rule the Muslims also enjoyed privileged positions in the administration and some of them were big landowners. The habits and customs created by these positions of security and comfort were not conducive to their responding to the challenges offered by the new economic activities offered by the British rule, in the same degree as the Hindus responded. This resulted in the Muslims becoming educationally, economically and therefore, socially more backward than the Hindus. The political consequences of this situation was that while the Hindus were ready for radical action against the British authority, the Muslims were interested in keeping up with the Hindus in the field of education and other social matters. When this development was coupled with the deliberate policy on the part of individual Englishmen and the British government to please the community which was comparatively less radical politically, the political differences were accentuated.

In this connection the influence of the superstructure of Islamic ideas and institutions can also not be underestimated. In a period when the non-Muslims of India were gradually trying to evolve the concept of Indian nationality, the Muslims were under the strong spell of influence of some religious principles which emphasised the unity of the Islamic world not only in religious but also in temporal matters. In the beginning of the twentieth century, this was at first concerned with the unity of Indian Muslims against the non-Muslims of India. Later, particularly beween 1912-21, this idea found its expression in a sense of solidarity with the Muslims all over the world.

The agencies which used to spread these messages was as much important as their content. The Ulema and the mosques were extensively used for this purpose, As a result of all these developments, many Indian Muslims began to feel that they were a separate political entity and that religion and politics were interrelated.

The Khilafat agitation was the highest watermark of Hindu-Muslim unity between 1885-1921. But as far as the Muslims were concerned, the stamp of religion and pan-Islamism were marked on it. The Hindu-Muslim unity it envisaged was not one of the two communities merging into one political body but an alliance between two groups each organised within its fold.

Another landmark of Hindu-Muslim unity in the period was the Lucknow Pact of 1916 between the Congress and the Muslim League. As the system of separate electorates and weightage granted to the Muslims in the Pact indicated, it again was not based on a concept of a common nationality comprising of the Hindus and the Muslims, but on the principle that the Muslims, who were a minority in the country, must be protected against the domination of the Hindus by special safeguards given to them. There were, of course, a few leaders like M. A. Jinnah who accepted the system of separate electorate as a temporary measure which should be given up later. But at that time they were only regarded as able scholars and constitutional experts and not as leaders who had great mass appeal to the Indian Muslims.

Maulana Azad was another great individual who never made any separatist demands. But he tried to awaken the Indian Muslims politically by appealing to their religious instincts and interests.

To sum up. During 1885-1921 the following four political trends existed among Indian Muslims: (1) The separatist elements which refused to cooperate with the non-Muslims in the political world. At first this section of the Muslims were non-political and emphasised the importance of loyalty to the established government. Later, they entered the political field with specific demands to safeguard the interests of Muslim community; (2) one section of the Muslims saw the wisdom of cooperating with the non-Muslims in the limited sphere of constitutional agitation and drawing schemes for constitutional reforms; (3) a revolutionary group who was as keen as any other section of the Indian people in the overthrow of foreign domination of the country; and (4) an active group of leaders and a large section of the Muslim masses who were enthusiastic of waging a struggle against the British government in India, in the company of the non-Muslims, for what they considered to be the interests of their co-religionists abroad. Sir Syed Ahmad Khan, the members of the Simla Deputation of 1906 and the founders of the Muslim League were the symbols of the first trend; the Muslim Congressmen and particularly M. A. Jinnah represented the second one; Abul Kalam Azad was the symbol of the third and Muhamad Ali, of the fourth. Although this kind of division of Muslim political thinking into four categories is broadly correct, one must remember that they cannot be kept in watertight compartments and that each one of them was not devoid of the influence of others.

## GANDHI BREAKS NEW GROUND

Towards the end of the period under survey in this study, Mohandas Karamchand Gandhi—popularly known in India as Mahatma Gandhi—emerged as the most important political leader. As in regard to many other spheres, in relation to the role of religion in politics also, Gandhi tried simultaneously to make a synthesis of all other strands of thought which preceded him and break new ground. In the Indian political field he was incessantly active until his death in 1948. For a proper assessment of his political philosophy one must study India's political history up to that year. It is outside the scope of this research project; here we are concerned only with the ideas he promulgated and the legacy of the political movements he led up to 1921.

Many of the maxims Gandhi put forward in regard to the role of religion in politics led to various interpretations and controversies. There is, however, no doubt that at least during 1916-21 he thought that religion had something to do with politics. Speaking before the Missionary Conference at Madras on 14 February 1916, Gandhi declared: 'I do not believe that religion has nothing to do with politics. The latter divorced from religion is like a corpse only fit to be buried.'[62] In another speech at Allahabad he declared:

India was pre-eminently the land of religion. It was the first and last duty of an Indian to maintain it as such. They

62 D. G. Tendulkar, *Mahatma* (Bombay, 1951) I, 227.

should draw their strength from the soul, from God. If they adhered to that path, Swarajya which they were aspiring to and working for, would become their handmaid.[63]

In spite of the similarity between some of these broad statements made by Gandhi and the Extremists there were many differences between him and the latter. While the Extremist leaders maintained that they were primarily inspired by the *Bhagvad Gita* and other Hindu religious texts, Gandhi acknowledged his indebtedness to the scriptures of other religions also. He once observed:

It was the New Testament which really awakened me to the rightness and value of Passive Resistance. When I read in the 'Sermon on the Mount' such passages as 'Resist not him that is evil but whosoever smiteth thee on thy right cheek turn to him the other also' and 'Love your enemies and pray for them that persecute you, that ye may be sons of your Father which is in heaven,' I was simply overjoyed and found my opinion confirmed where I least expected it. The *Bhagavad Gita* deepened the impression....[64]

Moreover, unlike the Extremists, Gandhi did not popularise certain religious festivals or 'pujas' of some Hindu gods or goddesses. Many of the meetings he convened began with prayers or the reciting of some religious hymns; but they were drawn from such various sources as the Quran, the Gita, the Bible, some Gujarati hymns, Bengali songs and Newman's 'Lead kindly light'.

Gandhi's attempt to blend religion, morals and politics was aimed at making an appeal to the masses of the Indian people as a whole and not to a particular sect or community. Another one of its objectives was to give the movement a unique sense of self-discipline which was necessary for the success of a non-violent, non-cooperation movement on a national scale. Gandhi's concept of the role of religion in politics was thus more broad-based than that of the Extremists. Consequently, his weapons were different from those of the Extremists. He rarely made use of such terms as 'Hindu nation' and 'Hindu solidarity'. But many of his expressions such as 'Ram Rajya' had an appeal to

63  M. K. Gandhi, *Speeches and Writings* (Madras, 1917) 299.
64  Joseph J. Doke, *M. K. Gandhi: An Indian Patriot in South Africa* (Madras, 1909) 88.

only the Hindu masses; his programmes and utterances, however, never antagonised the Muslim masses during 1916-21.

## GANDHI'S CONCEPT OF HINDU-MUSLIM UNITY

On the other hand, he tried his level best to promote Hindu-
Muslim unity and, to a very great extent, succeeded in his attempts during this period. But the unity he envisaged was not
based on the concept that Hindus and Muslims should lose
their separate identities and merge into one political stream,
but on the view that Hindus and Muslims, though separate
entities, could join in an alliance for some forms of social and
political action. Gandhi's opinions regarding the protection of
cows and the Khilafat substantiate this point. Believing as he
did that it was the duty of the Hindus to protect the cow,
he suggested to the Hindus that 'The best and only way to save
the cow is to save the Khilafat.'[65]   On the Khilafat itself he
wrote elsewhere:

> It is expedient to suffer for my Mahomedan brother to the
> utmost in a just cause and I should therefore travel with him
> along the whole road so long as the means employed by him
> are as honourable as his end.[66]

Gandhi did not realise, at any rate during 1918-21, that
strong bonds of friendship between the Hindus and the Muslims could be established only by members of each community
dropping their orthodoxy and not on the basis of a temporary
alliance in accordance with which the Hindus would support
Muslims on the Khilafat and the Muslims would agree not to
harm the cow which was sacred to the Hindus. As later history
showed, such a temporary alliance bore within itself the seeds
of the destruction of the unity achieved by it.

The combination of a religious approach and revolutionary
political programme, which Gandhi represented during 1919-21,
was not peculiar to him. It was present in many Indian leaders
of thought and action and in some cases, it contributed to their
success in arousing enthusiasm for a political movement under
their leadership, Perhaps in the Indian political context of

65  Mahatma Gandhi, *Young India* (Madras, 1922) 413.
66  *Ibid.*, 170.

1919-21, only the type of views which Gandhi held would have made a leader a national figure commanding allegiance from all sections of the people. For the success of his political mission he had to accept the fact that the political thinking of the people was to some extent moulded by the revivalist legacy of the Hindu Extremists and the pan-Islamic outlook of many Muslims. He had also to open a new chapter in Indian politics. Gandhi did all this when he extended his support to the Khilafat agitation and launched the non-cooperation movement.

In the next chapter we will examine the philosophical basis of Gandhism and the non-cooperation movement.

# CHAPTER V

# GANDHI AND NON-COOPERATION MOVEMENT

MOHANDAS KARAMCHAND GANDHI (1869-1948) entered the Indian political scene as a prominent figure only in 1918; but by 1919 he had emerged as the most important national leader. His writings and speeches of this period and of the subsequent years cover many subjects such as non-cooperation, training for self-government, modern civilization, concept of swadeshi, non-violence as a dogma, policy and principle, passive resistance and soul-force, Hindu-Muslim unity, economics of cottage industries and benefits of an indigenous system of education. His views on all these subjects were a part of his total philosophy which was often referred to as Gandhism. In this study we are concerned only with his political philosophy and that too of the period prior to 1922. In politics, as in regard to other matters, he was making experiments. By making a study of the political activities prior to 1922 we get only a glimpse of his political philosophy as it evolved later. But in the history of India's struggle for freedom, the non-cooperation movement which the Indian National Congress launched under Gandhi's leadership during 1920-21 was a landmark and in the period which we are covering in this study, i.e., 1905-21, it came as a climax to all other earlier political movements.

## GANDHI'S EMERGENCE AS THE NATIONAL LEADER

Gandhi was not associated with the political movements of India before 1918. After a long period of residence in the Union of South Africa he returned to India in 1915. In that country he experimented with *satyagraha*—literally, the pursuit of truth—in connection with the passive resistance which he organised against racial discrimination practised against the 'non-whites'.[1] The reports of his campaigns in South Africa reached India and earned him a high reputation among his countrymen for his courage and selfless work. Immediately after his return to India Gandhi did not enter active politics, but tried to make a study of the Indian political situation.

In 1915 there was a lull in the political life of the country. With the annulment of the partition of Bengal, the tension too died out. The struggle between the Moderates and the Extremists for the leadership of the national movement had weakened the Congress from which the Extremists had gone out. Neither the Moderates nor the Extremists were in a position to assert themselves as national leaders. Another political party, which was gradually emerging as a force, was the Muslim League which strengthened the separatist trends among the Indian Muslims.

The task of a national leader under such circumstances was to initiate a movement which could be national in a real sense and the philosophy which could assimilate the fundamental tenets of the various political groups inside the country, thereby making it acceptable to a considerable section of the people. For the success of such a movement it was necessary that it should be so designed—consciously or unconsciously—to satisfy diverse groups with conflicting ideas and even clashing interests. Gandhi achieved success to a remarkable extent in performing this Herculean task. We see in his writings and speeches the liberalism and the economic content of the philosophy of the Moderates, the political radicalism and religious outlook which characterized the Extremists and a readiness to accept the orthodox Muslim's interpretation of the events concerning Turkey and Arabia. One can also see the traces of the influence of the Home Rule League movements led by Annie Besant in the political agitation led by Gandhi during 1919-20.[2] While, on the one hand Gandhi was trying to combine the

1 An exhaustive account of the work of Gandhi in the Union of South Africa is given by H. S. L. Polak in M. K. Gandhi: *Speeches and Writings* (Madras, 1917).

2 Mrs Besant was interned under the Defence of India Rules in June 1917 and her arrest created widespread resentment against the government in the country.

various strands of thought which influenced the people before he appeared on the Indian political scene, on the other, he was opening a new chapter in modern India's political history when he led and organised the non-cooperation movement of 1920-21. As the first campaign of mass civil disobedience against the alien government on a national scale, it set in motion new political trends in the country.

Before Gandhi launched the non-cooperation movement he had added to his rich experience of conducting such a movement in South Africa by associating himself with the agitations in Champaran[3] and Kaira.[4] They were local struggles concerned with local issues. The movement of 1920-21 was concerned with issues of national importance and as such it raised some fundamental issues.

## IMMEDIATE CAUSES FOR THE NON-COOPERATION MOVEMENT

As we noted earlier, in one sense the non-cooperation movement was the climax of earlier movements. There were also some immediate causes for it being launched in 1919 and for the shape it took at that time. Most prominent among them were the Rowlatt Act, the Jallianwala Bagh tragedy and the Khilafat agitation. As a result of these developments and the impact of the war and of other international developments the political situation in the country was ripe for starting a campaign against the alien government.

During the world war of 1914-18, the politically conscious section of the people of the country gave unconditional support to the war efforts of the government and hoped that, after the war, the people of India would move towards self-government rapidly. As one of Gandhi's followers, who later became a prominent political leader, noted:

The war aims which were declared to be nothing less than making the world safe for democracy, the protection of weak nationalities, and the conferment of the boon of self-determi-

3 For details of the Champaran movement refer to D. G. Tendulkar, *Mahatma* (Ahmedabad, 1951) I, 242-61.
4 The story of the movement in Kaira—a district in Gujarat—has been described by Gandhi himself in a speech delivered in Bombay in 1918 (Gandhi, n. 1, 279-81).

nation on all peoples naturally roused great hopes in the minds of the people of India who began to see in the world-devastating war a chance of their deliverance from the humiliating position of a subject people and a hope of the elevation of their country to the status of an equal partner in the British Commonwealth.[5]

But after the war those who hoped that India would move rapidly towards self-government were disappointed. Many events such as the arrest of some of their leaders gave them a rude shock. They were further agitated by the report of the committee, headed by Sir Sydney Rowlatt, which investigated the revolutionary movements in the country and suggested how the government should meet it.

The Report which was published on 19 July 1918 recommended the continuation of all the provisions of the Defence of India Act which, in practice, meant the denial of civil rights and liberties to the people. The Defence of India Act was not very much resented during the war because it was a temporary measure intended to deal with an extraordinary situation. The Bills, based on the Report of Rowlatt, were meant to make a permanent change in the criminal law of the land. These Bills were brought forward before the Imperial Legislature on 6 February 1919. Gandhi not only condemned the Bills in an outright manner, but also warned the British government that the nation as such was not going to abide by any act which would deny its people civil rights. He stated:

When the Rowlatt Bills were published, I felt that they were so restrictive of human liberty that they must be resisted to the utmost. I observed too that the opposition to them was universal among Indians. I submit that no state, however despotic, has the right to enact laws which are repugnant to the whole body of the people, much less a government guided by constitutional usage and precedent such as the Indian government.[6]

Notwithstanding the public agitation and the opposition from the non-official members of the Legislature, the Bills were en-

5 Rajendra Prasad in M. K. Gandhi, *Young India* 1919-22 (Madras, 1922) xxv-xxvi.
6. Gandhi, n. 5, 13.

acted with the support of the official majority. Commenting on the government's decision, Gandhi said:

> If my occasional resistance be a lighted match, the Rowlatt Legislation and the persistance in retaining it on the statute book is a thousand matches scattered throughout India. The only way to avoid civic resistance altogether is to withdraw that legislation.[7]

Gandhi's criticism of this arbitrary measure was in line with the liberal thinking of the Moderates, but his programme of protesting against it was far from being liberal.

Implementation of Gandhi's programme to protest against the Rowlatt Act led to another important development—the Jallianwala Bagh tragedy—which was another reason for launching the non-cooperation movement in 1919. On 23 March 1919 Gandhi appealed to the people to observe 6 April as an all-India *hartal,* to demonstrate resentment of the people against the Rowlatt Act. The *hartal* was very successful. Later many meetings were held in different parts of the country and in the Punjab a few minor riots also took place. The Government of the Punjab, which was headed by Sir Michael O'Dwyer took strong action against the popular leaders who organised protest meetings in that province. Gandhi was served with an order not to enter the Punjab. When he refused to comply with it he was arrested. Dr Kitchlew and Satyapal, two popular leaders of the province, were later arrested. There were also firing at the demonstrators. There was high tension in the Punjab and on 13 April 1919 it reached a climax. On that day a meeting was held in the Jallianwala Bagh in Amritsar. The following account gives the story of what was referred to as the Amritsar Massacre and the Jallianwala Bagh tragedy:

> On the 13th a meeting was advertised to be held at a vacant space known as Jallianwala Bagh. General Dyer prohibited any gathering of men on pain of death and hearing that a meeting was going to be held at Jallianwala proceeded to the spot with his troops and machine guns. The place was full of men, women and children as it was an important Hindu festival day. Within 30 seconds of his arrival he opened fire which continued for 10 minutes directing it where the crowd was thickest. The fire continued till ammunition was

7. D. G. Tendulkar, n. 3, 320.

exhausted. Some 5 to 6 hundred people were killed outright and three times the number wounded. The place being surrounded on all sides by high walls no one could escape. There was no warning given before firing and no care taken of the dead and wounded after it. Subsequently, Martial law was declared in Amritsar, Lahore, Gujrat and Layalpur districts and what may be fitly described as a reign of terror followed.[8]

No other single incident in the history of modern India caused as much dissatisfaction against the government as the Jallianwala Bagh tragedy. Even the government was compelled to yield to the public demand to enquire into the justness and propriety of the police firing and a committee under the chairmanship of Sir Hunter was appointed for the purpose. But before the committee began its proceedings, the government passed an Indemnity Act for the protection of its officers. The Hunter Committee was divided in its findings and its report failed to satisfy Indian public opinion. All these developments related to the Amritsar firing added a stimulus to the non-cooperation movement when it was launched later.

We have dealt with many aspects of the Khilafat question in the last chapter. The Khilafat agitation was another source of strength to the non-cooperation movement. The terms of the peace treaty with reference to the Khilafat were interpreted by many Indian Muslim leaders as a betrayal of the promise given by the British to them. The news of the Peace Treaty reached India on the same day when the Hunter Committee's Report was published. Both intensified the widespread discontent against the British government.

In a letter to the Viceroy, Gandhi referred to the Khilafat and the Punjab question (the Amritsar firing) and explained in the following manner how they have changed his attitude towards the government:

Events that have happened during the past month have confirmed me in the opinion that the Imperial Government have acted in the Khilafat matter in an unscrupulous, immoral and unjust manner and have been moving from wrong to wrong in order to defend their immorality. I can retain neither respect, nor affection for such Government.
The attitude of the Imperial and Your Excellency's Govern-

8 Rajendra Prasad, n. 5, xxxi-xxxii.

ment on the Punjab question has given me additional cause for grave dissatisfaction.... Your Excellency's light-hearted treatment of the official crime, your exoneration of Sir Michael O'Dwyer, Mr. Montagu's dispatch and, above all the shameful ignorance of the Punjab events and callous disregard of the feelings of Indians betrayed by the House of Lords, have filled me with the gravest misgivings regarding the future of the Empire, have estranged me completely from the present Government and have disabled me from tendering, as I have hitherto tendered, my loyal cooperation.[9]

## THE NON-COOPERATION MOVEMENT AND ITS PROGRAMME

The stage was thus set for inaugurating a new political campaign in India. Although the events noted above gave immediate stimulus to the non-cooperation movement, there was no doubt that the movement itself was not only a protest against the Rowlatt Act, the Khilafat and the Amritsar firing, but an expression of the general lack of faith in the justness of the British rule and of the consequent demand for *swaraj* by Indians.

In his letter to the Viceroy, which was referred to earlier, Gandhi made his intention of starting the non-cooperation movement clear. He said:

In my humble opinion the ordinary method of agitating by way of petitions, deputations and the like is no remedy for moving to repentence a Government so hopelessly indifferent to the welfare of its charge as the Government of India has proved to be.... I have, therefore, ventured to suggest the remedy of Non-Cooperation which enables those who wish, to dissociate themselves from the Government and which, if it is unattended by violence and undertaken in an ordered manner, must compel it to retrace its steps and undo the wrongs committed.[10]

In the last chapter we have referred to the Khilafat agitation. The Khilafat Committee, which was concerned with it, accepted Gandhi's non-cooperation programme on 28 May 1920. On 30 June there was a joint Hindu-Muslim conference at Allahabad and it decided to resort to non-cooperation after giving a month's notice to the Viceroy. The 31st of August was observed as the Khilafat Day. Gandhi and Maulana Shaukat Ali toured

9 Gandhi, n. 5, 219-20.
10 *Ibid.*

different parts of the country and tried to gather support for the programme of non-cooperation. When a special session of the Indian National Congress met in Calcutta, in September 1920, and adopted a resolution favouring non-cooperation, the movement gathered momentum and strength. The annual session of the Congress which was held at Nagpur in the same year reaffirmed the resolution of non-violent non-cooperation passed at the Calcutta session. The programme of the non-cooperation movement revealed that its ultimate aim was the removal of the British rule in India and such specific slogans as the repeal of the Rowlatt Act and the redress of the Punjab grievances were meant to arouse the consciousness of the masses and gather support from them.

This was evident from the fact that the Indian National Congress in its resolution accepted by the session held in Calcutta in September 1920 declared: ... the only effectual means to vindicate national honour and to prevent a repetition of similar wrongs in the future is the establishment of Swarajya.'[11] The Congress also maintained that there was 'no course left for the people or India but to approve of and adopt the policy of progressive, non-violent, Non-cooperation inaugurated by Mr Gandhi until the said wrongs are righted and Swarajya is established.'[12]

The next session of the Congress held in Nagpur in 1920 congratulated the nation upon the progress made until then in working out the programme of non-cooperation. It also declared that the entire or any part of the scheme of non-violent non-cooperation, with the renunciation of the voluntary association with the present government at one end and the refusal to pay taxes on the other, should be put in force at a time to be determined by either the Indian National Congress or the All India Congress Committee. To prepare the country for successful non-cooperation with the British government the Congress suggested taking effective steps in that behalf by the boycott of the schools controlled by the government and by the boycott of law courts by the lawyers and the litigants. In order to make India economically independent and self-contained, the Congress called

11 *The Indian National Congress 1920-23* (Allahabad, 1924) 7.
12 *Ibid.*

upon the merchants and traders to carry out a gradual boycott of foreign trade relations and to encourage handspinning and handweaving.[13]

## PASSIVE RESISTANCE AND SATYAGRAHA

Such a programme envisaging non-cooperation with the authorities in many fields was an innovation in the Indian national movement. Gandhi, as the leader who inaugurated it, often explained its philosophical basis. In a statement read out before the court during his trial, he said:

I hold it to be a virtue to be disaffected towards a Government which in its totality has done more harm to India than any previous system. India is less manly under the British rule than she ever was before. Holding such a belief, I consider it to be a sin to have affection for the system.... In my humble opinion, Non-co-operation with evil is as much a duty as is co-operation with good.[14]

Gandhi acknowledged his indebtedness to many great teachers and books as far as the evolution of the idea of non-cooperation with, and resistance to, evil is concerned. He was inspired by the philosophy of passive resistance evolved by others. To quote Gandhi himself:

It was the New Testament which really awakened me to the rightness and value of Passive Resistance.... The *Bhagavad Gita* deepened the impression and Tolstoi's 'The Kingdom of God is Within You' gave it permanent form.[15]

According to one of Gandhi's biographers:

Ruskin and Thoreau have both had some share in forming his [Gandhi's] opinions, Ruskin's 'Crown of Wild Olive' being an especial favourite. Last, but not least, the Passive Resistance Movement in England with regard to education has proved an object lesson, not only to him but to his people, of singular force and interest.[16]

Gandhi's contribution in this field was that he tried to make the method of passive civil resistance work on a national scale.

13 *Ibid.*, 29.
14 Gandhi, n. 5, 1053.
15 Joseph J. Doke, *M. K. Gandhi — An Indian Patriot in South Africa* (Madras, 1909) 88.
16 *Ibid.*

His programme of action also went beyond the traditional passive resistance. Once he said:

> The English expression 'Passive Resistance' hardly denotes the force about which I propose to write. But *Satyagraha*, i.e., truth-force, correctly conveys the meaning. Truth-force is soul-force and is the opposite of the force of arms.[17]

About its applicability he said:,

> It is a force that may be used by individuals as well as by communities. It may be used as well in political as in domestic affairs. Its universal applicability is a demonstration of its permanence and invincibility.[18]

In the words of Gandhi:

> Passive resistance has been conceived and is regarded as the weapon of the weak  Whilst it avoids violence, being not open to the weak, it does not exclude its use if, in the opinion of the passive resister, the occasion demands it.[19]

Not so satyagraha. It was not the weapon of the weak but of those who were more fearless and courageous than the soldiers in the battlefield. Explaining this view Gandhi said:

> Non-violence in its dynamic condition means conscious suffering. It does not mean meek submission to the will of the evil-doer, but it means the putting one's whole soul against the will of the tyrant. Working under this law of our being, it is possible for a single individual to defy the whole might of an unjust empire to save his honour, his religion, his soul and lay the foundation for that empire's fall or its regeneration.[20]

## NON-VIOLENCE AS A DOGMA, POLICY AND CREED

To what extent was non-violence an essential feature of the programme of the non-cooperation movement? It is doubtful that many of Gandhi's followers and the Indian National Congress fully subscribed to his ideas in regard to this matter. On the one hand the resolution of the Congress on non-cooperation stated:

17 Mahatma Gandhi, *Speeches and Writings* (Madras, 1929) 192.
18 *Ibid.*, 187.
19 Gandhi, n. 5, 222.
20 Gandhi, n. 5, 262.

This Congress desires to lay emphasis on Non-violence being the integral part of the non-co-operation resolution and invites the attention of the people to the fact that Non-violence in word and deed is as essential between people themselves, as in respect of the Government.[21]

On the other hand it did not give an ethical reason for taking this stand but only maintained that 'the spirit of violence is not only contrary to the growth of a true spirit of democracy, but actually retards the enforcement (if necessary) of the other stages of non-cooperation.'[22]

Maulana Muhammad Ali, who was a colleague of Gandhi, explaining his view on the question of the role of non-violence in politics said in 1923:

Warfare, according to the Quran, is an evil;... but persecution is a worse evil, and may be put down with the weapons of war. When persecution ceases, and every man is free to act with the sole motive of securing divine goodwill, warfare must cease. These are the limits of Violence in Islam, as I understand it, and I cannot go beyond these limits without infringing the Law of God. But I have agreed to work with Mahatma Gandhi, and our compact is that as long as I am associated with him I shall not resort to the use of force even for purposes of self-defence. And I have willingly entered into this compact because I think we can achieve victory without violence; that the use of violence for a nation of three hundred and twenty millions of people should be a matter of reproach to it.[23]

Many other followers of Gandhi—both Hindus and Muslims—shared Muhammad Ali's view that violence was justified under some circumstances, but there were some advantages in accepting non-violence as a tactics.

Gandhi was not entirely unaware of this fact even in 1920. He wrote:

I want India to recognise that she has a soul that cannot perish and that can rise triumphant above every physical weakness and defy the physical combination of a whole world.... However, being a practical man, I do not wait till

21 *Indian National Congress*, n. 11, 31.
22 *Ibid*.
23 Afzal Iqbal,. comp. and ed., *Select Writings And Speeches of Maulana Mohammad Ali* (Lahore, 1944) 279.

India recognises the practicability of the spiritual life in the political world. India considers herself to be powerless and paralysed before the machine-guns, the tanks and the aeroplanes of the English. And she takes up Non-cooperation out of her weakness. It must still serve the same purpose, namely, bring her delivery from the crushing weight of British injustice, if a sufficient number of people practise it.[24]

A large number of people practised it. But a few resorted to violence also. There were scattered incidents of violence throughout the non-cooperation movement. But when it led to the death of some policemen at Chauri Chaura in February 1922, Gandhi suspended the movement. He gave the following reasons:

The tragedy of Chauri Chaura is really the index finger. It shows the way India may easily go, if drastic precautions be not taken. If we are not to evolve violence out of non-violence, it is quite clear that we must hastily retrace our steps and re-establish an atmosphere of peace, re-arrange our programme and not think of starting mass Civil Disobedience until we are sure of peace being retained in spite of mass Civil Disobedience being started and in spite of Government provocation.[25]

Gandhi also hoped that by the suspension of the movement, 'every Congressman or woman will not only feel disappointed but he or she will feel relieved of the burden of unreality and of national sin.'[26] But the fact that many were disappointed and were angry when they heard of the suspension of the movement, showed that they did not subscribe to Gandhi's ideas on non-violence.

The biographer of Pandit Motilal Nehru sums up the reaction of many of Gandhi's followers to the suspension of the movement in the following words:

These decisions were like a clap of thunder to the Mahatma's adherents. Probably no one was closer to him than his faithful secretary, Mahadev Desai; but even Desai wrote from Agra gaol (February 15th) that the shock had 'absolutely unhinged' him. Lajpat Rai addressed a circular letter to the Congress Working Committee in which he described Gandhi as 'one

24 Gandhi, n. 5, 262.
25 *Ibid.*, 997.
26 *Ibid.*, 998.

of the greatest men of all ages, all times and all countries.... Our defeat is in proportion to the greatness of our leader... Mahatmaji pitched his standard too high.... To change the heart of mobs in such a way as to make it impossible for them to indulge in such brutalities without changing the hearts of Governments, that rule over them, is an impossibility. ... In Lucknow gaol the reactions of the Nehrus were equally violent. Motilal was beside himself with anger, while his son vented his despair in a letter which Gandhi described 'as a freezing dose'.[27]

Many others who participated in the non-cooperation movement were more disillusioned than these leaders. It will not, therefore, be wrong to conclude that the majority of those who participated in the non-cooperation movement did not owe allegiance to the concept of non-violent struggle as interpreted by Gandhi. They accepted it only as an expedient measure.

But it is equally significant that Gandhi continued to be the most important political leader of India even after his taking this decisive step which went against the dominant mood of the country. His ability to retain the leadership of the country can be partly attributed to his magnetic personality; but it is also due to the realisation on the part of many people in the country that some degree of restraint on the part of the political agitators would be helpful to the success of the national movement. In this period Britain was a Great Power in the world and the British government in India possessed overwhelming military strength. The participation of the Indian masses in the national movement was still in the rudimentary stage, except in some parts of the country. It was, therefore, necessary to make tactical withdrawals during the struggle for freedom. From this standpoint the suspension of the non-cooperation movement was not an unwise step Making such withdrawals and the necessary compromise for the purpose was another legacy of the political movements led by Gandhi. But the reasons he gave for it were couched in metaphysical and ethical terms and were not accepted by the vast number of his followers. In the realm of ideas he did not, therefore, bequeath a liberal political philosophy although in the field of action he occasionally functioned as a liberal.

27 B. R. Nanda, *The Nehrus: Motilal and Jawaharlal* (London, 1962) 201.

## BOYCOTT OF SCHOOLS, COURTS AND FOREIGN GOODS

Another item of the programme of non-cooperation which was at first accepted by many of Gandhi's followers but which was rejected by them later was the boycott of schools and courts. The annual session of the Congress which met at Nagpur in 1920 called upon the students of the age of sixteen and above to withdraw without delay, irrespective of consequence, from institutions owned, aided or in any way controlled by government and advised them to devote themselves to some special service in connection with the non-cooperation movement or to continue their education in national institutions. It also called upon lawyers to make greater efforts to suspend their practice and to devote their attention to national service including boycott of law courts by litigants and fellow lawyers and the settlement of disputes by private arbitration. There was also a call to give up the titles of honour given by the government and to boycott legislative bodies. The official historian of the Congress later summed the response to these calls:

> The No-vote campaign had been a remarkable success. Less successful was the boycott of courts and colleges, though their prestige was greatly damaged. Numerous lawyers had left their profession throughout the country and thrown themselves heart and soul into the movement. An unexpected measure of response, however, was noticeable in the field of National Education. Though the number of students that non-cooperated was not large, there was an earnest move towards National Education.[28]

Even this claim regarding the success of the boycott of educational institutions was highly exaggerated. The reality was nearer to the following observation made by C. Y. Chintamani, a critic of the programme of non-cooperation:

> It was admitted [in the Report of the Civil Disobedience Enquiry Committee consisted of Congressmen] that, so far as effort was directed to the weaning of students from Government schools and colleges, it has met with poor success, and that the majority of the students who had come out of Government schools were obliged to return gradually to their old schools; which does not appear exactly to support the claim

28 B. P. Sitaramayya, *The History of the Indian National Congress* (Bombay, 1947) I, 211.

later made in the report that the non-cooperation movement has destroyed the prestige of Government institutions.[29]

The boycott of courts was also not very successful. The number of lawyers who suspended practice in courts was insignificant compared to their full strength. Some of them went back to their profession later.

The successful boycott was the one concerned with foreign goods. Emphasising the importance of this boycott Gandhi said:

India cannot be free so long as India voluntarily encourages or tolerates the economic drain which has been going on for the past century and a half. Boycott of foreign goods means no more and no less than boycott of foreign cloth.... India has the ability to manufacture all her cloth if her children will work for it.[30]

This boycott was connected with the 'swadeshi' movement which was aimed at promoting indigenous goods: Gandhi associated it with the development of cottage industries also. Referring to the success of Gandhi's programme in this field one of his followers wrote:

In the matter of the organisation of Swadeshi, the result achieved in popularising spinning wheels and the use of Khaddar (hand spun and hand woven cloth) has been marvellous. In homes which had altogether forgotten even the name of Charka (spinning wheel) its musical hum can now be heard. It has invaded even the parlour of the rich, while it has given a source of livelihood to lakhs of poor women in the country.[31]

Although the success of the spinning wheel was spectacular, it was the growth of Indian industries, which used all the modern methods of production which led to the ultimate success of the swadeshi movement.

While suspending the non-cooperation movement, the Working Committee of the Congress called upon all Congress organisations to concentrate their efforts on creating an atmosphere of non-violence and further strengthening the Congress organi-

29 C. Y. Chintamani, *Indian Politics Since the Mutiny* (Allahabad, 1947) 140.
30 Gandhi, n. 5, 513.
31 Rajendra Prasad, n. 5, cxlv.

sation by improving the panchayats and national education
institutions and by stimulating the use of spinning wheel and
production of khaddar. These aspects of the Congress programme were not as popular as those connected with non-cooperation
and political campaigns. And even among those who used
khaddar many did so because it was a political uniform of the
Congressmen and not because they had any faith in Gandhi's
programme of cottage industries and spinning wheel.

### GANDHI'S OPPOSITION TO MODERN CIVILISATION

This gap between the thinking of Gandhi and that of a vast
number of his political followers arose from the fact that
they did not agree with his approach towards modern civilisation. In as early as 1908 Gandhi had thus made clear his understanding of the difference between Indian and western civilisation:

> ... the aim of the Indian civilisation is to elevate the moral
> being, that of the Western civilisation to propagate immorality.
> The latter is godless, the former is based on a belief in God.
> So understanding and so believing it behoves on every lover
> of India to the old Indian civilisation.[32]

Gandhi did not always make this distinction between Indian
civilisation and western civilisation; but he consistently maintained his oppositon to 'modern civilisation'. In a letter to a
friend he wrote in 1909:

> There is no impassable barrier between East and West. (2)
> There is no such thing as Western or European civilisation,
> but there is a modern civilisation which is purely material.
> (3) The people of Europe, before they were touched by
> modern civilisation, had much in common with the people
> of the East;... (4) It is not the British people who are ruling
> India, but it is modern civilisation, through its railways, tele-
> graph, telephone, and almost every invention which has been
> claimed to be a triumph of civilisation. (5) Bombay, Calcutta
> and the other chief cities of India are the real plague spots. (6)
> If British rule were replaced tomorrow by Indian rule based
> on modern methods, India would be no better, except that
> she would be able to retain some of the money that is drained
> away to England....[33]

32 M. K. Gandhi, *Hind Swaraj* (Ahmedabad, 1909) 2.
33 Tendulker, n. 3, 129-30.

Many of Gandhi's followers did not share these views of their leader. Their aim was obviously to establish a modern state and society in India. The sense of direction of the Indian national movement in general, in spite of some deviations, was towards the fulfilment of the aspiration of the politically conscious people to make India modern in every sense of the term. A question may be asked: then why did they accept the leadership of Gandhi who rejected these aspirations? They did because Gandhi did not demand from his political followers unqualified allegiance to all his views. During the period of a struggle he did demand implicit obedience and discipline of the highest order in his ranks. But that was a different matter.

In this connection it is worth noting that Gandhi often referred to Gokhale as his political *Guru* (teacher) and Jawaharlal Nehru as his political heir and that both these leaders were far from being the champions of ancient civilisation. They openly acclaimed the merits of modern civilisation, acknowledged their indebtedness to the West and stated that their aim was to reorganise Indian society, economy and state on modern lines.

SPIRITUAL BASIS OF THE POLITICAL ACTIVITY

It is also doubtful that the vast number of Gandhi's political followers shared his views on 'spiritualization of politics'. Gandhi once said: 'You and I have to act on the political platform from a spiritual side and if this is done, we should then conquer the conqueror'.[34] Gandhi maintained that the non-cooperation movement was 'a struggle of good against evil and the force behind it was soul force.'[35] It is in this context that Gandhi considered self-purification to be the first step in the political struggles. On one occasion he said:

I have found that we have not yet reached a conscious recognition of our national state. We have not had the discipline necessary for a realization of that state and venture to say that there is nothing so powerful as fasting and prayer that would give us the requisite discipline, spirit of self-sacrifice, humility and resoluteness of will without which there can be no real progress.[36]

34 Gandhi, n. 1, 211.
35 Doke, n. 15, 89.
36 Gandhi, n. 5, 58.

Gandhi himself displayed a unique sense of self-discipline by his austere way of life and inspired others to make sacrifices for their country. In the type of struggle he conducted, in which an unarmed people was struggling to be free from a mighty imperial Power, Gandhi's appeal to austerity and self-discipline had some place. And perhaps the most effective way of enforcing austerity and self-discipline among the masses of the Indian people at that time was through such practices as prayer and fasting because of their deep association with religion.

The immediate effects of Gandhi's statements connected with 'modern and western civilizations' and 'spiritualization of politics' were to raise the pride of the people in their country and to give them some kind of spiritual stamina in the struggle for freedom from foreign rule. One of the long-term effects of these aspects of Gandhian philosophy was the encouragement of obscurantist thinking among some sections of the people. As some of the symbols Gandhi used had a greater appeal to the Hindus than to the Muslims, they also gave a 'Hindu colour' to the national movement under his leadership. But during 1919-20 they were not so obvious because of Gandhi's support to the Khilafat agitation and the decision of the majority of the Muslim leaders to support the non-cooperation movement.

### FOR AN INDIGENOUS AND PRACTICAL SCHEME OF EDUCATION

Although the call to boycott schools sponsored and supported by the government did not meet with great success, some ideas of Gandhi on education did make an impact on the Indian mind. Gandhi said: 'Education through English had created a wide gulf between the educated few and the masses. It had created gulf in the families also. An English educated man had no community of feelings and ideas with the ladies of the family.'[37] According to Gandhi, the then existing system of education was undesirable on the following grounds:

It is based upon foreign culture to the almost entire exclusion of indigenous culture. (2) It ignores the culture of the heart

37 Gandhi, n. 1, 297-8.

and the hand and confines itself simply to the head. (3) Real education is impossible through a foreign medium.[38]

Gandhi advocated the establishment of educational institutions which could be symbolic of India's 'protest against the British injustice and as a vindication of national honour' and drawing its 'inspiration from the national ideals of a united India'. They stood for a 'synthesis of the different cultures that have come to stay in India, that have influenced Indian life, and that, in their turn, have themselves been influenced by the spirit of the soil.'[39] In this respect Gandhi's ideas on education were similar to those of the Extremists.

But while the latter emphasised the importance of imparting technical education which would be necessary to facilitate the industrialisation of India on a large scale, Gandhi ignored it. He focussed attention, in addition to religion, politics and history, on vocational training. The vocational training, which Gandhi envisaged, was suited to the economy of a predominantly agricultural society in which cottage industries, but no heavy industries, fulfilled an important role.

Although his educational plans had these limitations, it must be said to his credit that his criticism of the unrealistic and bookish system of education was justified. He maintained that the

> introduction of manual training will serve a double purpose in a poor country like ours. It will pay for the education of our children and teach them an occupation on which they can fall back in after-life, if they choose, for earning a living. Such a system must make our children self-reliant. Nothing will demoralise the nation so much as that we should learn to despise labour.[40]

Another aspect of Gandhi's thinking on this matter was his uncompromising opposition to the use of the foreign language as the medium of education. Enumerating its defects, he said:

> Foreign medium has caused brain-fag, put an undue strain upon the nerves of our children, made them crammers and imitators, unfitted them for original work and thought and disabled them for filtrating their learning to the family or

38 Gandhi, n. 5, 386-7.
39 *Ibid.*, 384-5.
40 Gandhi, n. 5, 388.

the masses.... The foreign medium has prevented the growth of our vernaculars.[41]

This did not mean that condemnation of English language as such. Gandhi conceded that it has a role to play as a language of international commerce and diplomacy.

## A POPULAR BASE FOR THE NATIONAL MOVEMENT

Gandhi's views on such subjects as education and cottage industries were part of his total philosophy which was aimed at creating a decentralised and democratic society in which the gulf between the minority of a few learned and rich people and the majority of uneducated and poor people would not exist. He also realised that the influence of religious and other traditions on the masses of the people were very strong and that the implementation of any programme, which would not take into consideration those traditions, would become an isolated action on the part of a few leaders who belonged to a minority. So, unlike many other political leaders, he thought of new schemes of educational, social and economic development and related all of them to political agitation on the part of the masses of the people in a manner which was understandable to them and for the redress of such specific grievances as the Amritsar tragedy, Rowlatt Act and the Khilafat. The ultimate effect of some of his speeches and writings and his first programme of non-co-operation was to give a popular base to the Indian national movement. Although Gandhi did not quote from the writings of European political philosophers on democracy, as the earlier Indian leaders did, his successful attempt in bringing a large mass of the people to the national movement was a great step towards democratising the political life of the country.

## DIRECTION TOWARDS FREEDOM

The sense of direction of the national movement under Gandhi's leadership was also undoubtedly towards strengthening the political forces which championed freedom—freedom of the individual and of the nation.

When restrictions were made by the government on the freedom of speech, Gandhi wrote in *Young India*:

41 *Ibid.*, 389.

Swaraj, the Khilafat, the Punjab occupy a subordinate place to the issue sprung upon the country by the Government. We must first make good the right of free speech and free association before we can make any further progress towards our goal. The Government would kill us if it could by a flank attack. To accept defeat in the matter of free speech and free association is to court disaster. If the Government is allowed to destroy non-violent activities in the country, however dangerous they may be to its existence, even the moderates' work must come to a standstill. In the general interest, therefore, we must defend these elementary rights with our lives...The safest and the quickest way to defend these rights is to ignore the restriction. We must speek the truth under a shower of bullets. We must band together in the face of bayonets. No cost is too great for purchasing these fundamental rights.[42]

Gandhi's great contribution to the national movement was that by making such fervent appeals to the people, he could arouse great enthusiasm among them for the cause of freedom. He could also inspire them for making great sacrifices in furtherance of that cause. He himself led the way. When he was prosecuted by the Government, instead of trying to defend himself, he said :

Non-violence implies voluntary submission to the penalty for Non-cooperation with evil. I am here, therefore, to invite and submit cheerfully to the highest penalty that can be inflicted upon me for what in law is a deliberate crime and what appears to me to be the highest duty of a citizen.[43]

This statement reflected a departure from the attitude of the political leaders who preceded Gandhi. With this open defiance of authority entered a new spirit in the Indian national movement and politics. No more was it easy to curb the desire of the people for freedom.

Even Gandhi's liking for law and order and his loyalty to non-violence were qualified by his desire to fight for freedom. On one occasion he said : '...anarchy under Home Rule was better than orderly foreign rule.'[44] He also said that he 'would have India to become free even by violence rather than that she

42 *Ibid.*, 942-3.
43 *Ibid.*, 1054.
44 Gandhi, n. 32, 157.

should remain in bondage. In slavery she is a helpless partner in the violence of the slave holder.'[45]

As this statement makes it clear the dominant objective of Gandhi's political activities was the achievement of the freedom of the country and it was this objective which brought forth the favourable response of a large section of the people to his appeals to participate in the political struggle. The political campaigns led by Gandhi opened a new chapter in the history of the national movement by making the spirit of resistance to authority an important factor in public life. As the official historian of the Congress notes :

Fear had been cast off by the people. A sense of self-respect developed in the Nation. Congressmen realized that service and self-sacrifice were the only means of winning public confidence. The prestige too of Government was materially shaken, and people had received good lessons regarding the ideology of Swaraj.[46]

It seemed that by the inauguration of the non-cooperation movement of 1919-21, the Indian National Congress reached the point of no return as far as its march towards its ultimate objective of the freedom of the country was concerned.

## TOTAL IMPACT OF GANDHI'S IDEOLOGY AND PROGRAMME

It is difficult to assess the impact of Gandhi's ideology and programme on the Indian national movement during 1919-21 without taking into consideration how he influenced it later. It can safely be asserted that he was the dominant figure in Indian political field from 1919 up to his death in 1948. During this period Gandhi shifted his emphasis from one point of view to another as occasion demanded and the response of the politically conscious people of India to Gandhi's ideology and programme also varied from one period to another. But the non-cooperation movement of 1919-21 and Gandhi's utterances of this period are significant, because both had a determining influence on the character of the Indian national movement and its political philosophy.

45. Gandhi, n. 5, 290.
46. Sitaramayya, *The History of the Indian National Congress* (Allahabad, 1935) 377.

It will be wrong to assume that just because a large number of people accepted Gandhi's political leadership, they accepted all his views. We noted above some divergence in the thinking of Gandhi and some of his followers on such fundamental questions as non-violence, spiritual basis of political action, modern civilisation and the role of cottage industries in the economic development of the country. But there was a wide area of agreement between Gandhi and his followers on the political objectives of the national movement and the programme of action for realising them.

According to Gandhi and his followers the ultimate objective of the national movement was the freedom of the country and the immediate objectives of such political programme as the non-cooperation movement was to redress the specific grievances connected with the Rowlatt Act, Jallianwala Bagh firings and the Khilafat.

A militant struggle—though non-violent in form—was the nature of the political agitation he led. Here, again, he received the unqualified allegiance of his followers who displayed great courage and willingness to make great sacrifices for the country.

But the minds of some of them rebelled against Gandhi's decision to suspend the non-cooperation movement on the ground that some people became violent and killed some policemen. They had no faith in the inherent virtue of non-violent methods. But as tactical withdrawals and a display of restraint in the struggle against a mighty empire by an unarmed people were not unwise steps, this action of Gandhi did not lead to the rejection of Gandhi's leadership by his followers. In other words, while Gandhi adhered to non-violence as a principle, many of his followers accepted it as a tactics.

Gandhi's opposition to modern civilisation, sometimes referred to as western civilisation, was not supported by some of his followers because they wanted to reconstruct Indian state, economy and society on modern lines. But it appealed to a large section of the people of India, because by glorifying the ancient Indian civilisation and holding it as superior to the modern western civilisation, such an attitude of opposition to the civilisation of the alien rulers gave great self-confidence and sense of pride to them. Even those who differed with Gandhi on this issue realised the immense mass appeal of the slogans based on such an attitude. The realisation of this fact by them and Gandhi's tolerance of those who differed from him so long as they accepted his leadership in the political sphere, facilitated his emergence as the supreme national leader during 1919-21, because unlike the 'Moderates' and the 'Extremists', his appeal was not confined either to those who looked to the West for inspiration or to the earlier period of Indian history for the same purpose.

Gandhi's use of symbols like 'Ramrajya' and his emphasis on prayer and fasting made an appeal primarily to the Hindu masses. But before 1921 it did not antagonise many educated Hindus, who have no use for them, because they were impressed by the fact that they gave discipline and spiritual stamina to many of those who participated in the political struggle.

Some of Gandhi's writings and speeches on these matters had no appeal to the Muslims. But a vast number of them accepted Gandhi's lead because he gave unqualified support to them on such issues as the Khilafat, with which they were concerned. As we noted in the earlier chapter, Gandhi's ideas and programme did promote Hindu-Muslim unity during 1918-21 ; however, that unity was not based on the concept that Hindus and Muslims should lose their separate identities and merge into one political stream, but on the view that Hindus and Muslims, though separate entities, could join in an alliance for some joint political action.

Some political workers and leaders, who were very active before 1918, could not associate themselves with the national movement under Gandhi's leadership, because they could not accept his ideas or the wisdom of the political campaigns he launched. Some of the most prominent among them were Surendranath Banerjea, Bipin Chandra Pal, C. Y. Chintamony and Muhammad Ali Jinnah. Rabindranath Tagore, an eminent poet, who once associated himself with the political movements of Bengal, was another critic of Gandhi. Their criticisms was mostly concerned with the intolerance set in motion by Gandhi's militant campaigns, his anarchist ideas, the chauvinist elements in his opposition to modern western civilisation and the unscientific nature of his views regarding the large-scale application of modern industrial methods in the economic field.

Although the critics of Gandhi were well-known people who possessed tremendous intellectual powers, Gandhi could still carry the masses with him because he became a symbol of the aspirations of the people for freedom and a rallying point for people of different social background and cultural levels. Gandhi's views on social and economic questions and the philosophical basis of his political actions might have had many drawbacks ; but during 1918-21, all of them fitted in with his essential scheme of drawing all the political currents, which preceded him, into the one stream of the national movement and leading it in the form of a militant, though non-violent, struggle against the alien government.

Gandhi was primarily a man of action and not a philosopher or political theorist. The legacy of his political actions in the ideological field had both positive and negative sides. More than any other leader, Gandhi strengthened the cause of freedom of the individual and the country by fighting for it and he promoted the democratic spirit by reducing the gulf between the leader and the followers by many items of his political programme. But some of his ideas were also conducive to the strengthening of obscurantism and some degree of revivalism in the country. They militated against the spirit of scientific enquiry and the ideas of the Ages of Enlightenment and Reason. Many of those, who accepted Gandhi's leadership in the political sphere, were not committed to his total philosophy. So the non-cooperation movement of 1919-21 did not show the full impact of all aspects of Gandhism.

# CHAPTER VI

# CONCLUSION

ALTHOUGH political theory and practice are interrelated, there is a difference between the approach of the practical politician and statesman on the one hand and that of a political theoretician on the other.

> The practical statesman is interested in theory and knowledge only, in so far as they can be immediately applied as weapons in the struggle for political power. For this reason he directs his appeal primarily to human emotions and human will. The political theorist on the other hand is interested in an idea for its own intrinsic value, and not like the practical statesman for its utility in political conflict or for its propagandistic influence on human activity. For the thinker in the field of political science, no less than elsewhere, knowledge should not be an instrument of political domination but an intellectual construct endowed with significance; retaining its independent validity despite the changing configurations of the actual political arena. The aspirations for power of the political thinker have to be subordinated to his aspirations for knowledge, and for this reason he must appeal primarily to man's capacity for intellectual judgement rather than to his more or less ethical and emotional capacity for enthusiasm.[1]

In this study we are concerned with the ideas of practical statesmen and politicians only and that too with those engaged in the limited task of conducting the nationalist movement. As the oft-repeated maxim that a dependent country has but one kind of politics, i.e., to fight the alien government and pave the way for self-government, applies to India of the period under survey. A study of the political philosophy of her national

1. Herman Heller, 'Political Science', *Encyclopaedia of the Social Sciences* (New York, 1949) XII, 210.

movement becomes in  one sense, the study of the most important
political trends of the country.

## INFLUENCES ON INDIAN POLITICAL THINKING

The organisation which led the movement during 1885-1921
was the Indian National Congress; but other parties too were
connected with it. The All India Muslim League was one such.
The role of the League in the later phase of the national movement, particularly in the nineteen-forties when it began to advocate the creation of Pakistan, cast some doubt about its right
to be regarded as a part of the *Indian* national movement.  But
prior to 1921, although it did champion the separate demands
of the Muslims, it was not, in any sense, outside the national
stream. Moreover, individuals like M.A. Jinnah played an important part in the working of both the Muslim League and
of the Indian National Congress.  The two parties came to an
agreement in 1916 and placed before the government joint
political demands.  In view of all these developments, the political ideas of the Muslim League leaders were not excluded from
this study. The 'Moderates' and the 'Extremists', whose political
ideas were analysed here, were also not the members of the
Congress Party throughout the period.  The Extremists left it
in 1907 after the Surat split and rejoined it only in 1916.  The
Moderates left the organisation in 1818.  But as both the Extremists and the Moderates represented significant political forces
of the country even when they were outside the Congress, the
views they expounded on various occasions made their impact
on the people.  This study of the political philosophy of the
Indian national movement is, therefore, concerned with the
different, and often conflicting, views expressed by the leaders
who were at one time members of the Congress party and at
other times outside it; and with the views of those who were
connected with organisations like the Muslim League. This fact
gives it a certain lack of cohesion; but this is inherent in the
subject under study.

There was another reason giving rise to the intellectual in-
coherence in Indian political thinking. As we noted in the earlier
chapters, the political and other ideas to which the Indian
leaders owed allegiance were of diverse origin.  The political ideas

of liberalism, which made an impact on the mind of the educated Indians during the early phase of the national movement, came from the West. So did the doctrine of socialism which began to attract the attention of some Indian leaders towards the close of the period under survey. In between there was the influence of some Indian leaders who referred to the ancient Indian heritage and its influence on their thinking. Then there were some Muslim leaders of the country who spoke their indebtedness to Islam and the lagacy of the Muslim countries of the Middle East. The Indian national movement between 1885 and 1921 reveals the influence of these various strands of thought which were acting and interacting on each other, but not necessarily leading to a synthesis.

Another factor which made its impact on the thinking of the people is the political and social background. Even when the educated Indians accepted the validity of the political ideas of the West, they have to work within a social and political background which was different from that of the western countries. They had, therefore, to modify some of these ideas and reject some others to suit the needs of the country. The most important instance is the form in which the Moderate leaders accepted liberalism. As the dominant political doctrine of the West it made a profound impression on those who were given a western education in the 19th and early 20th centuries. From 1885, the year of its inception, up to 1905 the Indian National Congress was dominated by this class of people who were referred to as 'liberals'. The challenge to their leadership came first from the 'Extremists' who emerged as a major political force at the beginning of the 20th century. Since then these earlier leaders were referred to as the 'Moderates'. At first, within the Congress, they could hold their own against the Extremists. These leaders, no doubt, accepted many of the political tenets of liberalism, but not all. In economic matters they often departed from liberalism, because the economic conditions of India demanded a radical approach. This was one of the many cases in which the unique features of the Indian situation made themselves felt on the political opinions of the leaders of the country.

There was, however, no doubt that the basic approach of the early leaders of the Congress was based on the political ideas

of the West which they imbibed through English education and
the knowledge of the history of the western countries. The very
concept 'nation', as understood in the West, was unknown to
India. The first important political work of the Congress leaders
was to popularise the view that India was a nation. Even before
the establishment of the Indian National Congress, Surendranath
Banerjea, in one of his speeches, referred to the great work of
Mazzini in promoting Italian unity and appealed to the people
of India to 'weld together into a compact mass'.[2] By 1888
Dadabhai Naoroji also began to remind the Parsees that they
should not dissociate themselves from the Hindus or the Muslims and that all Indians would sink or swim together as one
people. As the Congress succeeded in fulfilling this function of
popularising the concept of an Indian nation to a limited extent,
Gokhale in his presidential address to the annual session of the
Congress held in 1905 was in a position to claim that the minds
of the people had been familiarised with the ideas of a united
India and that close bonds of sympathy had knit together the
different provinces.

Banerjea, Dadabhi and Gokhale held and propagated the
view that one race was not inferior to another. When they
championed the right of Indians to enter the civil service, they
maintained that what they wanted was not a few more posts
for their countrymen, but the acceptance by the government of
their right to develop resourcefulness and the capacity to take
the initiative.

## THE MODERATES AND LIBERALISM

The political philosophy of many of the early leaders of the
Congress and the 'Moderates' of 1905-21 was also influenced
by their methods of agitation, which was constitutional in
character. This, in its turn, was influenced by their belief in the
providential character of the British rule in India and their
inability or unwillingness to arouse mass enthusiasm for a political agitation against the British rule. They realised that the
success of the constitutional agitation envisaged prolonged
preparation and patient waiting for a very long time. They
were prepared to pay such high prices rather than try to achieve

2 R. C. Palit, *Surendranath Banerjea's Speeches* (Calcutta, 1880) 21.

their political ends through a radical programme, which, they feared, might lead the country to violence, chaos and confusion.

The gradual evolution of India towards self-government under the guidance of the British government was their ulti- mate goal. Their immediate objective was to create the political atmosphere which would facilitate Indians acquiring the politi- cal and administrative experience necessary for governing the country themselves.

With the purpose in view they agitated for the increased re- presentation of the legislative councils and Indianisation of the civil service and demanded an extension of civil rights to the people by such measures as the removal of the restrictions on the press, the repeal of the laws of Preventive Detention and the Seditious Meetings Act and by such reforms as the separation of the judiciary from the executive and the reorganisation of the judicial services. In their utterances these Moderate leaders often quoted with approval many maxims from the writings and speeches of European liberals. Combined with the impact of the spread of modern education, the development of press and of the constitutional reforms, the political ideas propagated by the Moderate leaders and the prolonged character of their agitation resulted in liberalism making a powerful appeal to a significant section of the educated people in the country. Even when poli- tical radicalism and socialism entered as major forces in Indian politics, they did not entirely supersede liberalism.

It is significant that these Indian leaders, who accepted some of the tenets of liberalism in regard to political matters, also realised that they could not be mechanically applied to India in regard to economic and social questions. In the opinion of the European liberals the state should not interfere in the eco- nomic life. But the Moderate leaders realised that the Indian situation demanded that the state should create tariff walls for the protection of Indian industries and should guide and help the economic development of the country by free use of its credit and superior organisation and by pioneering industrial undertaking and subsidizing private cooperative effort. It should, however, be noted that these views of the Moderates did not spring from an acceptance of such political doctrines as social- ism, but from their pragmatic appraisal of the economic pro- blems of the country.

It is difficult to sum up the political philosophy of the early leaders of the Congress and that of those who were later referred to as the Moderates. In one sense they were liberals; but they were liberals with a difference. They accepted those tenets of liberalism which promoted critical views of dogmatic beliefs and encouraged an experimental attitude towards problems of government and society. They emphasised individual liberty and demanded the extension of the freedom of the press. Their political demands were directed towards giving political training to the people of the country. But while claiming and agitating for these rights they wanted their followers to show tolerance towards their political opponents and accept the fact that they should undergo a period of apprenticeship before they could attain their goal of self-government. Although some of these ideas were successfully changed by some leaders in the later phase of the national movement, there is no doubt that they made an impact on the political developments of the counrty.

They also gave an economic content to the Indian national movement by making their followers aware of the economic problems of the country and by stating that their solutions were connected with the achievement of their political ends.

These early leaders of the Congress had a secular view of politics and wanted the reconstruction of Indian society on the basis of the ideas of the ages of enlightenment and of liberalism which were prevalent in Europe in the 18th and 19th centuries. They never defended any indigenous social institutions like caste. Far from giving any slogan for reviving the past, these leaders frankly advocated industrialising the country on modern lines. They wanted India to enter the international community of commercial and industrial nations as a full-fledged member. In spite of the fact that the Indian national movement did not owe uninterrupted allegiance to the political philosophy of the early leaders of the Congress, it is undeniable that it was a major factor in the shaping of the policies and programme of the movement. The constitution of Indian republic and the social and economic programmes of the different parties in free India, and particularly those of the party in power, bear testimony to the political legacy of the early leaders of the Congress.

When these leaders put forward their political ideas, their appeal was limited to a small section of the people; but by the time they were embodied in the constitution of free India, they had become part and parcel of the traditions of the national movement which had a mass base. How did this transformation take place? The answer to this question lies in the history of the national movement, in between its origins and its last phase, when it was dominated by leaders who thought that the people of India, in their struggle for freedom, need not have to confine themselves to the methods of agitation implicit in the tenets of European liberalism. Some of them contributed to the success of the national movement by supplying it such sources of strength as the mass support which the movement lacked when its leadership was confined to the Moderates.

## THE PHILOSOPHY OF EXTREMISTS

The Extremist leaders, who came to prominence at the beginning of the 20th century, were the first to fulfil this function. Their understanding of the aims of the national movement was clearer than that of the early leaders. They realised that the fundamental issue in Indian politics was not concerned with such specific questions as the Indianisation of the civil services and the reduction of the Indian military expenditure, but with the basic question of Indians getting a large share in the administration and with putting an end to Britain's economic exploitation of the country. In their opinion this could be achieved only by India becoming completely free—in their own words, by her attaining 'swaraj'. This awareness, on the part of the Extremists, of the conflict of interests between the British government in India and the Indian nationalist movement stood in glaring contrast with the faith of the Moderates in the providential character of the British rule in the country.

From this followed other differences between the two groups of leaders. As the Extremists had no hope of influencing the public opinion in England and the authorities in India by arguments and negotiations, they declared that their motto was self-reliance and not mendicancy. Their programme was formulated with a view to bring pressure on the government by such methods as the economic boycott of British goods and passive resistance to the authorities. A political agitation with such

methods could be carried out only with widespread and enthusiastic support from the people.   The Extremist leaders, therefore, wanted to organise such forms of struggle and agitations
as would make a powerful appeal to the emotions and sentiments of the people.   With this aim they made frequent refer-
ences to India's past glories and to the political record of such
historical figures like Shivaji.   In consonance with the religious
traditions of the Hindus, who constituted the majority of the
people, they represented India as a Mother Goddess and made
use of *puja*, the worship of Hindu goddesses, and the Ganesh
festival, connected with a Hindu god, to instil enthusiasm in the
people for political causes.   They advocated the implementation
of a scheme of national education in which emphasis was given to
the study of the traditions and history of the country.   They also
stressed the need for enriching the Indian languages.   Unlike
the Moderates, many of the Extremists wrote and spoke extensively in Indian languages and by so doing, drew a large
number of people into the national movement.

As far as the national movement and its political philosophy
were concerned, this kind of activities of the Extremist leaders
did both good and harm.   They bridged the gulf between the
leaders and their followers,  because the  former,  unlike the
Moderates, did not speak the language that was foreign to the
latter.   The fact that the Extremists based their political action
on the belief that its success depended upon mass action and
not on the will and pleasure of the British anthorities had the
same effect.

The propagation of the idea that the citizens had the right
to resist the arbitrary actions of the authorities was another
good feature of the programme of the Extremists.   In all these
respects they strengthened the forces of democracy in the
country.

But in some respects they weakened them.   The resort to the
*puja* ritual, and the Shivaji and Ganesh festivals for political purposes did not naturally appeal to the Muslims.   During the early
phase of the Indian National Congress some Muslim leaders
kept away from the political agitations, because they wanted the
Muslims to reach the level of the Hindus in such fields as education before they entered the political field.   But during the
second phase, when the Extremists began to play a prominent

CONCLUSION                                                                           189

part in Indian politics, one section of the Muslims became positively hostile to the national movement. The political philosophy of the Extremists was one of the many factors which contributed to this development. The Muslims, as a rule, could not accept the Hindu gods and goddesses as national symbols. Nor could they consider India as a mother goddess. They were also antagonised by the statement of some of the leaders who spoke of a Hindu nation. This interrelation of religion and politics was one of the harmful features of the political thought and activities of the Extremists. In a country like India where a significant section of the people owed allegiance to a religion different from that of the majority it sowed the seeds of political disunity.

Implied in the concept that India was a mother goddess worthy of being worshipped was the emphasis on the collective freedom of the nation, as distinct from, if not apposed to, the freedom of the individual. According to some of the Extremist leaders the nation was an organism, and the individuals were its organs. They maintained that as organs found the fulfilment of their ends, not in themselves but in the collective life of the organism to which they belonged, the interests of the individual could be identified with those of the nation. In a vague sense many of the Extremist leaders accepted idealism as a doctrine and rejected those aspects of liberalism which emphasised civil and other rights of the individual.

At least one Extremist leader, Aurobindo Ghose, took his followers away from another aspect of liberalism. He gave a theological explanation to history and politics and substituted a scientific approach to political philosophy by a mystic one. This promoted a certain degree of obscurantism in the political thinking of many Indians.

As we noted earlier, the Extremist leaders, as a group, did not subscribe to a systematically worked out political philosophy. In many details they differed from one another. Moreover, the view of each individual changed from time to time. These leaders were primarily interested in conducting the struggle for freedom from the British rule and they tried to evolve a strategy and some tactics which would be effective for that purpose. And in that process they formulated many political ideas, which had become the heritage of modern India. It is difficult to generalise on them. Such a statement as that their political philosophy is a combination of political radicalism, reaction and religious revivalism does indicate some of its salient features; but as a simplification of a highly complex phenomenon it can be misleading.

## MUSLIM ATTITUDES

No generalisation can be made on the political ideas of the Indian Muslims also. On political questions many of them thought on the same lines as the Hindus, but many others did not do so because religion was a major factor in their political thinking.

During 1885-1921 there were various schools of thought among the Indian Muslims. In the late 19th century and in early 20th, some of their leaders advocated that the Muslims should keep away from politics, at least, until they made the same educational progress as the Hindus. Another group of leaders, less influential than the first, participated in the work of the Congress party and agitated for the extension of civil rights and political opportunities. They belonged to the Moderate school. With the emergence of the Extremists as a major force in Indian politics, new developments took place as far as the political attitude of the Muslims was concerned. The refusal to join the political movements, in which the leadership was in the hands of Hindus, took the shape of plain hostility towards it. As we noted earlier, one of the reasons for this, was the Hindu religious revivalism implicit in the political philosophy of the Extremists. The next step in the separatist tendencies of the Indian Muslims was the demand of some of their leaders for separate electorate and weightage for the Muslims in the legislatures. The All India Muslim League founded in 1906 supplied the organisational machinery for propagating these views. The effect of these political trends was to encourage the feeling among the Indian Muslims that they were a separate political entity and their interests would be promoted by cooperating with the British government in India and not by participating in the political struggles of other Indians. This was the most dominant view among the Indian Muslims in the first decade of the 20th century.

Later, however a new trend appeared. A majority of the politically conscious section of the Indian Muslims became disillusioned with the British government following its annulment of the partition of Bengal and also because it did not, in the view of Indian Muslim leaders, protect Muslim interests abroad. This led to their decision to cooperate with the non-Muslims in the political sphere and which, in turn, had two effects. One was the Congress-Muslim League Pact as a high watermark of collaboration between those Hindus and Muslims who believed in the constitutional method of agitation. Another was the emergence of political radicalism among the Indian Muslims which reached the climax in the Khilafat agitation of 1920-21. A significant fact which emerged from our analysis of these trends was that both in the decision of the Muslims to cooperate with the Hindus against the government and in their decision to keep away from the political movements of the country and cooperate with the British government, their religion played a major part. At no time did they give up the idea that their political interests were different from those of others; at one stage they even thought that it was their duty to protect Muslim interests abroad. From this, one can conclude that in the period under survey, the political philosophy of the Indian Muslims, with few exceptions, was based on the concept that religion was a major factor in politics. In the later phase of the Indian national movement when this concept found fertile ground, some Muslim leaders could develop the theory that the Hindus and the Muslims were separate nations and that the Muslims should have a separate home of their own in the Indian sub-continent.

## POLITICAL PHILOSOPHY OF GANDHI

The next subject dealt with in this study is the political philosophy of the non-cooperation movement of 1920-21 and of Gandhi who led it. This is an appropriate conclusion to this survey of the political philosophy of the Indian national movement from 1885 to 1921 not only because, chronologically speaking, the non-cooperation movement took place last but because, in one sense, it was the culmination of all the movements which preceded it. It was also the result of an attempt on the part of Gandhi to make a synthesis of all the movements which influenced the Indian national movement. These strands of thought were not easily reconcilable. Gandhi did not, therefore, succeed in making a complete synthesis out of them. But if he had ignored the impact made by any one of them, he would not have become the symbol of the national movement which he became during 1919-21.

Gandhi himself accepted his indebtedness to the leaders who preceded him. He claimed Gokhale to be his spiritual *Guru* (teacher). Like Gokhale, he was also a champion of civil rights. He made the abolition of the Rowlatt Act, which infringed on civil rights, an issue in the non-cooperation movement. Like the Moderates, he was also prepared for peaceful and prolonged negotiation with the government. But unlike them, and like the Extremists, he was a rebel against the arbitrary actions of the government and he did not rule out the desirability of organising passive resistance to authority when occasion demanded.

Another feature, common to the political programme of Gandhi and that of the Extremists, was the fact that in both, religion played a role. But the nature of its role in both was not the same. Unlike the Extremists, Gandhi never spoke of a Hindu nation. Moreover, he said that he drew his inspiration from the scriptures of other religious as well. But some of the concepts he propagated such as *Ram Rajya* appealed only to the Hindus.

Like the Extremists, again, Gandhi emphasised the importance of enriching Indian languages and developing a national language for India. In all these respects, Gandhi continued the great work begun by the Extremists to further the process of democratising the national movement and building it on the foundations of the traditions of the country and on the strength of the support of the people to it.

Some aspects of his philosophy introduced an element of mysticism in his political activities and to that extent it took the national movement, which he dominated, away from a rational outlook.

The same effect was produced by Gandhi's condemnation of modern civilisation in all its aspects such as industrialisation and modern education.

CC 12

While these aspects of Gandhi's philosophy were in conflict with the faith of the Moderates in the ideas of the 'Ages of Enlightenment and Reason' of Europe, there were other aspects which were at variance with liberalism to which they owed allegiance. To take an example. He declared that anarchy was better than foreign rule even if the latter could maintain law and order. Many of the Moderate leaders maintained that he was strengthening the forces of anarchy by making such statements and by organising civil disobedience to the government.

Some of the Moderate leaders also accused Gandhi of creating those political conditions which encouraged intolerance towards non-conformists. It is difficult to prove that Gandhi himself consciously promoted any such tendencies ; but there was no doubt that these were some of the effects of the emotions and passions aroused by the mass movements which he led.

Gandhi's plea to reject modern civilisation on the ground that it was inferior to the ancient Indian civilisation gave self-confidence to the people of the country who were struggling for freedom from a mighty foreign power ; but it also promoted some degree of national chauvinism ; and in this respect Gandhi's political programme had the same effect as that of the Extremists and it differed sharply from that produced by the political agitation of the Moderates and by that of the socialists like Pandit Nehru, both of whom emphasised the fact that the Indian national movement must be viewed in the background of world developments.

Among the events outside India only the dismemberment of the Khilafat and other questions connected with Turkey and the Arab world attracted Gandhi's attention during 1919-21. And in regard to these, his attitude was as follows : 'I cannot regulate the Muhammedan feeling : I must accept his statement that the Khilafat is with him a religious question in the sense that it binds him to reach the goal even at the cost of his own life'.[3] This refusal to examine this question critically and accept the point of view of his Muslim friend in the expectation that they would concede to the Hindus on matters such as the protection of cows was not conducive to the spirit of enquiry

3.   Mahatma Gandhi, *Young India* 1919-1922 (Madras, 1922) 170.

which was gradually taking roots in India. The Hindu-Muslim unity created by the decision of the Hindus to support the Khilafat agitation of the Muslims was also not of a permanent nature. Instead of leading to a situation in which the Hindus and Muslims would merge in one political stream, it promoted the feeling that Hindus and Muslims, though separate political entities, could join in an alliance for some united action. This was not a basis on which an Indian nation, comprising of all communities, could be built up.

To sum up Gandhi's views. In the realm of ideas his contribution to the national movement during 1919-21 had both negative and positive results. The political campaigns he led did encourage some anarchist tendencies and a certain degree of intolerance towards non-conformists. There was some obscurantist and non-scientific, if not unscientific, elements in his philosophy. National chauvinism was inherent in his opposition to modern civilisation and its different manifestations. Some of his economic programmes, like *swadeshi* and boycott emphasised the indigenous methods of production and cottage industries to such an extent that they later became powerful weapons in the hands of those who wanted to resist the re-organisation of India's economic life on modern and scientific lines.

But as against these, Gandhi could claim that he instilled self-confidence in the people of the country. He also made them fearless and capable of resisting the arbitrary actions of those who were in authority. By bringing a large number of people into the national movement, he made its character very broad-based. He also succeeded in bringing some unity between the Muslims and the Hindus though it did not last long. Although he did not oppose the caste system, and even defended it occasionally, he undermined it by vigorously attacking the practice of untouchability. The total effect of his activities in regard to these matters, was to strengthen the forces of democracy and liberalism in this country.

There was a contradiction in many of Gandhi's aims and the methods pursued by him ; because while advocating a return to the past he was in fact laying the foundations of a new society. This was not peculiar to Gandhi. Leaders of many parts of the world and of different periods in history had often appealed to the religious and other traditions of the people to make their reformist and revolutionary movements a success.

The return to the classics dominated bourgeois Renaissance. Rome influenced Napoleon and the Revolution. The return to the natural uncorrupted man was the ideal of eighteenth century revolutionaries. Yet it is the new whose tension men feel in their minds and hearts at such times...He may think it is the past he is born to save or re-establish on earth and only when it is done it is seen that the future has come into being. The reformer 'returning' to primitive Christianity brings bourgeois Protestantism into being.[4]

Pointing attention to the similarity between these reformers and Gandhi an Indian scholar observed :

Gandhi imagined that he was engaged in an effort to reproduce Ram Raj of the Golden age of the Hindus, while, in reality, he was attempting to evolve a modern democratic capitalist national state existence for India.[5]

The statement is true in so far as it refers to the ultimate effect of Gandhi's political activities, but it is doubtful that Gandhi himself imagined that he was engaged in an effort to reproduce Ram Raj of the Golden Age of the Hindus. There were reasons to believe that he was conscious of the fact that he was engaged in the task of creating something new and not return- ing to the past. It is significant that he considered Gokhale, who accepted the most important features of liberalism and other advanced ideas of his times, as his teacher and that he 'nominated' Pandit Jawaharlal Nehru—again a leader who owed allegiance to socialism, an advanced political philosophy of his times—as his political heir. There were no religious revivalism and obscurantism in the thinking of these two leaders while they were present in the political philosophies of many other leaders who proceeded and succeeded Gandhi to whom he neither acknowledged his indebtedness or tried to give his mantle of leadership. As this study stops with 1921, this is not an appro- priate place to make an assessment of Gandhi who led a very active life until his death in 1948. We may, however, note that

4.  Christopher Caudwell *Studies in a Dying Culture* (London, 1938) 27-8.

5.  A. R. Desai, *Social Background of Indian Nationalism* (Bombay, 1954) 249.

even a survey of Gandhi's political activities until 1921 indicates that by functioning as a link between the exponents of two western political doctrines such as liberalism and socialism which exercised considerable influence on the Indian national movement, and, simultaneously, by broadbasing and Indianising it, he fulfilled an important role.

SOCIALISM, ASIAN RESURGENCE AND INTERNATIONALISM

We may close this study by making a brief reference to the new political ideas which appeared on the Indian political horizon before 1921, but which became the philosophy of major political groups and important leaders only later. These ideas were expressed in such words and phrases as 'socialism', 'Asian resurgence' and 'internationalism'. Rabindranath Tagore, the poet, was the ablest advocate of internationalism in this period. As early as in 1921 he said :

> At this dawn of the world's awakening, if our national endeavour holds no intimations of a universal message, the poverty of our spirit will be laid piteously bare... Universal humanity has sent us its urgent call. Let our mind answer in its own language...The dust of angry passion will only obscure the greater world from our view. And we shall exhibit a sorry image of our country if we fail to see for ourselves the vast dimensions of India in its world context.[6]

Aurobindo Ghose, who was a leader of the Extremist camp, became a votary of Asian resurgence by 1918. He wrote :

> It is difficult to believe that Asia once free to think, act and live for herself will be for long content merely to imitate the past or the present evolution of Europe. The temperament of her peoples is marked off by too deep-seated a difference, the build and movement of their minds is of another character. As present, however, the movement of resurgence in Asia is finding expression more by a preface, an attempt to vindicate her bare right to live for herself, than by any pregnant effort of independent creative thought or action.[7]

Aurobindo Ghose also refers to the emergence of socialism as

---

6. Rabindranath Tagore, *Towards Universal Man* (Bombay, 1961) 272.
7. Sri Aurobindo Ghose, *War and Self-Determination* (Pondicherry, 1957) 102-3.

a force in the political field. But, among the well-known leaders, it was Lajpat Rai who championed the cause of organised labour most effectively. Presiding over the first session of the All India Trade Union Congress he said :

> For the present our greatest need in this country is to organise, agitate and educate. We must organise our workers, make them class conscious, and educate them in the ways and means of commonweal.[8]

These three concepts of socialism, Asian resurgence and internationalism became very constant themes in the speeches and writings of Indian leaders in the nineteen-twenties and thirties. Pandit Jawaharlal Nehru was the outstanding exponent of socialism and internationalism. Even before India became free, he spoke and wrote extensively on the dangers of fascism, nazism and Japanese militarism and on the need for maintaining international peace and security through collective action on the part of all nations. He often referred to the struggle for freedom in other Asian countries also, though he did not view the Asian resurgence as a movement against European nations. Apart from Nehru, the members of the Congress Socialist party, the Communist party and many splinter groups popularised socialist doctrines and the concept of internationalism with varying interpretations. As far as the political philosophy of the Indian national movement was concerned, these ideas assumed an importance after 1921 which they did not have before that year because, consequent on the economic development in the country, urban labourers, who became an important factor, were receptive to them. So were the increasing number of educated people in the country. The socialist ideas found a fertile field in these groups of people and the trade unions and peasant organisations founded by some of them. Their history belongs to a period outside the scope of this study. A brief reference is made here to the support given by some Indian leaders to socialism, Asian resurgence and internationalism, because these ideas appeared on the Indian political horizon towards the end of the period under review, i.e., 1885-1921, when other political ideas dominated the national movement of the country.

---

8.   Lala Lajpat Rai, *India's Will to Freedom* (Madras, 1921) 179.

# CHAPTER VII

# EPILOGUE—THE GANDHIAN ERA

By 1920, Gandhi emerged as the most important leader of the Indian nationalists. Until 1945, he dominated the Indian National Congress. The period from 1920-1945 can be broadly referred to as the Gandhian era. Not that there were no critics and opponents of Gandhi on the Indian political stage in this period. There were many. But Gandhi could eclipse most of them. A leader like Pandit Jawaharlal Nehru often criticised Gandhi and put forward economic and social ideas different from those of the Mahatma. But until 1945, he implicitly accepted Gandhi's leadership in the field of action. After 1945, when the negotiations with the British for the transfer of power to Indian hands began, Nehru and his colleagues in the Congress began to chalk out a plan for themselves. Although they occasionally went to Gandhi for his advice until his death in 1948, they refused to accept his social and economic ideas as far as the reconstruction of the country was concerned. Gandhi was not unaware of his differences with his followers in the Congress party. But he decided to work with them because he knew that some of his ideas were too idealistic to get supporters during his life. Moreover, these differences were not related to the basic issue in Indian politics—the struggle for freedom for the country.

Gandhi and his colleagues in the Congress had, however, basic differences with the Muslim League on the fundamental question of the political unity of the sub-continent and on the matter of the political structure of the country with special reference to the place of Muslims in it. These differences were never resolved and ultimately when the British withdrew, a separate state named Pakistan was created and it incorporated in it the Muslim majority areas of North Western and North-Eastern parts of India. Mohammed Ali Jinnah was the leader of the Muslim League in the later phase of the Gandhian era; and as far as a large section of the Muslims was concerned, Gandhi could never eclipse him.

Other dissidents in the Gandhian era were the socialists and the communists. Their influence in the country as a whole was limited. But they placed their distinctive stamp on Indian politics by the time the country became free.

## COMBINATION OF DIFFERENT ROLES IN GANDHI

It is difficult to assess Gandhi's role as an Indian nationalist leader, because he combined in himself the role of a prophet, that of a Hindu religious reformer, that of an Indian social reformer and that of an Indian nationalist leader. It is difficult to isolate Gandhi's role in one field from that in another. It also seems that Gandhi's functions in the capacity of a Hindu religious reformer clashed with those in the capacity of an Indian nationalist leader. On the other hand, there are many students of Indian politics who maintain that he succeeded in one field to the extent that he did, because he was also active in other fields.

The functions of a world prophet were not necessarily antagonistic to those of a nationalist leader. But Gandhi often found it difficult to combine them. Even when he could do so, many of his followers could not appreciate his attempt to do so. His Indian followers complained that his emphasis on non-violence and right means compromised with the interests of the nationalist movement. In Nehru's words: "Always there has been that inner conflict within him and in our national politics, between Gandhi as a national leader and Gandhi as a man with a prophetic message which was not confined to India, but was for humanity and the world. It is never easy to reconcile a strict adherence to truth as one sees it with exigencies and expediencies of life, especially of political life. Normally, people do not even worry themselves over this problem. They keep truth apart in some corner of their minds, if they keep it at all anywhere and accept expediency as a measure of action. In politics that has been the universal rule not only because they cannot act purely on a purely personal plane. They have to make others act and they have to consider the limitations of others and their understanding and receptivity to truth.

And because of that, they have to make compromises with that truth, and adapt it to prevailing circumstances." Nehru conceded that Gandhi often made the necessary compromise : "But from time to time he pulls himself up, as if he were afraid that he had gone too far in his compromisings and returns to his moorings. In the midst of action, he seems to be in tune with the man's mind, responsive to its capacity and, therefore, adapting itself to it to some extent, at other times he becomes more theoretical and apparently less adaptable. There is also the same difference obser-vable in his action and his writings."

Another friendly critic of Gandhi thought that Gandhi's deep concern with Indian interests compromised with his world mission. He pointed out : "If you demonstrate your message in the language only of the East and in terms only of the Indian contingencies, is there not the grave danger that inessentials will be confused with fundamentals, that some features which correspond to extreme situations in India will be wrongly understood to be vital in the universal scene." Gandhi did not consider that there was any clash of these two roles. He rejected that patriotism which was not consistent with the broadest good of humanity at large. In his words : "The life of the world has become such a thing, that national interests cannot be really understood nor served except from the point of view of the universal interests of all humanity." He hoped that through the realisation of freedom of India by non-violent means, he could carry on and realise the mission of the brotherhood of men. He explained why he confined himself to the narrow and limited field of India and her problems : "I am in a position of a scientist who is in the midst of a very incomplete experiment and who, therefore, is unable to forecast large result and larger corrolaries in a language capable of being understood." Gandhi also felt that if he would be effective in India, the rest of the world would accept his message of non-violence later.

## POLITICAL CAMPAIGNS FOR FREEDOM

The non-cooperation movement of 1920-1921, which was re-ferred to in an earlier chapter, was one of the political landmarks in the Gandhian era. Others were the civil disobedience move-ment of 1930-1931, the Individual Civil Disobedience of 1940 and the Quit India Movement of 1942-1945. All these movements and many other political campaigns Gandhi led from 1920-1945 were a combination of legal and extra-legal measures. Gandhi and his followers frankly questioned the moral authority of the British government to rule India and they courted arrest by openly violating the laws. But they also did not rule out negotiations with their political opponents. Very often the political agitations, which went beyond the constitutional methods, were used by the Indian nationalists to bring pressure on the authorities to get concessions from them rather than to replace the then existing administrative system and state apparatus by entirely new ones.

Another characteristic of the political movements was its stress on non-violence. Gandhi himself explicitly stated that he owed allegiance to non-violence as a creed. But he realized that many of his followers did not share his own views on this matter. He placed it before them as a politically expedient measure and pointed out to them that it was wise to accept non-violence as a tactics because the British Government in India possessed superior force. At least once Gandhi withdrew a political movement because it led to violence. But as a rule, Gandhi maintained that the British government was responsible for violence and chaos. And he was not prepared to withdraw or suspend all movements just because they led to violence. This was particularly true of "Quit India Movement" of August 1942.

From 1920 to 1942 the demands of the Indian nationalist movement were varied. At first they were very specific and confined to such matters as the injustice done to political agitators in Amritsar, the Khilafat and the Rowlatt Act. Then they included the right to manufacture salt without paying duty in 1931 and the right of the freedom of speech in 1940. By 1942 the demands themselves were general and they included that Britain must "quit India."

Another important feature of the Indian nationalist movement was the relations between Gandhi, the supreme leader, and his followers, including the senior Congress leaders. Although Gandhi can be compared to Lenin and Mao in regard to his capacity to arouse the masses for social action, his concept of power was different from the other two leaders. He never tried to control and dominate the party organisation to the same degree as the other two leaders did. Moreover, the Indian National Congress, unlike the communist parties of the Soviet Union and China, was never a closely-knit organisation. In other words, even if Gandhi wanted it, he could not have succeeded in dominating the party completely. Moreover, Gandhi's aims and style of functioning were very different. This became very clear when India was at the threshold of freedom. After 1945, it was clear that very soon Indians would be acquiring full power and that a substantive share of this power would be controlled by the Congress leaders. At that time Gandhi decided to keep away from power and his colleagues like Nehru and Patel became senior members of the Government since September 1946. In August 1947, the South Asian sub-continent was partitioned into two completely independent—sovereign—states of India and Pakistan. Since August 1947, Gandhi was not associated with the day-to-day operations of the ruling Congress party and those of the government of independent India.

In spite of these aspects of the political movements led by Gandhi, his impact on the Indian nationalist movement was considerable.

## A Unique Leader

Another aspect of the work of Gandhi which raised great controversy was his attempt to function simultaneously as the religious and social reformer and nationalist leader. Like all creative reformers, Gandhi was simultaneously a revivalist and revolutionary. After accepting the framework of Hindu philosophical traditions, conceding the role of heredity in human life and using such idioms as Ram Rajya which made an appeal to the Hindu masses, Gandhi made an outright and uncompromising attack on the social behaviour of the Hindus such as untouchability and the concept of superiority of one caste over another. His last and relentless struggle was against the intolerance of Hindus towards the Muslims. More than any other leader, he succeeded in these battles although all the causes for which he fought were not entirely won during his life. His success in some of these fields were partly due to the fact that he worked within the framework of Hinduism.

But in the political field he and the Indian nationalist movement had to pay heavily for these activities of India's most dominant political leader. Many non-Hindus, and particularly many Muslims, were not enthused by Gandhi's style of functioning in public life. To them, Gandhi appeared to be a Hindu leader. The contradiction was inherent in the Indian situation of that time. If Gandhi had to attack the Hindu intolerance and Hindu orthodoxy effectively, he could do so only in the garb of a Hindu saint. But for having appeared in the public life of India as a Mahatma—a Hindu saint—his hold on the Muslim masses was considerably less than his hold on the Hindu masses. When the former moved towards accepting the leadership of those Muslim leaders who demanded the creation of Pakistan on the basis that the Muslims were a separate nation, he could not stem the new tide. It is difficult to answer the following question : What would have happened if Gandhi had acted differently? There would still have been a Pakistan because the schism between the Hindus and the Muslims had deep roots in history. And if Gandhi had not fought against Hindu orthodoxy effectively and had not ultimately courted martyrdom by being murdered by a Hindu fanatic, India would not have been a secular state in theory and to some extent secular in practice, as it is today. Assessing Gandhi's role in this respect, an Indian communist writes : 'Here once again, as in the case of Tilak, the criticism is made that the language of Gandhiji, his prayer meetings, his insistence on non-violence and the rest helped to spread communalism or atleast brought grist to the mill of the communalists (Hindu and Muslim religious sectarians). This appeared to be unbalanced criticism. The main result of the work in preaching of Gandhiji was the partial turning of the awakened Hindu masses to secularism and nationalism and away from communalism and casteism. He did not succeed completely by any means, as the partition tragedy only too grimly showed. Nevertheless, more than any other single individual and on a massive scale he was able to place a picture of secular India and of communal unity. The fact that India chose to remain a secular republic is in large measure due to him. The Hindu communalist (sectarian) felt at an enormous disadvantage in combating him since it was impossible to contest the Indianness or the "Hinduness" of the man or to dispute that what he was telling the people sprang from the very depths of the traditions of India'.[1]

1. Mohit Sen, *The Indian Revolution* (New Delhi, 1970), p. 20,

GANDHI—THE DEMOCRAT AND MODERNISER

Whatever might have been the idioms Gandhi used and the style in which he functioned  politically, he was India's greatest  moderniser and  democrat.  V. S.  Naipaul,  a writer of the West Indies, makes the significant observation that Gandhi was the least  Indian of Indian leaders and adds: "He looked at India as no Indian  was able to; his vision was direct, and this directness was, and is, revolutionary.  He sees exactly what the visitor sees; he does not ignore the obvious.  He sees the beggars and the  shameless  pundits and the filth of Benaras; he sees the atrocious sanitary habits of doctors, lawyers  and  journalists.  He  sees  the  Indian  callousness,  the Indian refusal to see.  No Indian attitude escapes him,  no Indian problem,  he  looks  down  to  the  roots  of  the  static,  decayed society."[1]  Gandhi's success in the field was due to  the  fact  that he  had  a  social  base  in India and that he knew the mind of the vast  masses  of  the  people  of  the  country.  No other leader of modern India had the same degree of social base as  Gandhi  had. A  few  leaders  belonging  to  different regions were more popular than Gandhi in their respective regions.  But they had  practically no  influence outside their regions.  The influence of leaders of the Muslim  League  and  the  Scheduled  Castes  Federation  cut across different regions, but was confined to their respective communities. The liberals, the socialists and the communists, who  thought  that their  ideologies  were  more  advanced  than those of Gandhi, had practically no support from the people in  the  rural  areas  of  the country.  Unlike them, Gandhi realized that in India of his times, the Indian masses meant primarily the people of the  villages.  But he  also  knew that the rural  masses alone would deliver the goods in India.  As the author of 'The Soul  of India' notes : 'It was inevitable  that an unspoken alliance would be established between the  frustrated  turning  away from European culture, the encircled middle classes who owed their increment of wealth and  power  to the  war,  who  were flexing their muscles and wanted to taste their political power  and  finally,  the  mute  but  discontented  masses. Such  an  alliance,  however, could not remain a formal link, a cold contract  binding  more  interest groups.  It had  to be achieved within the person of one man, who would  be  accepted  as undis-

---

1. V. S. Naipaul, *An Area of Darkness* (New York, 1964), p. 78.

puted leader of the whole movement, who would synthesise it and give it emotional impulse that was still lacking.' Gandhi was such a person and as such he became the symbol of Indian unity.

## GANDHI AS A REVOLUTIONARY

Gandhi was a revolutionary because he led many militant, though non-violent, struggles against the alien rulers. At first he wanted specific grievances to be redressed; later he took his stand on Indian freedom and asked the British to "Quit India". His adherence to non-violence did not mean any compromise on fundamentals. He never allowed "a coward to take shelter behind non-violence so called". He said that he had no attraction for the peace of the grave and that he would rather have India resort to arms to defend her honour than she would, in a cowardly manner, become or remain a helpless witness to her own dishonour. Gandhi also realised that although non-violence was a creed to him, it was only a policy to many of his followers.

The most important element in Gandhi's political campaigns such as Civil Disobedience and Non-Violent, Non-Cooperation was the open rebellion and challenge to established authority. He once told the court which was trying him : "I am here to invite and submit cheerfully to the highest penalty that can be inflicted upon me for what in law is a deliberate crime and what appears to me to be the highest duty of a citizen". Gandhi was more than once convicted for long terms of imprisonment. But his campaigns were not performances of an individual. He released the mass energy of India by putting before them specific programmes of action to challenge the British power in the country.

The civil disobedience and the non-cooperation movements Gandhi led were militant struggles embodying the use of force, although no enemy was physically hurt. Boycott of foreign goods and attempts at paralysing the government were included in the programme. On the eve of the civil disobedience movement of 1930-31, Gandhi wrote to the British Viceroy : "It is not a matter of carrying conviction by argument. The matter revolves itself into one of matching forces. Conviction or no conviction, Great Britain would defend her Indian commerce and interests by all the forces at her command. India must equally evolve force enough to free herself from that embrace of death." In 1942 when Gandhi asked the British to quit, he gave a call to his countrymen: "Do or Die."

Gandhi championed the development of a "national economy for India." He maintained that only "Swadeshi (Indian-made) goods should be used and foreign goods should be boycotted. He did not have the control of the state apparatus to raise an iron curtain around the country. And his methods were also not of a dictator. But he successfully raised a bamboo curta'n around the country by insisting that his followers must not use foreign goods however cheap and durable they were.

While leading the nationalist movement for freedom, Gandhi tried to reconstruct Indian society on modern lines. With this aim, he concentrated his attacks on feudalism, superstitions, and social behaviour which were a brake on progress and those bottlenecks in society which retarded production in the economic field. He was a liberal; but instead of mechanically repeating Western liberal concepts, he modified them so that he could creatively apply them to Indian situations.

The total impact of Gandhi's political campaigns was in the direction of democracy and individual and national freedom. It was not an accident that Gandhi claimed Gokhale to be his political leader and Nehru to be his political heir, although these two leaders did not link religion with politics as he did. An Indian communist, who considered Gandhism to be the ideological reflex of the peasant petty bourgeoisie, says that the outcome of his activity was beneficial to the nation as a whole and particularly it was so to the national bourgeoisie. He adds : "It is to be regretted that the more farsighted representatives of the capitalist class in India had a clearer understanding of the potential of peasant Gandhi than did the representatives of the working class who adopted, taking the period as a whole, rather sectarian and supercilious approach."[1] The communists were misled by some "mystical" statements of Gandhi and by his condemnation of modern civilisation in all its aspects such as industrialization and modern education. The Indian capitalists, who often financed him and the political movements he led, did not have any such wrong assessment. They knew that the ultimate effect of the movement he led was a highly industrialised and nationalist India. The Hindu fanatic, who murdered him also knew this well. He realised that

1. *Ibid.*, p. 19.

Gandhi was a great danger to feudalism and Hindu orthodoxy. But his calculations went wrong in another aspect. He thought that by murdering the Mahatma he would weaken his ideas; on the other hand as far as the reconstruction of Indian economy and society were concerned, Gandhi's martyrdom had the effect of further strengthening the forces of secularism and modernism.

Although Gandhi was considered by many Marxist thinkers as the leader of Indian bourgeoisie, they did not maintain that he functioned always as the representative of that class. Many of the battles he conducted for the poorer classes of the society had a revolutionary significance which went beyond the interests of that class. His strict adherence to some basic ideals, even when that was not in the interests of the bourgeoisie, had also the same effect. E.M.S. Namboodiripad, one of the foremost communist leaders of India, reflecting on the gulf between Gandhi and other nationalist leaders on the eve of India's achievement of freedom and during the years immediately following it, argued that this gulf was the manifestation of the reality that Gandhiji's insistence on certain moral values had once been helpful to the bourgeoisie, but became in the last days of his life, a hinderance. Namboodiripad adds : "It was this change in the position of the bourgeoisie as a class and its individual representatives that brought it into conflict with Gandhiji, the man who still clung to the ideals which he had been preaching in the days of anti-imperialist struggle. The moral values which he had preached in the days of anti-imperialist struggle now became a hinderance to the politicians who came to power. Gandhiji, on the other hand, remained true to them and could not reconcile himself to the sudden change which occurred to his former colleagues and lieutenants. Particularly was this so on the question of Hindu-Muslim unity and on the corruption in the ranks of the Congress. We may conclude by saying that Gandhiji became the Father of the Nation, precisely because the idealism to which he adhered to in the years of anti-imperialist struggle became a practically useful political weapon in the hands of the bourgeoisie in the latter days of his life, because his idealism did in the post-independent years become a hinderance to the self-interest of the bourgeoisie."[1]

1. E.M.S. Namboodiripad, *The Mahatma and the Ism* (New Delhi, 1959), p. 117.

## Nehru, the Socialist and the Communist Enrich Gandhi's Contributions

Gandhi's role in regard to broadening the social base of the nationalist movement and giving social and economic content to it was enriched by leaders like Pandit Jawaharlal Nehru and parties and groups committed to socialism. Nehru's contributions were in regard to (1) maintaining that India should unhesitatingly and unequivocally accept industrialization and re-organise her society on that basis; (2) popularising the ideas that urban intellectuals and organised proletariat, with their commitment to social and economic justice, should be brought into the national political stream and (3) in asserting that the political development in the domestic scene in India should be viewed in the context of international events. Nehru occasionally also spoke of socialism although he was very vague about it. He had no organisation of his own. He functioned within the framework of the Indian National Congress which until 1945, was dominated by Gandhi and those who owed allegiance to him.

The non-communal approach to politics, which was a part of Gandhi's philosophy, was spread by Nehru in modern secular terms.

In the later half of the nineteen-twenties, some individuals who owed allegiance to communism, tried to spread their ideas in the country. But they were not very effective. In 1933 a Communist Party of India was established. It had limited support from some trade unions and from some groups like the intellectuals and students in urban areas. In some scattered parts of the country some of the communists were popular in rural areas also.

The Congress Socialist Party, which was established in 1934, functioned within the Congress Party. It was also an urban phenomenon. Unlike the communists, the socialists were not isolated from the nationalist movement. But their party apparatus was not as well organised as that of the communists.

The total impact of the work of these communists and the socialists and individuals like Nehru, though very limited, was to give a social and economic content to the Indian Nationalist Movement and to give an international bias to it. It also gave some precision to the slogans used in regard to the social and economic aspirations of the people. Some of these aspirations were later incorporated in the "Directive Principles" of the Constitution of Indian Republic.

## RELIGIOUS SECTARIANISM CHALLENGES GANDHI

Another trend in Indian politics, instead of enriching Gandhi's contribution, went contrary to the spirit of his ideas and his work. It was based on religious sectarianism, often referred to in India as "Communalism". In the Indian context this was the meaning of the term : "Communalism supposes the existence of a community, a group of adherents of the same religion, but it gets the edge of its meaning through the parallelism with the other term; it is something like nationalism, in which the nation, so to speak, is replaced by the community. In other words, communalism is the affirmation of the religious community as a political group." The Hindus who were in a majority did not support Hindu communalism in a big way, because, broadly speaking, they realised that their interests lay in Indian nationalism. But the Muslim middle class which was the politically conscious section of their community, did not feel that their interests were safe in the hands of the leaders of the Indian nationalist movement.

Towards the close of the nineteenth century itself the Muslim middle class accepted a communal approach to Indian politics. The communal spirit of the Indian Muslims was not in proportion to their adherence to the tenets of their religion, but to their affirmation of the community of Muslims as a social, economic and political group and to the degree of their antagonism to the Hindus, whose domination they feared. Referring to the demand for the creation of Pakistan, one prominent Pakistani scholar and jurist said later : "Below the surface there was a medley of racial, cultural and religious groupings and patterns which began to be agitated as soon as the prospects of the devolution of political authority on the people of India became a possibility : As the process of the transfer of political authority proceeded, this agitation increased and sharp conflicts developed. The main struggle took shape between the two largest sections of the population, Hindu and Muslim. The objective was political ; the urge was economic, the dividing line was cultural. As the two conflicting cultures were both based, or purported to be based, upon religion, the conflict assumed the character of a religious struggle, particularly on the Muslim side." As the Muslim side was effectively supported by the British government, the ultimate result was the creation of Pakistan. The demand for the creation of Pakistan was for the first time put forward by the All India Muslim League on 23rd March 1940. And in August 1947 Pakistan came into being as a sovereign state.

## THE INTERNATIONAL OUTLOOK

One important feature of the Indian nationalist movement was that it gradually developed an international outlook. In this, it was in contrast with many other nationalists of some Asian and African countries which were obsessed with its struggle for freedom to such an extent that it took no interest in developments outside the country. The fact that leaders like Gandhi and poets like Rabindranath Tagore had an international outlook was a factor in favour of this development. But the adoption of clear-cut view by the Indian National Congress on specific issues or events outside the country was primarily due to Jawaharlal Nehru.

In the nineteen-thirties Nehru consistently demanded that the Indian National Congress must line up with Republican Spain, China, Ethiopia and Czechoslovakia in their struggle against imperialism and fascism. The Indian National Congress, under Nehru's guidance, also denounced the aggressive policies of Japan, Italy and Germany and the Western Powers' acquiescence in it.

During the World War II, the Congress Party was in dilemma. On the one hand it was opposed to British imperialism and on the other it was concerned with the expansion of Nazism and Fascism in Europe and Japanese militarism in Asia. The dilemma was reflected in a series of resolutions of the Indian National Congress. The party's executive stated on 15 September 1939 : "If Great Britain fights for the maintenance and extension of democracy, then she must necessarily end imperialism in her own possessions. A free democratic India will gladly associate herself with other free nations for mutual defence against aggression and for economic cooperation." Britain was in no mood to accept this view. On the other hand Churchill and his other colleagues made it clear that they would do their level best to preserve their colonies. On 9 August 1942 the All India Congress Committee demanded the immediate withdrawal of the British Power from India and made it clear that if the withdrawal would take place, Free India would become an ally of the United Nations and would fight for the success of freedom and democracy. The Congress resolution added : "A Free India will assure that success by throwing all her great resources in the struggle for freedom and against the aggression of Nazism, Fascism and Imperialism. The British took this attitude of the Congress as a challenge to their authority and arrested Gandhi and all the prominent leaders of the Congress on 9 August 1942. This was followed by widespread arrests throughout the country. The people spontaneously rose in revolt and for a short time the government was paralyzed in some parts of the country. The authorities took very vigorous and drastic measures and ruthlessly suppressed the revolt.

It is significant that even these developments did not make the people of India sympathetic towards the European fascists and the Japanese militarists. This was partly because, the training Gandhi gave to them was based on self-reliance and not on dependence on foreigners. This was also because of the anti-fascist campaigns organised by leaders like Nehru and organisations like the Communist Party. The communists were, to some extent, isolated from the main stream of the nationalist movement after the 'Quit India' movement was launched in August 1942 because of the unconditional support they gave to Britain's war efforts on the ground that the war had become a people's war after the Soviet Union was attacked by Germans.

Subhas Chandra Bose was an extreme nationalist who was unhappy by Gandhi's leadership of the Indian National Congress during 1938-39. During the war he left India for Germany and later he reached Japan from where he organised an 'Indian National Army.' Bose's efforts were not of great military significance. But after the war when the British Government tried the Indian Army officers who joined the Indian National Army, there was a widespread manifestation of emotional support to them. It was of great political significance. Even Gandhi and Nehru expressed their admiration for the patriotism and the spirit of self-sacrifice displayed by Bose and his followers.

The purpose of this epilogue is not to give an exhaustive treatment of the Gandhian era in Indian politics. Such a treatment cannot be done in one single chapter. In view of the various and often conflicting trends of thought, it is realised that justice could be done to them only if they are dealt at length in five or six chapters and only if it occupies as much space as the five chapters preceding this chapter. This will be attempted in another study. In this study on the political philosophy of the Indian nationalist movement between 1885-1920, this general survey of the later phase of the Indian nationalist movement is added because it is felt that this focussing attention on what happened later will help the understanding of what went before 1920.

## BIBLIOGRAPHY

### Primary Sources

ABBAS, M. H., *All about the Khilafat, with the views of Mahatma Gandhi and others, together with full details of the Indian Khilafat Delegation in Europe headed by Maulana Mohammed Ali*, four parts, Calcutta, 1923.

AFZAL IQBAL, Ed., *Mohammed Ali, My life, a Fragment : An Autobiographical Sketch*, Lahore, 1946.

——, *Select Writings and Speeches of Maulana Mohammed Ali*, Lahore, 1944.

AGA KHAN, THE, *India in Transition*, London, 1918.

——, *The Memoirs of the Aga Khan*, London, 1954.

AHMAD, KAZI SIRAJ-UD-DIN, Comp., *The Truth about the Khilafat*, Lahore, 1916.

*All India Moderates' Conference*, 1918, Bombay, 1918.

*All India Muslim League*, India Office Library Tract, 1908.

ANDREWS, CHARLES FREER, *The Indian Problem*, Madras, 1923.

——, *Non-Cooperation*, Madras, 1922.

ARUNDALE, G. S., *National Education*, Madras, 1916.

AUROBINDO, SRI, *Uttarapura Speech*, Calcutta, 1943.

AZAD, ABUL KALAM, *India Wins Freedom*, Calcutta, 1959.

BASU, BHUPENDRANATH, *Why India is Heart and Soul with Great Britain*, London, 1914.

BANERJEE, SIR SURENDRA NATH, *Speeches and Writings*, Madras, n.d.

——, *Presidential Address at the All India Moderates' Conference*, Bombay, 1918.

——, *A Nation in Making*, London, 1925.

BONNERJEE, W. C., Ed., *Indian Politics (A Collection of Essays and Addresses)*, Madras, 1898.

BESANT, ANNIE, *The Birth of New India*, Madras, 1917.

——, *Congress Speeches*, Adyar, 1917.

——, *India : a nation; a plea for self-government*, London, 1916.

——, *India and empire, a lecture and various papers on Indian grievances*, London, 1914.

——, *The future of Indian politics, a contribution to the under-standing of present day problems*, London, 1922.

BOMBAY GOVERNMENT RECORDS, *Source Material for a History of the Freedom Movement in India*, Vol. I, 1818-1885, Vol., II, 1885-1920, Bombay, 1958.

CHAKRAVARTHI, DHIRESH CHANDRA AND BHATTACHARYA, C., Comp., *Congress in Evolution (Being a Collection of Congress Resolutions from 1885 to 1940)*, Calcutta, 1935.

CHINTAMANI, SIR C. Y., ED., *Indian Social Reforms, a collection of essays, addresses, speeches*, Madras, 1901.

CHATTERJEE, *Towards Home Rule*, Pt. I, Calcutta, 1917.

CURZON, GEORGE N., *Speeches*, 4 vols., Calcutta, 1900-6.

DAS, CHITTARANJAN, *Freedom through Disobedience*, Madras, 1922.

——, *Deshabandhu Chitta Ranjan : brief survey of life and work, Provincial Conference Speeches, Congress Speeches*, Calcutta, 1927.

DESAI, MAHADEO, ED., *Lord Macaulay's Legislative Minutes*, Calcutta, 1946.

DUGREKAR, H. V., Ed., *Bhagwan Tilak's Messages to His Country-men*, Pt. I, Benaras 1917.

DUTT, ROMESH CHANDER, *Open Letters to Lord Curzon and Speeches and, Papers, Calcutta*, 1905.

——, *Speeches and Papers on Indian Questions*, 2 vols., Calcutta, 1902.

——, *England and India : A Record of Progress during a Hundred Years (1785-1885)*, London, 1897.

GANDHI, MOHANDAS KARAMCHAND, *Gokhale, My Political Guru*, Ahmedabad, 1955.

——, *Speeches and Writings*, Madras, 1917.

——, *Freedom's Battle, being a comprehensive collection of writings and speeches on the present situation*, Madras, 1922.

——, *Young India 1919-22...with a brief introduction of the non-cooperation movement by Babu Rajendra Prasad*, Madras, 1922.

——, *India Home Rule*, 5th edn., Madras, 1922.

——, *Swarajya in One Year*, 2nd edn., Madras, 1921.

——, *Hind Swaraj*, Ahmedabad, 1909.

——, *The Story of my Experiments with Truth*, Ahmedabad, 1929.

GHOSE, AUROBINDO, *Speeches*, Pondicherry, 1952.

——, *Bankim-Tilak-Dayanand*, 2nd edn., Calcutta, 1947.

——, *Doyanand : the Man and his Work*, 1917.

——, *The Doctrine of Passive Resistance*, Pondicherry, 1948.

——, *The Renaissance in India*, Calcutta, 1946.

GHOSE, RASHBEHARI, *Speeches and Writings of Dr. Sir Rashbehari Ghose*, Madras, 1921.

——, *The Honourable Dr. Rash Behary Ghose : His Life Sketch and Speeches*, Madras, 1907.

GOKHALE, GOPAL KRISHNA, *Speeches*, Madras, 1920.

——, *Public life in India, its needs and responsibilities* (*A speech*), Bombay, 1922.

GREAT BRITAIN, INDIA OFFICE, *East India* (*Constitutional Reforms*)— *Report on Indian Constitutional Reforms*, London, 1918.

GREAT BRITAIN, INDIA OFFICE, HOUSE OF LORDS, *Indian Constitutional Report, Speeches delivered in the House of Lords on October 23rd and 24th 1918, by the Marquess of Lansdowne, and Earl of Selbourne* (*sic*) *Lord Curzon and others*, London, 1918.


HASHIMY, DR. S. Y., Ed., *Muhammed Iqbal : Iqbal's Maiden English Lecture—Islam as an Ethical and Political Ideal : Delivered in 1928*, Lahore, 1955.

HUME, ALLAN OCTAVIAN, *A Speech on the Indian National Congress —its origin, aims and objects, delivered at Allahabad*, Calcutta, 1888.


IMAM, SYED ALI, *Speech as President of the All India Muslim League*, Bankipur, 1908.

INDIA, *The Government of India Act 1919*, London, 1921.

——, *The Sedition Committee Report*, Calcutta, 1919.

——, *India in 1921—East India* (*Progress and Condition*), London, 1922.

INDIAN NATIONAL CONGRESS, *A Scheme of Reforms Passed by the Indian National Congress...And by the All India Muslim League, 1916*, Poona, 1917.

——, *The Indian National Congress, containing an account of its origin and growth, full texts of all Presidential addresses; reprint of all the Congress resolutions, extracts from all the welcome addresses, notable utterances of the movement, portraits of all the Congress Presidents*, Madras, 1917.

——, *United Provinces Congress Committee ; Memorandum in support of the joint scheme of reforms proposed by the Indian National Congress and All India Muslim League submitted to the Right Honourable the Secretary of State for India and His Excellency the Viceroy and Governor General of India on behalf of the Provincial Congress Committee of the United Provinces of Agra and Oudh*, Allahabad, 1917.

——, *From Calcutta Special to Gaya : The development of non-co-operation as unheld by the Indian National Congress, 1920-1922,* Masulipattam, 1923.

——, 32nd Session, Calcutta, 1917. *The Case for India : The Presidential address by Annie Besant,* London, 1918.

INDIAN NATIONAL CONGRESS, BRITISH COMMITTEE, *The Rowlatt Bills* (*a criticism*), London, 1919.

——, *Demands of the Indian National Congress as presented to the Joint Select Committee of both Houses of Parliament on the Government of India Bill, by the Honourable V. J. Patel...Mr. V. P. Madhava Rao...and B. G. Tilak*, London, 1919.

JAEGEEBHOY, J. R. B., Ed., *Some unpublished and later speeches and writings of the Hon. Sir Pherozeshah Mehta*, Bombay, 1918.

KARIM RAZAUL, *Muslims and the Congress* (*being a symposium of Addresses of the Muslim Presidents of the Congress from 1885 to 1940*), Calcutta, 1941.

KETTH, A. B. Ed., *Speeches and Documents on India Policy,* London, 1922.

KELKAR, N. C., *Indian Home Rule League Pamphlet No. 1*, 1916.

KHANDEKAR, D. G., Ed., *India in 1906 : collection of presidential addresses delivered at the National Congress, 1906*, Poona, 1907.

LAJPAT RAI, LALA, *Young India : an interpretation and a history of the nationalist movement from within*, New York, 1916.

——, *Ideals of non-cooperation*, Madras 1924.

——, *The political future of India*, New York, 1921.

——, *The United States of America*, Calcutta, 1917.

——, *India's will to freedom : writings and speeches on the present situation*, Madras, 1921.

——, *Reflections on the political situation in India, with a personal note and extracts : Indian and English newspapers et cetra,* Lahore, 1915.

——, *The Man in his word,* Madras, 1907.

——, *The Message of the Bhagavat Gita,* Allahabad, 1908.

——, *The Problem of National Education in India,* London, 1920.


MAZUMDAR, AMBIKA CHARAN, *Separation of judicial from executive functions, His speech with Congress resolutions,* Adyar, 1915.

MAJUMDAR, JATINDRA KUMAR Ed., *Indian Speeches and Documents on British Rule 1821-1918,* London, 1937.

MAJUMDAR, PROKASH CHANDRA, *A defence of the Congress-League Scheme (a study in comparative politics), being a reply to the criticisms with reference to the constitutions of Colonies, and European and American countries,* Calcutta, 1918.

MALAVIYA, MADAN MOHAN, *Speeches and Writings,* Madras, 1919.

——, *A critique of the Montague-Chelmsford proposal of Indian Constitutional Reforms,* Allahabad, 1918.

MEMUR-UD-DIN, SHEIKH, *The Indian Muslim Attitude towards the British Government,* Cuttack, 1915.

MITTER, B. L., *Extremists and Moderates—a Study,* Calcutta, 1918.

MONTAGU, EDWIN SAMUEL, *The Rt. Hon., Mr. E. S. Montagu on Indian affairs : Speeches,* Madras, 1917.

——, *Speeches on Indian questions,* Madras, 1917.

MONTAGU, VENETIA, Ed., *Edwin S. Montagu, An Indian Diary,* London, 1930.

MORLEY, VISCOUNT, *Indian Speeches 1907-1909* London, 1909.

MUKHERJI, PANCHANANDAS, Comp., and Ed., *Indian Constitutional Documents* (1773-1915), Calcutta, 1918.


NAIDU, SAROJINI, *Speeches and Writings,* 2nd edn., Madras, 1919.

NAIR, C. SANKARAN, *Two Notable Speeches,* Calicut, 1900 (?)

NAOROJI, DADABHAI, *Poverty and un-British Rule in India,* London, 1901.

——, *Speeches and Writings,* Madras, 1909.

NATESAN, G. A., Ed., *The Indian demands, a symposium on the memorandum of the nineteen and speeches at the Congress and Moslem League on their scheme of self-government for India,* Madras, 1917.

——, *Congress Presidential Addresses, 1911-1914,* Madras, 1934.

——, *Indian National Congress—Collection of the Presidential and Inaugural Speeches, delivered at the Indian National Congress*, Madras, 1917.

——, *Indian National Congress—Speeches and Documents connected with the Congress*, Madras, 1917.

——, *India's Goal* : *constructive criticisms by leading Indians on the Montagu-Chelmsford Scheme*, Madras, 1918.

PAL, BIPINCHANDRA, *Beginnings of Freedom Movement in Modern India*, Calcutta, 1954.

——, *Indian nationalism, its Principles and Personalities*, Madras, 1916.

——, *Nationality and Empire* : *a running study of some current Indian Problems*, Calcutta, 1916.

——, *Memories of My Life and Times*, 1932, 2 vols., Calcutta, 1951.

——, *On Bande Mataram, The spirit of Indian Nationalism*, London, 1910.

——, *Mr. Pal's lecture on the Rowlatt Bills*, 1919.

——, *Responsible Government*, Calcutta, 1917.

——, *Speeches*, Madras, 1907.

——, *Swadeshi and Swaraj*, Calcutta, 1954.

——, *The new spirit* : *a selection from the writings of Bipin Chandra Pal*, Calcutta, 1907.

——, *The World Situation and Ourselves*, Calcutta, 1919.

PALIT, R. C., Ed., *Surendranath Banerjea's Speeches*, Calcutta, 1880.

PAREKH, CHUNNILAL LALLUBHAI, Ed., *Naoroji, Dadabhai, Essays, Speeches, Addresses and Writings* (on Indian Politics), Bombay, 1887.

RALEIGH, SIR THOMAS, Ed., *Lord Curzon in India—Indian Speeches*, London, 1905.

RAO, RAJA, AND SINGH, IQBAL, Ed., *Changing India*, London, 1939.

RAY, PRITHWIS CHANDRA, Ed., *The separation of judicial and executive functions in British India—a compilation of authoritative opinions* (1783-1900), Calcutta, 1901.

SANKARAKRISHNA, K. C., Comp., *India's demands* : *Speeches delivered on the platforms of the Indian National Congress and the All India Muslim League*, Madras, 1917.

SATYAMOORTHI, S., *Rights of Gitizen*, Madras, 1919.

SINHA, S. C., Comp., *Indian Speeches of Lord Curzon* (1898-1901), 2 vols., Calcutta, 1900-02.

SITARAMAYYA, B. PATTABHI, *The History of the Congress* (1885-1935), Allahabad, 1935.

SRINIVASA SASTRI, V. S., *Self Government for India under the British flag*, Allahabad, 1916.

——, *The Congress-League Scheme, exposition*, Allahabad, 1917.

SUBRAMANYA IYER, G., *Some aspects of British Rule in India*, Madras, 1903.

TILAK, BAL GANGADHAR, *All about Lokmanya Tilak*, Madras, 1922.

——, *Tilak's masterpiece : being a verbatim report of his address to the Jury*, Surat, 1908.

——, *The trial of Bal Gangadhar Tilak, B.A.,LL.B., The Kesari prosecution*, Madras, 1908.

——, *Tilak's Speeches*, Poona, 1908.

——, *His Writings and Speeches*, Madras, 1918, 2nd ed., 1919.

——, *Mr. Tilak's Case*, Madras, 1916.

WEDDERBURN, SIR WILLIAM, *Allen Octavian Hume, C.B., Father of the Indian National Congress*, 1829 to 1912. London, 1913.

YOUNG, G. M., Ed., *Selected Speeches 1854 with his Minute on Indian Education by Lord Macaulay*, London, 1935.

## Secondary Sources

BERLIN, ISIAH, *The Age of Enlightenment*, New York, 1956.

BOLITHO, HECTOR, *Jinnah : Creator of Pakistan*, London, 1954.

BOSE, PRAMATHA NATH, *The Economic Aspect of the Montagu-Chelmsford Reform Scheme*, Calcutta, 1918.

BUCH, MAGANLAL AMRITLAL, *Rise and growth of Indian Liberalism*, London, 1937.

CHINTAMANI SIR C. Y., *Indian Politics since the Mutiny : Being an account of the development of public life and political institutions and of prominent political personalities*, Allahabad, 1937.

CHIROL, SIR VALENTINE, *India : Old and New*, London, 1921.

COUPLAND, R., *The Indian Problem 1833-1935*, Oxford, 1943.

CURTIS, LIONAL, *Letters to the people of India on Responsible Government*, Calcutta, 1917.

DAVIDSON, W. H., *Political Thought in England—Bentham to Mill*, Oxford, 1915.

DAYAL, BHAGWAN, *The Development of Modern Indian Education*, Calcutta, 1955.

DESAI, A. R., *Social Background of Indian Nationalism*, Bombay, 1954.

DESAI, MAHADEV HARIVAI, *Maulana Abul Kalam Azad, the President of the Indian National Congress, a biographical memoir*, 2nd ed., Agra, 1946.

DOKE, JOSEPH J., *M. K. Gandhi—An Indian Patriot in South Africa*, Madras, 1909.

GADGIL, D. R., *Industrial Evolution of India in Recent Times*, London, 1946.

GHOSE, P. C., *Indian National Congress 1892-1907*, thesis in London University.

GLEDHILL, A., *The Republic of India*, London, 1951.

GOKHALE, D. V. Ed., *The contempt of court case against Mr. N. C. Kelkar, editor, The Kesari*, Poona, 1924.

GOPALAKRISHNAN, P. K., *Development of Economic Ideas in India*, New Delhi, 1959.

GRIFFITHS, SIR PERCIVAL JOSEPH, *The British Impact on India*, London, 1952.

GUPTA, ATULCHANDRA, *Studies in the Bengal Renaissance*, Jadavpur, 1958.

HOYLAND, JOHN SOMERVELL, *Gopal Krishna Gokhale, his life and speeches*, Calcutta, 1948.

HUNTER, W. W., *The India of the Queen*, London, 1908.

HUSSAIN, AZIM, *Fazl-i-Hussain*, London, 1946.

ILBERT, SIR COURTENAY, *The Government of India, being a digest of the Statute Law relating thereto with historical introduction and explanatory matter*, Oxford, 1915.

INDIA, *Montagu-Chelmsford Report—Report on Indian Constitutional Reforms*, Delhi, 1918.

JAIN, M. P., *Outlines of Indian Legal History*, Delhi, 1952.

KEITH, A. B., *A Constitutional History of India*, London, 1936.

KELKAR, NARSINHA CHINTAMAN, *Life and times of Lokmanya Tilak* (D. V. Divakar, trans.,), Madras, 1928.

LASKI, HAROLD J., *The Age of European Liberalism*, London, 1947.
LOVETT, SIR VERNEY, *A History of Indian Nationalist Movement*, London, 1920.

MAJUMDAR, R. C., AND OTHERS, *Modern India, being Pt. III of an Advanced History of India*, London, 1949.
MASANI, R. P., *Dadabhai Naoroji : The Grand Old Man of India*, London, 1939.
MILL, J. S., *On Liberty and Considerations on Representative Government*, Oxford, 1948.
MITRA, HARENDRANATH, *India in parliament and abroad*, 1919-1920, Calcutta, 1920.
MORLEY, J. V., *Recollections*, London, 1917.
MUIR, RAMSAY, *The Making of British India*, London, 1915.
MUKERJI, D. P., *Modern Indian Culture—A Social Study*, Bombay, 1948.
MUKHERJI, H. AND MUKHERJEE, UMA, *Origins of the National Education Movement*, Calcutta, 1957.
——, *India's Fight for Freedom*, Calcutta, 1958.

NAIK, VASANT NARAYAN, *Indian Liberalism : A Study*, Bombay, 1945.
NAIR, SIR CHETTUR SANKARAN, *Gandhi and Anarchy*, Madras, 1922, 2nd ed., 1923.
NEVINSON, H. W., *The New Spirit in India*, London, 1908.

O'MALLEY, L. S. S., Ed., *Modern India and the West : Study of the inter-section of their civilization*, London, 1941.

PARVATE, T. V., *Bal Gangadhar Tilak*, Ahmedabad, 1958.
——, *Gopal Krishna Gokhale*, Ahmedabad, 1959.

RAO, M. V., KRISHNA, *The Growth of Indian Liberalism in the Nineteenth Century*, Mysore, 1951.
REYNOLDS, PAUL EARNEST, *History of British India under the Company and the Crown*, 3rd ed., London, 1952.
ROY, T. N., *The Present Situation*, Calcutta, 1918.

RUTHNASWAMY, M., *The Political Theory of the Government of India*, Madras, 1928.

SAIYID, M. H., *Mohammad Ali Jinnah : A Political Study*, Lahore, 1945.

SARMA, D. S., *Studies in the Renaissance of Hinduism in the Nineteenth and Twentieth Centuries*, Banaras, 1944.

SAYEED, KHALID BIN, *Pakistan, the Formative Phase*, Karachi, 1960.

SHAHANI, TEJKUMAL KARAMCHAND, *Gopal Krishna Gokhale : A Historical biography*, Bombay, 1929.

SMITH, VINCENT A., *The Oxford History of India*, Oxford, 1958.

SMITH, W. C., *Modern Islam in India*, London, 1946.

SRINIVAS SASTRI, V. S., *Life of Gopal Krishna Gokhale*, Bangalore City, 1937.

SRINIVASACHARI, C. S., *Social and religious movements in the nineteenth century*, Bombay, 1947.

STRACHY, SIR JOHN, *India : Its Administration and Progress*, London, 1911.

STOKES, ERIC, *The English Utilitarians and India*, Oxford, 1959.

TAHMANKAR, D. V., *Lokamanya Tilak*, London, 1956.

TARACHAND, *History of Freedom Movement in India*, Vol. I, Delhi, 1961.

TENDULKAR, D. G., *Mahatma* Vols. 1 and 2, Ahmedabad, 1951.

THOMPSON, E., AND GARRAT, G., *Rise and Fulfilment of British Rule in India*, London, 1934.

VARMA, V. P., *The Political Philosophy of Sri Aurobindo*, Bombay, 1960.

VYAS, M. A., *The Social Renaissance in India*, Bombay, 1957.

# INDEX

ADAN, 33
Aiyer, C. P. Ramaswami, 102
*Al Hilal*, 140, 143
Ali, Ameer, 120, 121
   on loyalty of Indian Muslims, 131
   speech at London League meeting, 137
Ali, Maulana Muhammad :
   on Simla Deputation, 127
   on Pan-Islamic sentiments, 141
   on revolt of Islam, 142
   on role of non-violence, 165
Ali, Shaukat, 143
Ali, Syed Ameer, 39, 41
All India Congress Committee, 162
All India Home Rule League, 101, 102
All India Khilafat Conference, 145
All India Muhammedan Confederacy, 128
All India Muslim League, 109, 123, 126, 128, 129, 130, 138, 181, 189
   resolution of 1919, 145
Ansari, Dr., 143
Arundale, G, S., 186
Arya College (Lahore), 89, 91, 92
Arya Samaj, 39, 40
Asian resurgence, 195, 196
Azad, Abul Kalam, 122, 143, 150
   on terrorist groups in Bengal, 139
   experience in Arab countries, 140
   on the Simla Deputation, 126
Azad, Mirza Ghulam, 39

BANDE MATARAM, 114
Banerjea, Gooro Das, 90
Benerjea, Surendranath, 59, 183

address at 1902 Congress session, 60
on abolition of customs duties, 61
autobiography, 81
criticism of Gandhi, 49
on British policy in India, 77
on swadeshi movement, 66
on Mazzani, 46
comment on Extremist challenge to Moderate leadership, 65, 66
on partition of Bengal, 79
on England's mission in the East, 64
on need for creation of National Fund, 45
Bankim Chandra, 131
Bengal British India Society, 44
Bengal India Association, 44
Bengal National College, 30
Besant, Mrs. Annie, 102, 103
*Bhagavad Gita*, 152
Bombay Association, 45
Bose, Subhas Chandra, 101
Brahmo Samaj, 38
British administrators, 18, 21
   policy, 25
   raj, 128

CALIPHATE, 121
Central National Muhammadan Association, 135
Chamberlain, Joseph, 22, 23
Champaran 157
Chand, Dr. Tara, 76
*Chandralok*, 135
Chatterji, Ramananda : on Home Rule, 103
Chinthamani, C. Y, 168
Civil Procedure Code, 31
Congress-League Pact, 121, 190
Crawford, John, 50

National Council of Education, 87, 89, 90
Nationalism, 105
Nehru, Motilal, 76

OBSCURATISM IN POLITICAL THINKING, 188
O'Dyer, Sir Michael, 159

PAL, BIPIN CHANDRA : ADDRESS ON PASSIVE RESISTANCE, 22
ideas on Durga Puja, 114
national education, definition of, 85
on the concept of Mother India 113
on swadeshi movement, 83
on celebration of Shivaji festivals, 116
on the political ideas of the Moderates, 72
on internationalism, 112
emphasis on collective freedom, 96
Prarthana Samaj, 39
Prasad, Dr. Rajendra, 155n
Press and Registration of Books Act, 1867, 33
Preventive Detention Act, 184

RAI, LAJPAT : ON SOCIAL ORGANISM OF A NATION, 96
on activities of terrorists, 98
criticism of early role of Congress leaders, 71
on protection of Hindu interests, 115
Promotion of Hindu nationalism, 115
on Gita, 111
on political extremism, 80
on national education, 86
Presidential Address at the AITUC session, 196
views on educational system, 90, 93
Rama Krishna Mission, 39
Ram Rajya, 152, 178, 191

Ranade, Mahadev Govind, 59
Rao, Krishna 72
Ray, P. C., 57
Rowlatt Act, 159, 161, 177, 191
Rowlatt, Sri Sydney, 158
Roy, Ram Mohan, 32, 38

SANJIVINI, 82
Saraswathi, Swami Dayanand, 39
Sayani, R. M.
Sayeed, Dr. Khalid Bin, 146
Seditions Committee, 135
on aims of Bengal terrorists, 99
Seditious Meetings Act, 184
Shibli, Maulana, 143
Shibli, Shams-ul-Ulema Allaf, 121
Simla, Deputation, the, 126-127
Smith, W. C. (Modern Islam in India), 143

TAGORE, RABINDRANATH, 90, 178
on internationalism, 195
Theosophical Society of India, 40, 101
Tilak, B. G.: views on Home Rule, 113
on aims of national education, 87
his Gita Rahasya, 110
on Shivaji festivals, 116
on objectives of Extermists, 70-71
on origin of the terms 'Extremists' and 'Moderates', 70
on passive resistance, 95
admiration for Bengal terrorists, 98
Tyabji, Badruddin, 121

VARMA, KRISHNA, 99
Vivekanand, Swami, 40
letter to a friend in Japan, 81
Vernacular Press Act, 33

WACHA, DINSHAW, 102
Wood, Sir Charles, 32

Zamindar, 143